ENCYCLOPEDIA

OF

Technology and Applied Sciences

9

Satellite – Tank

Marshall Cavendish

New York • London • Toronto • Sydney

ncyclopedia of technology and applied sciences

England

Robert W. Cahn, F.R.S., Professor and Honorary Distinguished Research
Fellow, Department of Materials Science and Metallurgy, University of
Cambridge, Cambridge, England

Martin Campbell-Kelly, Department of Computer Science, University of
Warwick, Coventry, England

Mark S. Coyne, Associate Professor, Department of Agronomy,
University of Kentucky, Lexington, Kentucky

R. Cengiz Ertekin, Professor, Department of Ocean Engineering,
University of Hawaii at Manoa, Honolulu, Hawaii

Donald R. Franceschetti, Ph.D., Distinguished Service Professor,
Departments of Physics and Chemistry, The University of Memphis,
Memphis, Tennessee

Colin Harding, Curator of Photographic Technology, National Museum of
Photography, Film, and Television, Bradford, England

Lee E. Harris, Ph.D., P.E., Associate Professor, Division of Marine and
Environmental Systems, Florida Institute of Technology,
Melbourne, Florida

Deborah Korenstein, Instructor in Medicine, Mount Sinai School of
Medicine, New York, New York

John Liffen, Associate Curator, The Science Museum, London, England

Robert C. Mebane, Ph.D., Professor, Department of Chemistry
University of Tennessee at Chattanooga, Chattanooga, Tennessee

Peter R. Morris, Visiting Fellow, Bath University, Bath, England

Christopher M. Pastore, Director of Research, Philadelphia College of
Textiles and Science, Philadelphia, Pennsylvania

Sunday Popo-Ola, Ph.D., Department of Civil Engineering, Imperial
College, London, England

Marc D. Rayman, Ph.D., Principal Engineer, National Aeronautics and
Space Administration (NASA) Jet Propulsion Laboratory at the
California Institute of Technology, Pasadena, California

John M. Ritz, Ph.D., Professor, Department of Occupational and
Technical Studies, Old Dominion University, Norfolk, Virginia

John Robinson, Former Curator, The Science Museum, London, England

Thomas R. Rybolt, Professor, Department of Chemistry, University
of Tennessee at Chattanooga, Chattanooga, Tennessee

Mark E. Sanders, Associate Professor, Department of Technology
Education, College of Human Resources and Education, Virginia Tech,
Blacksburg, Virginia

Anthony E. Schwaller, Ph.D., Professor, Department of Environmental
and Technological Studies, College of Science and Engineering,
St. Cloud State University, St. Cloud, Minnesota

J. Derek Smith, Ph.D., Department of Engineering, University of
Cambridge, Cambridge, England

Colin Uttley, Programmes Manager, The Science Museum, London,
England

Phil Whitfield, Professor, School of Life, Basic Medical, and Health
Sciences, King's College London, London, England

Marshall Cavendish Corporation
99 White Plains Road
Tarrytown, New York 10591-9001

© 2000 Marshall Cavendish Corporation

Created by **Brown Partworks Ltd.**

Library of Congress Cataloging-in-Publication Data

Encyclopedia of technology and applied sciences.
     p.   cm.
     Includes bibliographical references.
     Contents: 1. Abacus–Beverages—2. Bicycle–Codes and ciphers—3. Color–Engine—
4. Engineering–Gyroscope—5. Hand tools–Leather—6. Light and optics–Military communications
and control—7. Military vehicles–Plant hormone—8. Plastics–Sailing—9. Satellite–Tank—10.
Technology in ancient civilizations–Wood and woodworking—11. Indexes.
     ISBN 0-7614-7116-2 (set)
     1. Technology Encyclopedias, Juvenile. [1. Technology Encyclopedias.]
T48.E52   2000
603—dc21

                   99-14520
                   CIP

     ISBN 0-7614-7116-2 (set)
     ISBN 0-7614-7125-1 (vol. 9)
Printed in Malaysia
Bound in U.S.A.
     06 05 04 03 02 01 00 54321

PHOTOGRAPHIC CREDITS

Agence France Presse: *1170*
Corbis: *1158:* Corbis–Bettmann; *1163:* Corbis; *1165:* Dave G. Houser/Corbis; *1166:* Niall MacLeod/Corbis; *1169:* Robert Maass/Corbis; *1173:* Ed Young/Corbis; *1177:* Jim Sugar Photography/Corbis; *1189:* Jacqui Hurst/Corbis; *1190:* Corbis–Bettmann; *1191:* Paul A. Souders/Corbis; *1194:* Jeff Hilton/Corbis; *1197:* Charles and Josette Lenars/Corbis; *1198:* Joseph Sohm, ChromoSohm, Inc./Corbis; *1200:* Nathan Benn/Corbis; *1201:* Scott T. Smith/Corbis; *1202:* James Marshall/Corbis; *1203:* Layne Kennedy/Corbis; *1204:* Chris Rainier/Corbis; *1205:* D. Boone/Corbis; *1207:* David H. Wells/Corbis; *1209:* Richard T. Nowitz/Corbis; *1213:* Natalie Fobes/Corbis; *1214:* Joseph Sohm, ChromoSohm Inc./Corbis; *1215:* Layne Kennedy/Corbis; *1216:* Pablo Corral V./Corbis; *1218:* Jonathan Blair/Corbis; *1219:* Corbis; *1224:* Roger Ressmeyer/Corbis; *1226:* Corbis; *1240:* Roger Ressmeyer/Corbis; *1242:* James L. Amos/Corbis; *1243:* Ales Fevser/Corbis; *1244:* Wally McNamee/Corbis; *1245:* Ann Purcell/Corbis; *1249:* Dave G. Houser/Corbis; *1251:* Hulton–Deutsch/Corbis; *1255:* Stephanie Maze/Corbis; *1258:* Michael Boys/Corbis; *1262:* Genevieve Naylor/Corbis; *1263:* Philip Gould/Corbis; *1264:* Dean Conger/Corbis; *1267:* Corbis; *1268:* Joseph Sohm, ChromoSohm Inc./Corbis; *1269:* Gunter Marx/Corbis; *1270:* Joel W. Rogers/Corbis; *1271:* Jeffry W. Myers/Corbis; *1273:* Amos Nachoum/Corbis; *1274:* Corbis–Bettmann; *1275:* Dave Bartruff/Corbis; *1276:* Corbis; *1279:* Leif Skoogfors/Corbis; *1280:* Corbis; *1282:* Patrick Bennett/Corbis; *1285:* Christopher Cormack/Corbis; *1288:* Gunter Marx/Corbis; *1294:* Corbis
Hulton Getty Picture Collection: *1196, 1208, 1232, 1282, 1293*
Image Bank: *1157:* Chris Alan Wilton/Image Bank; *1162:* Image Makers/Image Bank; *1168:* Chris Close/Image Bank; *1181:* AEF/Image Bank; *1184:* Paul Slaughter/Image Bank; *1220:* Jan Caudron/Image Bank; *1230:* Max Dannenbaum/Image Bank
Image Select: *1159:* Image Select; *1193 & 1287:* Ann Ronan at Image Select
Mary Evans Picture Library: *1188, 1248, 1252, 1253, 1277*
NASA: *1160, 1223, 1227, 1228, 1229, 1231, 1233, 1234*
Science Photo Library: *1164:* Adam Hart–Davis/SPL; *1171:* Victor de Schwanberg/SPL; *1176:* U.S. Department of Energy/SPL; *1179:* Tommaso Guicciardini/SPL; *1180:* Rosenfeld Images/SPL; *1185:* David Nunuk/SPL; *1195:* John Mead/SPL; *1210:* Kaj R. Svensson/SPL; *1211:* Tony Craddock/SPL; *1217:* Dr. Tony Brain/SPL; *1221:* NASA/SPL; *1237:* Victor Habbick Visions/SPL; *1238:* Geoff Tompkinson/SPL; *1239:* Simon Fraser/SPL; *1241:* Clive Freeman/Royal Institution/SPL; *1283:* Geoff Tompkinson/SPL; *1284:* BSIP Boucharlat/SPL; *1286:* David Parker/SPL
Tony Stone Images: *1192:* Colin Prior/Tony Stone Images; *1206:* Poulides/Thatcher/Tony Stone Images; *1278:* Cosmo Cordina/Tony Stone Images
TRH Pictures: *1167:* NASA/TRH Pictures; *1186:* TRH Pictures; *1187:* Hoverspeed/TRH Pictures; *1257:* Nissan/TRH Pictures; *1260:* DOD/TRH Pictures; *1272:* U.S. Navy/TRH Pictures; *1290:* TRH Pictures

ILLUSTRATION CREDITS:

© **Marshall Cavendish Picture Library:** *1182 & 1247*

Cover illustration: illustration of a communications satellite
Title page illustration: a satellite passes over the United States and Europe as it orbits Earth. Chris Alan Wilton/Image Bank

CONTENTS

USEFUL INFORMATION

Use this table to convert the English system (or the imperial system), the system of units common in the United States (e.g., inches, miles, quarts), to the metric system (e.g., meters, kilometers, liters) or to convert the metric system to the English system. You can convert one measurement into another by multiplying. For example, to convert centimeters into inches, multiply the number of centimeters by 0.3937. To convert inches into centimeters, multiply the number of inches by 2.54.

To convert	into	multiply by
Acres	Square feet	43,560
	Square yards	4840
	Square miles	0.00156
	Square meters	4046.856
	Hectares	0.40468
Celsius	Fahrenheit	First multiply by 1.8 then add 32
Centimeters	Inches	0.3937
	Feet	0.0328
Cubic cm	Cubic inches	0.06102
Cubic feet	Cubic inches	1728
	Cubic yards	0.037037
	Gallons	7.48
	Cubic meters	0.028317
	Liters	28.32
Cubic inches	Fluid ounces	0.554113
	Cups	0.069264
	Quarts	0.017316
	Gallons	0.004329
	Liters	0.016387
	Milliliters	16.387064
Cubic meters	Cubic feet	35.3145
	Cubic yards	1.30795
Cubic yards	Cubic feet	27
	Cubic meters	0.76456
Cups, fluid	Quarts	0.25
	Pints	0.5
	Ounces	8
	Milliliters	237
	Tablespoons	16
	Teaspoons	48
Fahrenheit	Celsius	First subtract 32 then divide by 1.8
Feet	Centimeters	30.48
	Meters	0.3048
	Kilometers	0.0003
	Inches	12
	Yards	0.3333
	Miles	0.00019
Gallons	Quarts	4
	Pints	8
	Cups	16
	Ounces	128
	Liters	3.785
	Milliliters	3785
	Cubic inches	231
	Cubic feet	0.1337
	Cubic yards	0.00495
	Cubic meters	0.00379
	British gallons	0.8327
Grams	Ounces	0.03527
	Pounds	0.0022
Hectares	Square meters	10,000
	Acres	2.471
Horsepower	Foot-pounds per minute	33,000
	British thermal units (Btu) per minute	42.42
	British thermal units (Btu) per hour	2546
	Kilowatts	0.7457
	Metric horsepower	1.014
Inches	Feet	0.08333

To convert	into	multiply by
Inches (continued)	Yards	0.02778
	Centimeters	2.54
	Meters	0.0254
Kilograms	Grams	1000
	Ounces	35.274
	Pounds	2.2046
	Short tons	0.0011
	Long tons	0.00098
	Metric tons (tonnes)	0.001
Kilometers	Meters	1000
	Miles	0.62137
	Yards	1093.6
	Feet	3280.8
Kilowatts	British thermal units (Btu) per minute	56.9
	Horsepower	1.341
	Metric horsepower	1.397
Kilowatt-hours	British thermal units (Btu)	3413
Knots	Statute miles per hour	1.1508
Leagues	Miles	3
Liters	Milliliters	1000
	Fluid ounces	33.814
	Quarts	1.05669
	British gallons	0.21998
	Cubic inches	61.02374
	Cubic feet	0.13531
Meters	Inches	39.37
	Feet	3.28083
	Yards	1.09361
	Miles	0.000621
	Kilometers	0.001
	Centimeters	100
	Millimeters	1000
Miles	Inches	63,360
	Feet	5280
	Yards	1760
	Meters	1609.34
	Kilometers	1.60934
	Nautical miles	0.8684
Miles nautical, U.S. and International	Statute miles	1.1508
	Feet	6076.115
	Meters	1852
Miles per minute	Feet per second	88
	Knots	52.104
Milliliters	Fluid ounces	0.0338
	Cubic inches	0.061
	Liters	0.001
Millimeters	Centimeters	0.1
	Meters	0.001
	Inches	0.03937
Ounces, avoirdupois	Pounds	0.0625
	Grams	28.34952
	Kilograms	0.0283495
Ounces, fluid	Pints	0.0625
	Quarts	0.03125
	Cubic inches	1.80469
	Cubic feet	0.00104
	Milliliters	29.57353
	Liters	0.02957
Pints, fluid	Ounces, fluid	16
	Quarts, fluid	0.5

To convert	into	multiply by
Pints, fluid (continued)	Cubic inches	28.8745
	Cubic feet	0.01671
	Milliliters	473.17647
	Liters	0.473176
Pounds	Ounces	16
	Grams	453.59237
	Kilograms	0.45359
	Tons	0.0005
	Tons, long	0.000446
	Metric tons (tonnes)	0.0004536
Quarts, fluid	Ounces, fluid	32
	Pints, fluid	2
	Gallons	0.25
	Cubic inches	57.749
	Cubic feet	0.033421
	Liters	0.946358
	Milliliters	946.358
Square centimeters	Square inches	0.155
Square feet	Square inches	144
	Square meters	0.093
	Square yards	0.111
Square inches	Square centimeters	6.452
	Square feet	0.0069
Square kilometers	Hectares	100
	Square meters	1,000,000
	Square miles	0.3861
Square meters	Square feet	10.758
	Square yards	1.196
Square miles	Acres	640
	Square kilometers	2.59
Square yards	Square feet	9
	Square inches	1296
	Square meters	0.836
Tablespoons	Ounces, fluid	0.5
	Teaspoons	3
	Milliliters	14.7868
Teaspoons	Ounces, fluid	0.16667
	Tablespoons	0.3333
	Milliliters	4.9289
Tons, Long	Pounds	2240
	Kilograms	1016.047
	Short tons	1.12
	Metric tons (tonnes)	1.016
Tons, short	Pounds	2000
	Kilograms	907.185
	Long tons	0.89286
	Metric tonnes	0.907
Tons, Metric (tonnes)	Pounds	2204.62
	Kilograms	1000
	Long tons	0.984206
	Short tons	1.10231
Watts	British thermal units (Btu) per hour	3.415
	Horsepower	0.00134
Yards	Inches	36
	Feet	3
	Miles	0.0005681
	Centimeters	91.44
	Meters	0.9144

SATELLITE

Satellites are robotic spacecraft that orbit planets or stars as platforms for communications and science

This communications satellite passes over the United States and Europe as it orbits Earth.

Since the first artificial satellites were launched in the late 1950s, satellite technology has had a revolutionary effect on human life. Satellites have a huge range of applications, from military surveillance to navigation, astronomy, and geology. Their greatest effect has perhaps been in the field of communications, where they have turned Earth into a global village of shared telecommunications. Whatever function a satellite performs in orbit, it must be designed as a strong structure that is capable of operating in the harsh conditions of space.

SATELLITE PRINCIPLES

A satellite is any object that is held in orbit around a larger object by the force of gravity. This article looks at artificial satellites that orbit Earth. The Moon is Earth's natural satellite, but since the launch of *Sputnik 1* by the Soviet Union in 1957, it has been joined by a swarm of smaller artificial satellites, numbering around 5000. In addition to these deliberate satellites, the space near Earth is filled with hundreds of thousands of pieces of space debris, ranging from discarded rocket sections to lost tools and even flecks of paint (see the box on page 1161).

Launching satellites

Satellites operate outside most of Earth's atmosphere at heights of at least 100 miles (160 km) above the surface. Rockets provide satellites with the boost they need to travel from the surface of Earth to their orbits in space (see ROCKET ENGINE; ROCKETRY). The principle of the rocket is used in a wide range of different launch vehicles, all of which use large amounts of propellant to put a fairly small payload (the load essential to the mission) into space. Most launch vehicles are made up of several different rocket stages designed to burn in parallel or one after another. As each stage exhausts its propellant, it falls away, reducing the weight of the remaining vehicle as it pushes farther into space (see LAUNCH VEHICLE).

Most launch vehicles—including the space shuttle—are designed to put payloads into orbit at an altitude of around 150 miles (250 km). If a particular satellite needs an extra boost in order to reach a higher orbit, it will be attached to another rocket engine called an upper stage. This separate smaller rocket engine will then be fired after the satellite has reached a low temporary orbit.

CORE FACTS

■ A satellite orbit is an elliptical path in which the satellite's speed away from Earth is always exactly balanced by the pull of Earth's gravity.

■ Satellites have several different subsystems, usually including structure, attitude control, power systems, communications, thermal control, propulsion, payload, and command and data handling.

■ Many satellites use their position outside the atmosphere to act as observation platforms for looking farther into space or back down at Earth.

■ Some satellites are used for sending and receiving communications or as reference points in navigation.

CONNECTIONS

● Satellites are widely used in **TELECOMMUNICATIONS** to carry information and data around the world.

● Satellites are used to transmit signals from **TELEVISION** stations around the world.

SATELLITE ORBITS

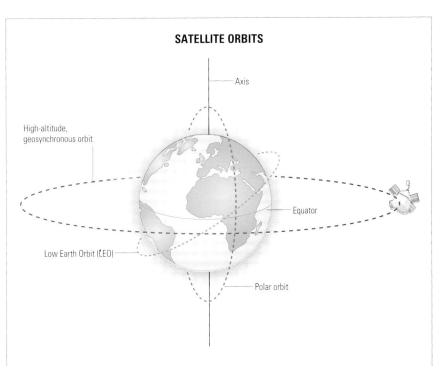

Axis

High-altitude, geosynchronous orbit

Equator

Low Earth Orbit (LEO)

Polar orbit

Satellites orbit Earth at different altitudes: a Low Earth Orbit (LEO) is several hundred miles above Earth; a polar orbit is also an LEO, but it passes directly over the North and South Poles; a high-altitude, geosynchronous orbit is at around 22,300 miles (35,900 km) above Earth.

Satellite orbits

An orbit is any path along which the pull of gravity on a satellite precisely balances its tendency to keep going in a straight line. The closer a satellite is to Earth, the faster it has to travel to stay in orbit (see MECHANICS; ROTATIONAL MOTION). Most satellites

An astronaut works on the Palapa B-2 satellite during its orbit of Earth.

orbit Earth at altitudes of around 150 to 600 miles (250 to 1000 km), and these orbits are called Low Earth Orbits (LEOs). LEO is very useful for a large number of different satellite applications. Polar orbits, for example, are at LEO altitude, but they are highly inclined (tilted) so that they pass over or close to both of Earth's poles (see the diagram at left). This means that the satellite can survey most of Earth as the planet slowly rotates below.

Another type of orbit is an elongated ellipse, where the satellite passes close to Earth at one point, called the perigee, and moves farther out into space at the other end of its orbit, called the apogee. Some satellites are positioned in elongated orbits and others move into elongated orbits while altering the position of their circular (or near-circular) orbits.

High-altitude circular orbits are useful for satellites that study large areas of Earth, because they can see more of the planet's surface at one time (see the diagram at left). The higher an orbit is, the longer the orbital period. This is because a satellite in higher orbit travels more slowly than one nearer to the ground because the pull of gravity is less—the effect of Earth's gravity decreases with altitude. In addition, because the orbit is farther from Earth, the distance around the orbit is longer.

At an altitude of about 22,300 miles (35,900 km), a satellite takes one day to orbit Earth—the same interval required for Earth to rotate once on its axis. A satellite in an east-west orbit at this height will be in a geosynchronous orbit, which means that it will remain in the same position above Earth. Geosynchronous orbits are particularly useful for communications satellites but have important uses in other applications as well.

SATELLITE SUBSYSTEMS

A satellite is designed to provide an orbiting platform for a payload of some sort, such as a camera, a communications relay station, or a telescope. The payload is the reason for putting the satellite in orbit, but the satellite itself has to be designed with other subsystems to ensure that it can do its job efficiently. The computer and other electronics that are needed to process the data collected are together called the command and data handling system.

Structure

The satellite's structure is often the simplest subsystem, but it is vital. A satellite must be designed and built using materials that are strong enough to resist the enormous stresses of launch but light enough to keep the launch costs low. In many cases, the structure must also be designed to avoid any interference with the satellite's instruments and moving parts.

The most popular materials used for satellite structures are carbon fiber laminates (see FIBERS AND YARNS) and lightweight metallic alloys (see ALLOY). These alloys usually contain lightweight metals such as aluminum or magnesium, mixed with small quantities of titanium or beryllium. The way in which these materials are used can also reduce weight and increase strength. Satellite casings are sometimes made in an extremely rigid honeycomb sandwich structure: the bulk of the panel is made up of empty hexagonal cells, which are sandwiched on either side with a thin sheet of solid material.

Attitude control

Once in orbit, a satellite must be able to orient itself so that it is pointing in the correct direction. In the low-gravity condition of orbit, this is actually a fairly difficult operation and involves a number of different approaches and methods.

The first step is to establish the satellite's current attitude (orientation). Some systems use electronic light detectors, which find the position of the Sun or bright stars and compare them to a computerized almanac of their changing positions. Sun sensors are relatively inexpensive instruments. Star detectors are more expensive, but they can help to orient the satellite far more accurately, and they work when the satellite is in Earth's shadow.

Another method of attitude sensing is to use an Earth sensor, which looks for the terrestrial horizon. A magnetometer, which is a device that measures the strength and direction of Earth's magnetic field, is also sometimes used. The inertial guidance system for attitude sensing is a casing containing a series of gyroscopes that are linked to electronic sensors (see GYROSCOPE). The gyroscopes record accelerations that act on the satellite in all directions, and a computer uses this to calculate, from its last-known position, the current position of the satellite (see NAVIGATION).

A variety of different devices can be used to correct a satellite's orientation once it has been accurately established. All the devices have to rely on the simple principle of action and reaction. Gas thrusters simply release high-pressure gas through nozzles arranged around the satellite, while most ion engines create an electrically charged gas, which is then expelled through an electric field. By expelling a gas in one direction, a reaction force is created to move the satellite in the opposite direction.

Reaction wheels are small, heavily weighted wheels aligned with the satellite's various axes of rotation, and they can be spun at high speeds (often several thousand revolutions per minute) by electric motors. As the reaction wheel spins in one direction, the satellite itself slowly rotates the other way. One advantage of reaction wheels is that they do not require propellants, and they can be used for as long as the satellite can generate electrical energy.

Power systems

Satellites usually have two sources of electrical power. Traditional chemical batteries are carried on board in order to provide energy during launch and in the early stages of the mission. However, batteries often have a limited life, and they add weight to the satellite. Once in space, most satellites therefore rely on solar cells, which are devices that convert light from the Sun into electrical energy. Solar cells

can be used to recharge certain batteries, to provide bursts of energy, or to power the satellite when it is in the shadow of Earth. Depending on the amount of power required, the solar cells can either be mounted in a cylinder around the satellite's outer casing or in large solar arrays that fold out from the satellite's body once it is in orbit (see SOLAR POWER).

Communications and data

Many satellites specialize in relaying and transmitting data, but all satellites must have command and data handling to process the information they gather, receive instructions, and transmit replies to Earth. All satellites therefore carry antennas and radio systems for sending and receiving their signals, as well as recording instruments on board.

Early satellites frequently recorded data on tape recorders, but the development of solid-state recording devices and of microelectronics has made tape recorders virtually obsolete.

Thermal control

One of the most hostile aspects of space is the extreme temperature variation between sunlight and shadow. With no atmosphere to help distribute heat and cushion the temperature differences, the materi-

Technicians prepare the Infrared Astronomical Satellite for launch at Vandenberg Air Force Base, California.

THE FIRST ARTIFICIAL SATELLITES

1870: U.S. writer Edward Everett Hale (1822–1909) proposes a crewed Earth satellite in a story called "The Brick Moon," raising possible applications for meteorology, navigation, and communications.

1926–1945: Rocket technology develops rapidly, from the first liquid rocket experiments by U.S. physicist Robert Goddard (1882–1945) to the V-2 missiles developed by German engineer Wernher von Braun (1912–1977) during World War II (1939–1945).

1945: British science-fiction writer Arthur C. Clarke (1917– ; see the box on page 1164) points out the possible use of a geosynchronous orbit as a location for radio-relay satellites.

1951: The British Interplanetary Society develops the principle of the minimum satellite vehicle, a lightweight satellite design.

1954: Project Orbiter is inaugurated, aiming to put a U.S. satellite in orbit using military missile technology.

1955: Project Vanguard, a satellite launch system based on rockets, is given priority over Project Orbiter, but runs into serious trouble during development.

1955: The Soviet Academy of Sciences establishes a commission to develop a satellite and to launch it during the International Geophysical Year of 1957–1958.

1957: On October 4, the Soviet Union launches *Sputnik 1*, a 184-lb (84-kg) satellite carrying a radio transmitter. Within a month, another satellite is launched, this time carrying a dog called Laika.

1958: After a series of failed Vanguard launches, Project Orbiter successfully puts the first U.S. satellite, *Explorer 1*, into orbit on January 31. It is the first scientific satellite carrying a radiation detector; it discovers the Van Allen radiation belts around Earth. At Christmas, Project Score broadcasts the first message from space, a greeting from U.S. president Dwight D. Eisenhower (1890–1969).

1960: The United States launches the first weather satellite, *TIROS* (*television infrared observation satellite*) *1*; *Transit 1B*, a navigation satellite; and *MIDAS* (*missile defense alarm system*) *2*, a spy satellite. The first communications satellite, *Courier 1B*, is launched.

1962: NASA launches the first in a series of astronomical satellites, collectively called the Orbiting Solar Observatory.

1963: NASA launches *Syncom 2*, the first geosynchronous communications satellite. A year later, *Syncom 3*, another geosynchronous satellite, broadcasts the opening ceremony of the Tokyo Olympic Games.

1965: The first commercial geosynchronous satellite, *Intelsat* (*international telecommunications satellite* organization) *1* is launched. In July, the Soviet Union launches the *Proton 1* automatic space laboratory, a 13.4-ton (12.2-tonne) satellite. France becomes the third nation independently to launch a satellite.

1970: Japan becomes the fourth nation to launch its own satellites, and China becomes the fifth.

1971: The Soviet Union launches *Saljut 1*, the first of seven crewed Saljut space stations that orbit the Earth.

Engineers prepare a communications satellite for launch.

1972: *Copernicus*, a NASA-launched astronomical satellite, studies ultraviolet radiation outside Earth's atmosphere.

1973: NASA launches *Skylab*, its only crewed space station.

1975: The European Space Agency (ESA) is formed.

1978: The *Einstein-Observatory* is launched by the United States. It is the first imaging X-ray telescope.

1981: The maiden flight of the U.S. space shuttle *Columbia* takes place. This and other space shuttles become the main way of delivering satellites to orbit. The ESA completes the development of the Ariane rocket, another important satellite-launching vehicle.

1986: The *Mir* space station is launched by the USSR.

1989: The ESA's *Hipparcos* program begins. A series of satellites collect data on the position and movement of a million stars.

1990: NASA launches the Hubble Space Telescope.

1998: Construction of the International Space Station, funded by the United States, Canada, Japan, Russia, and the ESA, begins.

HISTORY OF TECHNOLOGY

als in a satellite are subjected to tremendous stresses as they expand and contract with changes in temperature. Structural materials are selected with this problem in mind, but thermal control remains an important satellite subsystem and involves various methods of active and passive temperature control.

The simplest forms of thermal control are passive and involve wrapping certain parts of the satellite in heat-reflecting or -absorbing materials. The most common wrappings used are insulation blankets, which are layers of reflective foil that are interleaved with netting for strength. Active thermal control works by transferring heat from one part of the satellite to another. One way of doing this is to use a hollow pipe that is filled with a small amount of fluid that boils at the hot end and condenses at the cold end. The action of boiling absorbs heat from the surroundings, and the condensation releases it again. The fluid is then transferred back to the hot end of the pipe along a narrow, absorbent wick.

SATELLITE APPLICATIONS

Satellites have a huge range of applications: they have revolutionized many aspects of science and everyday life during the last few decades. Most satellites can be grouped into just a few different types.

Astronomy

The visible light that reaches us from space is just one small part of the much broader electromagnetic spectrum, nearly all of which is blocked out by the atmosphere (see ELECTROMAGNETIC RADIATION). Although the atmosphere protects life on Earth from harmful radiation, it also keeps astronomers from using other portions of the spectrum to learn about the Universe. Putting astronomical satellites, specially designed telescopes and detectors, in orbit above the atmosphere is a way around this problem.

Different types of telescopes must be used to detect different wavelengths in the spectrum (see TELESCOPE), and this has an effect on the design of the satellite itself. For instance, similar telescope designs can be used for infrared and ultraviolet, which are close in wavelength to visible light, with mirrors that focus the light. However, because infrared is low-energy heat radiation, orbiting infrared telescopes must be heavily shielded from strong sources of heat, such as sunlight, Earth, and even their own electronics. For this reason, infrared telescopes are cooled with systems that bring the temperatures down to near absolute zero. One such method is to fill the telescope casings with liquid helium kept at temperatures of $-441\,^\circ$F ($-263\,^\circ$C).

Attitude subsystems are extremely important on astronomical satellites, since the information they return is useless unless astronomers know precisely where they are focusing. The satellite's attitude will also frequently be altered, as ground-based controllers move the telescope to look at different objects. The instruments on board astronomical satellites are very sensitive and may burn out if exposed to the full strength of a bright light source such as the Sun, Moon, or Earth.

The Hubble Space Telescope (HST) is an astronomical satellite—the first large optical telescope in orbit. Although the largest Earth-based telescopes can detect more light than the HST, the space telescope avoids a problem that cripples ground-based astronomy: the rapid fluctuations of Earth's atmosphere refract starlight, making it twinkle, which limits the resolution of detail from any telescope on Earth (see LIGHT AND OPTICS; WAVE MOTION).

Earth remote sensing

Remote-sensing satellites use the same technologies that astronomers use to study outer space, but they turn the instruments around to look at Earth. The field of remote sensing was largely unforeseen by the pioneers of the space program but has many uses, ranging from mapmaking to prospecting.

Because a satellite in a low polar orbit can pass over huge tracts of Earth's surface in a very short time, it is an ideal tool for conducting large-scale sur-

SPACE DEBRIS

Since 1957, more than 5000 satellites have been launched into Earth orbit. Many of these launches have produced a large number of debris fragments, ranging from casing fragments and rocket stages that have been released deliberately to flecks of paint and dust. Although it is estimated that around 30,000 objects have been deliberately launched, there are hundreds of thousands of fragments of space debris all traveling at high speeds—some over 17,000 mph (27,000 km/h), or 5 miles (8 km) per second—thus carrying the danger of a serious collision.

At least one satellite is thought to have been destroyed by this type of collision, and others have been seriously damaged. NASA used the space shuttle to launch and retrieve the Long Duration Exposure Facility, which was a satellite used, among other studies, to measure the number and severity of collisions. Engineers are also attempting to map the debris using optical telescopes (see TELESCOPE) and radio telescopes to measure the radar reflections of these fragments (see RADAR). The threat is worst in Low Earth Orbit, where the majority of satellites travel. At heights of a few hundred miles, there are still some faint traces of atmospheric gases, which drag on the debris and eventually pull it down to burn up on reentry. However, despite policies of deorbiting satellites at the end of their useful lives, the threat of space collisions is still serious because the unused satellites may take many years to reenter.

A CLOSER LOOK

veys. One of the main techniques used in remote sensing is multispectral imaging—taking photographs of the same area in a variety of different wavelengths. The light reflected by Earth at different wavelengths can reveal many surprising details, such as regions planted with different crops, and even the difference between healthy and diseased crops. Multispectral images taken at different times can best be compared accurately if they have been taken under similar illumination from the Sun. Many remote-sensing satellites are therefore put into an orbit where they will always remain in the same position relative to both the Sun and Earth.

Photography is a passive form of remote sensing, but, more recently, active instruments have been developed. These often use radar, which uses radio waves that are fired from the satellite down to Earth's surface and then bounce back up. Some satellites, such as the European Space Agency's European Remote Sensing satellites *ERS-1* and *ERS-2*, are equipped with synthetic aperture radar. With this system, in the time it takes for the radio waves to travel from the satellite to the ground and then return to the satellite, the satellite will have traveled about 900 yards (800 m), so the 30-foot (10-m) radar antenna behaves like an antenna that is many times longer, able to send and receive low-frequency radio waves (see ANTENNA AND TRANSMITTER; RADAR). By combining the time it takes for the beam to return, the angle of its return, the signal strength, and other parameters, computers back on Earth can transform this information into maps showing ground elevation, slope, and surface characteristics.

An important function of a certain kind of Earth-observation satellite is measuring the height of the surface of the oceans. This can reveal important

This enhanced-color satellite image over Nepal shows the Himalayas.

information about the seafloor and about meteorological (weather) information. As well as looking down into the atmosphere, some satellites also monitor conditions in space around Earth.

Meteorology

Using satellites to photograph weather patterns is another application that was suggested long before the space age, but the distribution of cloud patterns is only one part of the overall weather system, and satellites usually carry instruments for measuring many other phenomena.

Weather satellites operate from either a low or a high orbit. High-altitude geosynchronous satellites are so far away that they can take pictures of one entire hemisphere of Earth. Because they remain in the same position above one point on the Earth, they can produce sequences of images that show weather systems developing and declining. Other weather satellites occupy low polar orbits about 600 miles (1000 km) high. At this distance, they can use a variety of active and passive instruments to measure other aspects of the weather.

One active instrument is the wind scatterometer. This is a form of radar used to measure wind strength and direction at the sea surface—an important weather factor, and one that cannot otherwise be measured accurately on a large scale. The scattero meter sends radar signals straight down, in front, and behind it. The change in strength and angle of the returning signals—called backscattering—depends on the direction and height of the ocean waves, which are in turn related to the wind conditions.

Passive instruments that are carried on board weather satellites usually include infrared cameras or spectrometers (see SPECTROSCOPY), which are used to measure the profile of infrared (heat) radiation given off by the atmosphere at different altitudes. Earth's atmosphere acts like a protective blanket, absorbing or reflecting different parts of the overall electromagnetic spectrum. Instruments that are tuned to these other wavelengths can map the distribution of specific chemicals in the atmosphere. For instance, the monitoring of the ozone layer is accomplished through the detection of the ultraviolet light it reflects back into space.

One major role of weather satellites is the collection of data from remote weather instruments, such as free-floating weather buoys or weather balloons. After collecting the data, the satellites transmit it to ground stations for analysis.

Military

Military spy satellites, which are remote-sensing satellites, have been used since the early days of the space age by competing powers keeping an eye on their rivals. Spy satellites proved to be an important deterrent to war during the cold war of the 1960s and 1970s, because neither side could make a military move that would not be detected by the enemy (see STRATEGIC DEFENSE SYSTEMS).

Spy satellites are developed with one central aim, which is to produce the most detailed images possible. Before the development of high-resolution electronic cameras, spy satellites used photographic film to record their images. They then jettisoned their film capsules back to Earth for recovery, often by a military aircraft, which snatched the descending film capsules in midair.

Film was soon replaced by electronic detectors such as television cameras, but at first the low resolution of these cameras meant that the satellites had to be put in the lowest orbits possible. The Big Bird satellites of the 1970s actually orbited on the outer limits of the atmosphere, and they were designed around a rocket, which periodically fired in order to counteract the effects of Earth's gravity and keep them safely in orbit.

Spy satellites are still a very important form of intelligence-gathering, so it is little wonder that their designs are kept secret. It is therefore hard to detail exactly how far they have progressed, but as far back as the early 1970s they were able to resolve objects that were just 1 foot (30 cm) wide. However, a huge collection of detailed high resolution images is useless without the ability to search through the huge volume of information for a few significant items (see INTELLIGENCE-GATHERING TECHNOLOGY).

It was for this reason that other types of military satellites were developed. Early-warning satellites now carry instruments capable of detecting the distinctive signatures of missiles being launched; they are also designed to give advance information about possible nuclear strikes. Electronic intelligence satellites, meanwhile, are designed to monitor radio transmissions and eavesdrop on communications that are possibly hostile. Although this type of spy technology exists, it is only of significant use when aimed at specific targets.

One final type of military satellite that went through intensive research in the 1980s is the space-based weapons system. Military strategists in the United States suggested that one way of breaking the cold war deadlock might be to put defensive weapons platforms in orbit, which would be linked to early-warning missile detectors. Satellites that were part of the Strategic Defense Initiative (nicknamed Star Wars) would then have fired missiles (or perhaps lasers) to intercept and destroy enemy nuclear missiles high in the atmosphere. However, the technical problems with the project were formidable, and interest declined as the cold war ended.

A number of communications and weather satellites are used for military functions as well as for civilian and commercial applications.

Navigation and distress

Satellites are not only useful as observation posts in space, however. The very ability to have an object in orbit outside Earth's atmosphere and in a fixed (or at least predictable) position can have a number of useful applications. A network of navigational satellites has been developed to take advantage of this. Using the Global Positioning System (GPS), it is now possible for any ship, aircraft, or even spacecraft to measure its distance from three or four of these satellites and then calculate a precise position on or above Earth's surface (see NAVIGATION). In many countries, GPS receivers are also available for cars and even hikers and other personal users. In addition, many satellites are used to listen for and relay emergency distress signals from ships or aircraft in trouble. Many lives have been saved through satellite-assisted search-and-rescue operations.

This satellite photograph shows a cyclonic cloud pattern over the Pacific Ocean. Meteorologists use photographs like this one to forecast the weather.

Communications

Perhaps the area of daily life that has been most affected by the satellite revolution is communications. Until the 1970s, broadcasting and most telephones were limited to areas where reliable cables or radio transmitters could be established, and talking to people on distant continents was unreliable, slow, and expensive.

The idea that satellites could be used in communications was proposed by British science-fiction writer Arthur C. Clarke (1917–) as early as 1945 (see the box on page 1164). He was the first to recognize the useful properties of the geosynchronous orbit, in which a ring of just three satellites placed at the correct height above the equator would remain stationary in the sky and at least one would be visible from anywhere on Earth. This would allow the satellites to act as communications relays, meaning that signals that were transmitted from a ground station on Earth could be bounced back down to any other ground station within the satellite's view, or they could be sent around the ring to the next satellite for retransmission to Earth.

The geosynchronous orbit is now filled with hundreds of communications satellites that relay signals in this way. One thing Clarke did not predict was the huge growth in international communications his concept would eventually trigger, and even with the development of highly efficient electronic systems, the demand for electronic communications—through telephone, fax, Internet, radio, television, and other media—means that new satellites are constantly being added to Earth's orbit.

ARTHUR C. CLARKE

Arthur C. Clarke, pictured at home in Sri Lanka in front of his satellite receiving dish.

Born in Somerset, England in 1917, Arthur C. Clarke is best known as a science-fiction writer, but he also has a successful record of suggesting future technologies. During World War II (1939–1945), Clarke joined the British Royal Air Force, where he worked as a radar operator. In 1945 he contacted the British Interplanetary Society with information about the existence of the geosynchronous orbit—an orbit in which an object moves at the same speed as Earth rotates, thus maintaining position above Earth's surface—at an altitude of around 22,300 miles (35,900 km) above the equator. Clarke suggested that this orbit might eventually be used for the siting of radio-relay stations—satellites that would send telephone calls and other signals around the world at the speed of light. Clarke thought these stations would have to be crewed with human operators, and at the time he failed to foresee the electronic revolution that made communications satellites a reality.

Clarke has, however, lived to see many of his predictions come true. Since the 1950s, he has become one of the world's most respected science-fiction writers, famously collaborating with U.S. film director Stanley Kubrick (1928–1999) on the 1968 film *2001: A Space Odyssey*.

PEOPLE

Communications satellites are launched either by national or commercial operations. A typical large geosynchronous communications satellite can carry more than 100,000 telephone calls and three television channels all at once. Once in orbit, the satellite deploys long arrays of solar cells to capture sunlight and generate power. The satellite's electronic systems are designed to maximize the rate at which signals can be received, amplified, and retransmitted to Earth. Different satellites are designed to handle different bands of radio signal. Commercial communications satellites use specific bands, receiving signals around one frequency and retransmitting them around another frequency. Similarly, military or navigation satellites are assigned bands of radio signal with different uplink (to the satellite) and downlink (to a ground-based receiver) frequencies.

However, not all communications satellites use high geosynchronous orbits. In the early days of the space age, rockets were simply not powerful enough to put satellites into this orbit, and countries at polar latitudes have their own problems. Because its orbit is directly above the equator, a geosynchronous satellite will appear closer to the horizon the farther north or south one goes, and it will have to transmit through a thicker layer of atmosphere than it would to a place directly below it. This can be a problem because the signals will be dispersed by the atmosphere in the same way sunlight is at dawn and dusk.

The former Soviet Union faced this problem, and so developed two separate satellite communications systems. For example, the *Ekran*, *Raduga*, and *Gorizont* satellites occupy traditional geosynchronous orbits, but the Molniya satellite series has an inclined elliptical orbit, with a high apogee nearly 25,000 miles (40,000 km) over Russia's far north and a much lower perigee about 300 miles (500 km) above the opposite side of Earth. This elliptical orbit ensures the satellite is visible in the northern skies for many hours at a time, and it is slow-moving, allowing ground stations to keep track of it. A series of three or more satellites placed in this orbit ensures that one satellite is always above the horizon.

In the 1990s, telecommunications companies began investigating the use of constellations of LEO satellites for communications. By using lower orbits than geosynchronous satellites inhabit, this design allowed shorter delays in calls and allowed lower power to be used on the handheld transmitters. But because the satellites are closer to Earth, each one covers a smaller area, which means that more are required in order to provide the desired coverage.

G. SPARROW

See also: SPACE FLIGHT; SPACE PROBES; SPACE STATION; SPACE TRAVEL AND TECHNOLOGY.

Further reading:
Beyond the Ionosphere: Fifty Years of Satellite Communication. Edited by A. Butrica. Washington, D.C.: National Aeronautics and Space Administration, 1997.

SCAFFOLDING AND FORMWORK

Scaffolding and formwork are temporary structures used to help construct or maintain buildings

Scaffolding erected around the Christ statue in Rio de Janeiro, Brazil, during its restoration in 1990.

Scaffolding is any temporary structure set up alongside a building undergoing construction or maintenance to provide a raised working platform of variable height. Formwork, or shuttering, is the use of wooden boards constructed temporarily to act as molds into which wet cement is poured and allowed to set hard.

Scaffolding for construction must be capable of being raised continuously to ever greater heights, and it must be able to support not only workers but also construction tools and materials. It also allows safe access to the higher parts of a structure for repair, cleaning, and painting. It is not the function of scaffolding to support the weight of a building. However, formwork provides support for concrete structures until they have set sufficiently to support themselves. Temporary supporting frameworks called falsework, or centering, hold complex structures such as arches in place during their construction.

CORE FACTS

- Scaffolding does not support the weight of a building; it provides a platform for builders and other workers to reach higher levels.
- Scaffolding can be made of wood, bamboo, or other locally available materials, but most modern scaffolding is made from tubular steel or alloys.
- Formwork involves the use of molds, usually of wood, into which wet cement or concrete is poured to produce the required shape when it hardens.

SCAFFOLDING

Scaffolding has been used throughout civilization by construction workers. For defensive purposes, towns were often surrounded by high fortified walls, which could not have been built without some form of scaffolding (see FORTIFICATION AND DEFENSE).

Sometimes, as in the construction of the Egyptian pyramids, this took the form of massive earth ramps. But building these was laborious and slow, and the ramps were soon replaced by reusable scaffolding similar to that used today. For centuries, only natural materials such as tree trunks and roughly dressed branches were available. Branches were cut a little way from the trunk to leave forks into which cross-pieces could be placed. Crude wooden ladders allowed workers carrying hods of brick, stone, or mortar to access high levels.

Timber scaffolding evolved into poles and planks that were cut to standard sizes and capable of being assembled into a rigid frame. In the eastern parts of Asia, bamboo, which is very strong and light and can grow to a height of 130 ft (40 m), was found to be an excellent and cheap material for scaffolding, even for tall buildings. Many of the multistory skyscrapers in Hong Kong were built using bamboo poles lashed together with natural fibers. In timber scaffolding used in the Western world, the standard vertical pole is made from larch wood and is 2.5–6 in (6–15 cm) in diameter. Components of this size are strong enough to carry the weight of workers and their equipment, but light enough to be easily carried and lifted to where they are needed.

CONNECTIONS

- The reliability of early scaffolding depended on the quality of available **WOOD AND WOODWORKING** tools and skills.

- Most accidents that occur during construction work can be prevented by implementing adequate **SAFETY SYSTEMS**.

A builder pours concrete into a wooden form at a construction site.

(see ELEVATOR). For the convenience and comfort of workers and to protect passersby, scaffolding structures are often enclosed in heavy plastic sheeting, which allows work to continue in adverse weather.

Scaffolding used for smaller jobs is often made of aluminum or magnesium alloy materials. Magnesium alloy is considerably lighter than steel and is easier to handle. It weighs around 110 lbs per cubic foot (1760 kg/m^3), which is less than a quarter the weight of steel, but it is expensive. These lighter alloys are also weaker and more flexible, so they are sometimes made in ribbed tubular sections to increase their rigidity (see ALLOY; STRUCTURES).

Sometimes scaffolding takes the form of rigid, free-standing structures that are fitted with casters for easy movement. Such structures may support tiered seating and are used to provide temporary seating accommodation for spectators at sports and other outdoor events.

FORMWORK

In many building projects, the main structure is produced using little more than scaffolding and formwork, especially for basements and concrete multilevel parking lots. Cooling towers for power stations are made using metal formwork, with the formwork being moved upward as the shell is built.

Like scaffolding, formwork has a long history. Crude mortar, consisting of fired chalk (quicklime), water, and sand was in use well over 2000 years ago, but around 100 B.C.E. the Romans developed a true form of concrete by adding to the mix volcanic material called pozzolana from Mount Vesuvius near Naples, Italy. The use of this valuable new building material, usually mixed with stones, led to considerable use of falsework and wooden forms.

In the construction of large buildings, such as the medieval English cathedrals, elaborate timber falsework was used. Safety standards were nonexistent and accidents were common. A detailed report exists of an incident in 1178 in which French architect William of Sens, while supervising repair work on England's Canterbury Cathedral, climbed the falsework to a height of 50 ft (15 m) to give instructions to the workers. The falsework gave way and William fell to the ground, sustaining serious injuries.

In modern formwork, steel reinforcing bars are placed in the forms before the wet concrete is added. When the layer of reinforced concrete has set, the reinforcing bars can be welded to the protruding tops of the previous reinforcement, and the forms reused for the next level. Wet concrete is raised to the point of application either by buckets on pulleys, conveyors and chutes, or pipelines and pumps.

R. YOUNGSON

Modern scaffolding structures are made using two or more sets of vertical poles called standards, linked by horizontal members called ledgers. One set of vertical standards is positioned close to the building wall and often secured to it; another set is placed parallel to the first, a few feet from the wall. The horizontal ledgers between the standards support wooden planks on which the workers stand. Diagonal bracing also improves rigidity by preventing the structure from collapsing sideways.

In the Western world, scaffolding is commonly made from lengths of tubular steel or lighter alloy, of 2 in (5 cm) outside diameter, which are secured with clips, brackets, and nuts and bolts. The bases of the vertical standards are often fitted with flat foot plates to increase stability and minimize the risk of the structure sinking into soft ground. Scaffolding kits consist of a number of interchangeable metal components; this means scaffolding can be quickly assembled. Scaffold boards are softwood planks used to make a platform. They are cut to a size of 9 by 1.5 in (23 by 4 cm) and are up to 12 ft (3.7 m) long.

Scaffolding for high buildings incorporates electrically operated elevators so that workers and materials may be rapidly raised to the required level

See also: BUILDING TECHNIQUES, MODERN; BUILDING TECHNIQUES, TRADITIONAL; CEMENT AND CONCRETE.

Further reading:
Scaffolding Introduction. Washington, D.C.: United Brotherhood of Carpenters, 1994.

SPECIAL FORMS OF SCAFFOLDING

A cradle, boat, or suspended scaffold is a narrow hanging receptacle used by window cleaners and painters working on tall buildings. A bricklayer's scaffold is connected between bearers called putlogs that are fixed to holes in the brickwork and to ledgers in the main scaffold. A mason's scaffold has well-braced steel sections supported on two rows of standards. It stands free of the wall being built. A saddle scaffold is set up over the ridge of a normal sloping roof. It may or may not be supported by standards on either side of the building. Saddle scaffolds are often used when chimneys have to be repaired.

A CLOSER LOOK

SEAPLANE AND FLYING BOAT

Seaplanes have floats that allow them to land or take off on water; flying boats have boat-shaped hulls

Early aviation pioneers, who required smooth, flat landing fields, soon realized the advantages of landing on water. U.S. airplane designer Glenn Curtiss (1878–1930) fitted floats to a biplane (a plane with two sets of wings, one above the other) and took off from water for the first time in 1911. Less than a year later, he produced the world's first flying boat, which had a central float formed from the fuselage, as well as two wingtip floats.

These planes were later developed for particular purposes. Naval spotter planes were launched from a deck-mounted catapult (see WARSHIP). On returning to the ship, they landed on floats and were lifted back on board by a crane. In the days before retractable landing gear, floats exerted an extra aerodynamic drag, but the flexibility of being able to land and take off from any stretch of water made seaplanes ideal for exploration flights and overwater airline services.

The great flying boats

Flying boats were large craft with boat-shaped hulls that carried passengers and cargo much more efficiently than floatplanes, which were conventional seaplanes with floats. In 1939, Boeing Clippers began transatlantic services, before land planes matched their range and payload. Meanwhile, British Empire flying boats flew to Africa and the East Asia and were able to touch down on convenient lakes and harbors long before suitable airfields were available.

During World War II (1939–1945), flying boats such as U.S. Navy Mariners flew long-range antisubmarine patrols over Atlantic convoys. The largest airplane ever built was a flying boat belonging to U.S. industrialist, film mogul, and aviator Howard Hughes (1905–1976). The enormous eight-engined *Spruce Goose* flew only once, in 1947, with Hughes himself at the controls. It was too expensive to operate regularly. The airplane had a 320-ft (97.5-m) wingspan—half as wide again as a Boeing 747—with a load capacity of 68 tons (62 tonnes).

After the war, flying boats became less attractive commercially, mainly because bigger planes were more difficult to moor on water, since their large vertical surfaces caught the wind. Taking off with a full load was difficult unless there were enough ripples to cause the aircraft to break free of the water, although steep waves could easily cause a crash.

Modern seaplanes

While flying boats are designed with complex hull shapes, many aircraft can be converted into seaplanes by adding floats. Today, light aircraft such as Cessnas and Pipers are made in floatplane versions for owners who want to fly to and from lakes and harbors rather than their nearest airport. Helicopters can also be operated from water by fitting them with floats instead of conventional wheels or skids.

The U.S. Convair YF2Y-1 Sea Dart is a twin-jet hydro-ski fighter.

Postwar flying boats also offer military advantages, since their landing areas cannot be put out of action by bombs or missiles. The British developed a flying boat fighter, the SR.A1, but the drag of its bulky hull meant its performance could not compete with land-based fighters. More promising was the U.S. Convair YF2Y-1 Sea Dart fighter, which used retractable skis to lift it off the water prior to takeoff, in a similar way to the wings of a hydrofoil. This plane first flew in 1953, becoming the first seaplane to fly faster than sound, but the project was dropped in favor of carrier-borne fighter aircraft.

The Martin P6M Seamaster flying boat bomber took over, with four jet engines fitted above the wings to prevent them from ingesting spray, and a watertight rotary bomb bay in the hull. The drooping wingtips served as floats that also hooked onto a buoy during docking. It was intended that this flying boat would be refueled at sea by submarines or warships, rather than operated from airfields or carriers, but the aircraft proved too expensive to operate. In the late 1990s, Japanese designers were experimenting with a similar design to be used for civil transport.

D. OWEN

See also: AERODYNAMICS; AIRCRAFT DESIGN AND CONSTRUCTION; BOATBUILDING AND SHIPBUILDING; FLIGHT, HISTORY OF; SHIP AND BOAT.

Further reading:

Mees, B. *Notes of a Seaplane Instructor: An Instructional Guide to Seaplane Flying.* San Andreas: Norcal Aviation, 1995.

CONNECTIONS

● Unlike a seaplane, a **HYDROFOIL** does not fly: it is a boat with underwater wings, which lift it clear of the water so that it can travel at high speed.

SECURITY EQUIPMENT

Security equipment protects people, buildings, and possessions against crime and hostile attack

This security camera surveys and records people entering buildings within its view.

CONNECTIONS

● Surveillance by **VIDEOGRAPHY** is becoming more widespread and thus more inexpensive.

● **COMPUTER** data is often valuable and secret, so access must be restricted by the use of passwords or other positive identification.

Security equipment has become a standard feature of modern life. Affluence has multiplied the number of attractive possessions and increased temptation to steal. This has triggered a technological response in the form of numerous devices intended both to discourage crime and to make it more difficult. Security equipment is also concerned with reducing a broader range of risks, including white-collar financial and computer crimes, industrial and military espionage, fires, accidents, sabotage, and terrorist attacks.

Development of security systems

Techniques for protecting the household, such as using locks and putting bars on windows, are ancient. As civilizations developed, however, the police and firefighting services began to take on responsibility for security. By the mid-19th century, private security companies began to build efficient large-scale security devices for businesses and government organizations for the purposes of intelligence, counterintelligence, internal security,

and investigation, and law enforcement. During World War I (1914–1918) and World War II (1939–1945), there was an increased awareness of security systems as protection against military espionage, sabotage, and subversion.

Since the 1960s, crime-related security systems have rapidly grown in most countries. One reason for this has been a large increase in the number of security-sensitive businesses, the increasing computerization of sensitive information, and the need for security against bombings and hijackings.

The development of security systems has been an uneven process worldwide. In developing countries, security technology generally exists only in rudimentary form, for example, only barred windows, locks, and elementary personal security measures exist. In many regions of these countries, however, facilities of large multinational corporations and sensitive government installations have installed sophisticated equipment.

Security systems are increasingly automated, and advances in miniaturization and electronics are reflected in equipment that is smaller, more reliable, and more easily installed and maintained.

Home security

Virtually all homes now contain valuable items, and in many cases home contents are worth hundreds of thousands of dollars. In consequence, a large number of private homes are now fitted with intruder alarms (see the box on page 1169) and other security systems. Video surveillance systems are also becoming more common and inexpensive. An effective system providing continuous surveillance with video recording can now be obtained for a few hundred dollars (see VIDEOGRAPHY). The simplest systems consist of a fixed camera mounted in one place, such as on the outside of a house, and connected by cable to a small monitor somewhere else, such as inside. More elab-

---

CORE FACTS

■ Simple video surveillance systems consist of a fixed camera mounted in one location and wired to a small monitor in another; more elaborate systems have moving cameras feeding multiple monitors and videocassette recorders (VCRs).

■ Goods in stores are now routinely protected by electronic tagging, which causes an alarm to sound if unpurchased goods are carried through an exit.

■ X-ray machines are routinely used in airports to detect handguns and other suspicious objects. Although plastic explosives cannot be detected by these machines, they can be detected by specially trained sniffer dogs.

■ Sensitive computer data is usually protected by passwords; the computer locks the system after two or three unauthorized access attempts.

orate systems have several moving cameras feeding multiple monitors and videocassette recorders (VCRs). These are forms of closed-circuit television (CCTV). Home security can also be enhanced by high-powered external lighting that is switched on automatically when an intruder enters a particular area. This acts as a major deterrent to burglary.

Much can be done to deter burglars by the conspicuous labeling of private possessions with an indelible identifying mark or name. Zip codes are often used for this purpose, since they localize ownership and make items less attractive to prospective buyers of stolen goods. Special pens are available that make marks invisible in normal lighting but readily visible under strong ultraviolet light. This method does not deter burglars, unless there is some indication that goods have been marked, but it improves the chances of recovering stolen items.

Workplace and store security

The main security concerns in the workplace are pilfering and other forms of employee crime, embezzlement and other white-collar crime, and shoplifting. Technology can, to some extent, help limit such forms of dishonesty. CCTV plays an important part in controlling workplace crime. Miniaturized video cameras, often too small to be readily recognized as such, can be placed in strategic positions so that the activities of staff, visitors, and customers can be monitored continuously. This "big brother is watching you" approach, although distasteful to some, has been forced on many organizations by heavy losses due to theft (see INTELLIGENCE-GATHERING TECHNOLOGY).

Goods on display in stores are now routinely protected by some form of electronic tagging. Unless the tag is removed after payment at the checkout, an alarm sounds when the goods are carried through an exit. Another simple system is the use of a continuous series cable, fitted with frequent connections, that is threaded through some part of each item. Goods can only be removed by breaking the circuit, which causes an alarm to sound. Sales staff have a special key to turn off the system so that they can remove items from the cable to sell them. Electrical continuity is then reestablished and the system is turned on again.

Airport security

The growing popularity of air travel from the 1950s on brought increasing threats from terrorists. Airport security measures are thus largely concerned with preventing passengers from taking weapons or explosives on board aircraft.

Questioning of individual passengers and manual searching of luggage has proved so time-consuming as to be impracticable, and technology has had to be devised to speed up the process. X-ray machines are routinely used at airports to detect handguns and other suspicious objects, but it is possible for terrorists to circumvent them using weapons made of plastic. X-ray machines do not detect plastic explo-

This X-ray machine checks the inside of travelers' suitcases for dangerous objects.

INTRUDER ALARMS

Intruder alarms are systems that are triggered when a property has been entered by an unauthorized person or by any person who has failed to take the correct action (such as typing in a pass number) on entry. They require a detector and a signaling device that indicates in one way or another that the detector has been triggered. Detectors respond to environmental changes caused by the intruder, and these may include significant variations in the levels of sound, pressure on floors or other structures, light intensity, and temperature.

Early systems relied on electrical contacts, which would break or complete an electrical circuit and turn on the alarm when an intruder opened a window or door. Such contacts could also be placed under floors to respond to pressure. Optical detectors are commonly used and may operate using invisible infrared light or low-powered lasers (see ELECTROMAGNETIC RADIATION; LASER AND MASER). They consist of a laser that emits a focused beam across a passageway or other area and strikes a photosensitive detector (see PHOTOCELL). As long as the light continues to reach the detector, the alarm is held off; if the light beam is broken, light no longer reaches the detector, and the alarm sounds. Angled mirrors can be used to expand the protected area.

Noises made by an intruder can be detected by sensitive microphones, which may be connected to sensors that respond by sounding an alarm (see MICROPHONE AND LOUDSPEAKER). Alternatively, ultrasound generators can produce continuous, silent signals detected by a microphone. The presence of an intruder alters the pattern of these signals, giving a change in the output of the detector and setting off an alarm (see TRANSDUCER AND SENSOR). Various other types of electronic and radio systems are also in use.

The alarm may sound in the immediate vicinity of the protected property or it may send a telephone alarm to a remote security agency that is capable of immediate response. In some cases, the presence of very obvious security systems on buildings or cars is sufficient to deter potential intruders. Occasionally dummy devices, such as dummy intruder alarm cases and CCTV cameras, are used for this purpose.

A CLOSER LOOK

COMPUTER VIRUSES

The creator of the Chernobyl computer virus, Chen Ing-hau, is arrested in Taipei, Taiwan, in April 1999. He made the virus after being angered by computer software companies that sold useless antivirus programs.

Computer viruses are small self-replicating programs that are surreptitiously introduced into software and deliberately released into the public domain. Viruses insert themselves into other programs and, sometimes on a particular date, produce effects ranging from the display of a harmless message to the destruction of data and essential software on a computer so as to render it entirely nonfunctional.

Viruses are spread on floppy disks or over the Internet. There are now thousands of different types behaving in many different ways, which makes their detection difficult. Virus detection programs can be run that identify and remove most of the viruses known at the time of writing or updating the programs. The best antivirus programs include an Internet link through which they can be regularly updated as new viruses are detected. Computer viruses can be avoided by using virus-checking files that are downloaded from the Internet to check floppy disks from other computers before they are used.

The motives for writing and releasing computer viruses remain unclear; often they are written just for fun. However, increasingly severe penalties are being imposed for this destructive and antisocial behavior.

A CLOSER LOOK

sives of the kind favored by terrorists. The plastic explosive known as Semtex can, for instance, be molded to fit inside an innocent-looking object such as a cassette recorder; this happened in the Lockerbie bombing of December 1988 (see ACCIDENTS AND DISASTERS). Although machines have been developed that can detect plastic explosives, they are extremely expensive and not yet routinely used. For example, in October 1995, a British company announced that it had developed an electronic sniffer called an Itemiser that could detect plastic explosives, including Semtex. A more affordable alternative, currently in wide use, is the deployment of dogs trained to detect explosives by smell.

Financial security

Personal or institutional wealth is no longer represented by gold coins locked in a chest or banknotes locked in a safe. Today, financial wealth is represented by microscopic spots of magnetism on disks or tapes in large computer databases. This seemingly insecure method of recording financial status is, however, adequately backed up both by further magnetic records and by paper printouts. Financial institutions also have backup computer systems in other cities or countries. But this type of system calls for a high level of security if it is not to be abused or to attract criminal attention.

There is vast electronic traffic involved in the transfer of funds and the interchange of financial information, and this too is liable to serious criminal interference. In the early days of financial computerization, a variety of criminal methods were used to take advantage of the relative crudeness of computer systems. Financial staff soon became familiar with the methods for transfer of funds, and, inevitably, there were some who moved other people's money into their own private accounts. One method said to have been used was known as salami-slicing, in which a tiny, insignificant amount of money was transferred from each of thousands of different accounts to that of the thief.

Preventing crime of this kind has been essentially a matter of writing software that keeps one step ahead of the criminal. Changing software is, however, expensive and can cause new problems by introducing bugs. Management also has a responsibility to limit the extent to which employees can undertake financial risk in their activities. The case of 28-year-old Nicholas Leeson, a trader at Baring's Bank whose unmonitored activities in Singapore caused accumulated losses of over $1 billion, sent tremors through the financial world in the 1990s. Management must also accept responsibility for the screening and selection of staff for positions especially vulnerable to financial crime.

Computer security

Computer crime involves both unauthorized access to computer systems and unauthorized activities by authorized users. Computer data (information) is valuable and often secret, and access to it must be

This security guard is observing surveillance monitors that show the areas of a shopping mall taken from different security cameras.

restricted. Serious harm can be done both by theft of vital data and by its loss through vandalism. Invasion of privacy, as in the case of personal medical data, is also a serious matter.

The main method of limiting access to any sensitive part of a computer system is through the use of passwords. If left to the user, these are often carelessly selected (for example, the person's first name) and easily guessed. Criminal hackers attempting to break into password-protected systems can run lists of every known name or even every known word through the system until the right one is found. Most current password systems now do not allow more than two or three tries before the system locks up. A further precaution is the automatic recording of the time of accessing of various sensitive computer files and the identities of the persons performing the access. Logs recording these activities are monitored by a human supervisor, or a computer programmed to recognize patterns (see PATTERN RECOGNITION).

Copying of files is so easy and speedy that precautions must be taken to prevent it. This is a trivial computer function done by setting the attributes (controlling properties) of the file to be read-only (without the ability to be changed). Computer supervisors must, however, ensure that employees do not have access to the normal means of changing the file attributes. The most sensitive and valuable data files are often kept in an encrypted (mathematically encoded) form so that normal access produces only incomprehensible material (see CODES AND CIPHERS). The key to the encryption is provided only to a few authorized personnel. In some cases, sensitive data is stored on disks or on tapes that are securely locked up and placed in the machines only when they are required.

R. YOUNGSON

See also: CODES AND CIPHERS; COMPUTER; FIREFIGHTING AND FIRE PROTECTION; INTELLIGENCE-GATHERING TECHNOLOGY; LOCK AND SAFE.

Further reading:
Hakim, S. *Securing Home and Business: A Guide to the Electronic Security Industry.* Boston: Butterworth-Heinemann, 1997.

PROTECTING ELECTRONIC COMMERCE

Computer systems have been a target for crime since banks and financial institutions first used them in the 1960s, but the growing use of the Internet for electronic commerce and banking has made the problem of computer security particularly acute. Traditionally, electronic transaction processing systems, as these are known, used private computer networks; however, the Internet uses the public telephone network and is therefore far less secure. Protecting electronic commerce will be a big security challenge for the 21st century.

In the mid-1990s, Internet stores and banks began to use a form of security known as secure sockets layer (SSL). This was a method of encrypting (mathematically coding) the transmissions between a web browser (the Internet software that runs on a person's home or office machine) and a web server (the main computer at the store or bank). In theory, this means anyone tapping into the public telephone network would not be able to work out details of an electronic transaction. A more advanced form of Internet security known as secure electronic transaction (SET) has been proposed as a worldwide standard for electronic commerce.

Scrambling information is only one of the requirements for protecting electronic commerce. The other main requirement is to be able to authenticate electronic transactions in the same way that a handwritten signature authenticates a paper transaction. Various systems, such as automated teller machines (ATMs), have been introduced that allow computer users to work with what are known as digital signatures or PIN (*personal* i*dentification* n*umber*) codes (see MONEY AND BANKING TECHNOLOGY).

HISTORY OF TECHNOLOGY

SEISMOGRAPHY

Seismography is the design and development of systems for recording movements in the ground

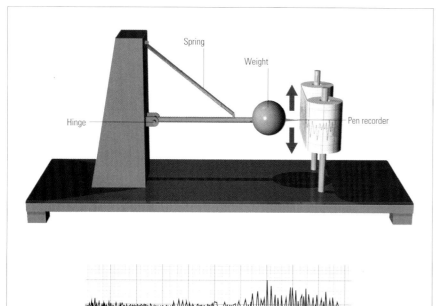

This inertial seismograph uses the displacement of a weight connected to a pen recorder to draw a seismogram of vertical ground motion. The seismogram shows the buildup of seismic waves associated with an earthquake.

Earthquakes are one of the most destructive forces of nature. They are capable of totally destroying human-made structures such as buildings, bridges, and railroads. The most common measure worldwide of earthquake intensity is the Richter scale, which is based on the accurate measurement of seismic waves (see the diagram). However, the United States and many other countries prefer the modified 12-grade Mercalli scale, which relies on witness observations. Alternative scales have been developed in Japan (7 grades) and Europe (12 grades).

Seismic waves

Seismic waves are vibrations in the ground that travel from a source, sometimes for thousands of miles. These vibrations originate from rock formations slipping over one another or from human sources such as nuclear weapons tests (see NUCLEAR WEAPONS).

At Earth's surface, seismic waves cause mechanical vibrations that result in ground motion. The amplitude of these vibrations varies from a few micrometers (thousandths of a meter) up to a few yards or meters. An earthquake can produce several different types of seismic waves. Some are compression waves; others oscillate from side to side (see WAVE MOTION). Because the different waves travel at different speeds, seismologists can measure the time intervals between the arrival of the different waves at their station to calculate how far away the source is.

CONNECTIONS

● Seismographic equipment is used in **PROSPECTING** for mineral deposits.

● Modern seismographs use electronic **AMPLIFIERS** to boost their signals.

Measuring seismic waves

Ground motion is recorded on a seismograph, and the actual ground-motion sensor is called a seismometer (or geophone in engineering seismology). A seismometer converts ground motions into some form of signal. The visual representation of the signal is called a seismogram. Since a seismograph gives information about vibrations in only one dimension (see the diagram), they are usually used in groups of three to record displacement in all three dimensions.

An inertial seismograph detects ground motion by comparing movement of the apparatus with a weight on a sprung hinge (see the diagram). Due to the effects of inertia (the tendency of masses to remain stationary), a displacement is produced between the weight and the rest of the apparatus when the seismograph is moved suddenly (see MECHANICS). This displacement may be very small, so in order to produce the seismogram directly, early seismographs used mechanical levers to magnify and inscribe the record on a moving strip of paper. Later seismographs converted ground motion to electrical signals by means of a transducer. This often took the form of a coil of wire that moved in a magnetic field every time there was displacement of the weight, inducing an electrical current (see ELECTRICITY AND MAGNETISM; TRANSDUCER AND SENSOR).

In modern seismographs, the signal is electronically amplified and processed by computer before being displayed for readings. The signals are converted into digital form and recorded on a magnetic tape or on a magnetic or optical disc (see COMPACT DISC; MAGNETIC STORAGE MEDIA). Data is collected in a seismological observatory and then transmitted via the Internet and archived in seismological data centers for further analysis (see INTERNET).

Uses of seismography

Oil exploration companies use seismic techniques and equipment to locate oil- and gas-bearing formations. An explosive charge is detonated and the pattern of waves produced gives information about the geology of the area (see OIL AND NATURAL GAS PRODUCTION). Using portable instruments, engineering seismologists study the effects of violent ground disturbances on buildings and other structures and advise on earthquake-resistant designs. Seismography also provides a remote-sensing technique for studying the structure of the planet and for monitoring earthquakes and nuclear testing.

M. BARMIN

See also: ACOUSTICS AND SOUND; ULTRASONICS.

Further reading:
Stein, S. *Introduction to Seismology: Earthquakes and Earth Structure.* Boston: Blackwell Publishers, 1994.

SEMICONDUCTOR AND SEMICONDUCTOR DEVICE

Semiconductor materials have an electrical conductivity between that of a conductor and an insulator

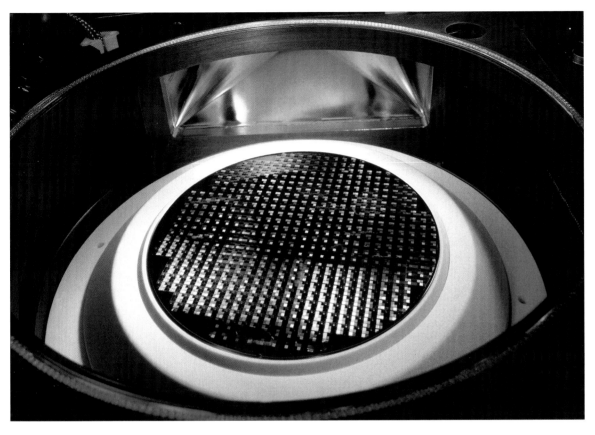

Modern technology is built around devices that use semiconductors. Televisions, telephones, and computers are filled with tiny semiconductor devices of elegant complexity. These devices have replaced mechanical parts in many applications. For example, as a driver steers an automobile down the highway, semiconductors monitor and control the engine temperature, manifold pressure, and fuel and air mixture supplied to the engine (see AUTOMOBILE).

Semiconductor devices are commonly used because they can be made extremely small, have a low weight, require little power, and possess no moving parts, which can wear out.

CORE FACTS

- The conducting properties of semiconductors are controlled by the introduction of specially chosen impurity atoms called dopants. Electron donor atoms produce n-type semiconductors; electron acceptor atoms produce p-type semiconductors.
- Electronic devices, such as diodes and transistors, are created by taking advantage of electron distributions created at junctions between n-type and p-type semiconductor material.
- The operation of most semiconductor devices requires that the semiconductor be formed from a single crystal lattice of high purity.

Intrinsic semiconductors

The most common semiconductor is silicon. Silicon atoms have four valence (outer) electrons that are able to form bonds with neighboring silicon atoms (see NUCLEAR ENERGY). The resulting structure is an orderly lattice of atoms arranged in a regular repeating structure (see the diagram on page 1174). At room temperature, thermal vibrations dislodge a few of the bond electrons, allowing them to travel throughout the entire silicon crystal. When an electron is removed from the bond between two silicon atoms, it leaves a hole. This hole is filled by an adjacent electron that in turn leaves a hole in an adjacent bond. In this way, the hole effectively migrates around the silicon lattice. The dislodged electrons carry negative charge, and, in effect, the migrating holes carry positive charge. These moving charges allow the semiconductor to conduct electricity.

The ease with which an electric current can move though a substance is described as the substance's conductivity. Good conductors, such as copper, have high conductivity. Insulators, such as glass, have low conductivity. Semiconductors have a conductivity that falls between these two extremes.

P-type and n-type semiconductors

It is sometimes necessary to make a semiconductor more conductive than normal. This can be done through the addition of impurity atoms during semiconductor growth. Impurity atoms, such as arsenic

CONNECTIONS

- Semiconductor devices have replaced the **ELECTRON TUBE** in many applications.

- Semiconductor devices operate according to the laws of **ELECTRICITY AND MAGNETISM**.

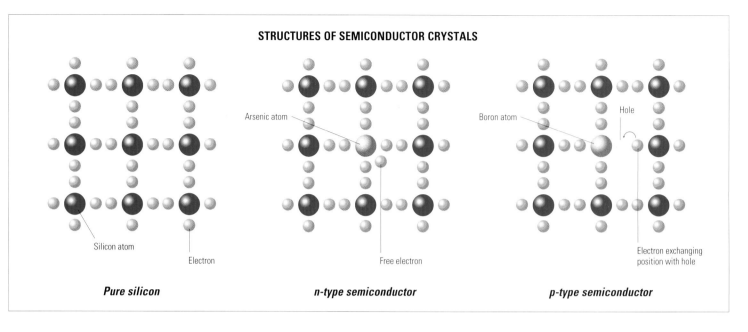

STRUCTURES OF SEMICONDUCTOR CRYSTALS

Silicon atom

Electron

Arsenic atom

Free electron

Boron atom

Hole

Electron exchanging position with hole

Pure silicon

n-type semiconductor

p-type semiconductor

and phosphorus, contain five valence electrons. Because only four electrons are used to bind the impurity atom to the silicon lattice, an extra electron is available for conduction. Semiconductors doped with these donor atoms are known as n-type, due to the negative charge of the extra electrons.

On the other hand, when impurities with only three valence electrons are added, such as boron or aluminum, each impurity atom has one too few electrons to complete all the bonds to the neighboring silicon atoms, and a hole is formed as a result. Semiconductors doped with acceptor impurities that cause excess holes are known as p-type.

Conductivity values are very sensitive to impurity concentrations. An n-type semiconductor in a typical semiconductor device may contain one atom of phosphorus for every 10 million silicon atoms.

Both n-type and p-type semiconductors are electrically neutral, however, because their atoms are electrically neutral. Describing a semiconductor as n-type only means that it contains many more mobile electrons than the corresponding intrinsic semiconductor. Similary, a p-type semiconductor has more holes than an intrinsic one.

Diodes

The simplest semiconductor device is a diode composed of an abrupt junction between n-type and p-type semiconductors (see the top diagram on page 1175). A pn junction allows an electrical current to flow through it in only one direction. This one-way conduction is the defining characteristic of a diode (see ELECTRONICS).

When a pn junction is formed, two competing effects occur simultaneously. The first effect is diffusion. The n-type material has vastly more mobile electrons than the p-type. These free electrons will diffuse into the p-type material as they move about during random thermal motion. Similarly, in effect, holes diffuse into the n-type material.

If it were not for the electric charge of the electrons and holes, this diffusion would continue until the semiconductors on each side of the junction contained equal numbers of electrons and holes. However, electrons and holes are eventually stopped from crossing the junction by the effects of the ones that have already crossed to the other side. This is because when an electron diffuses from the n-type material to the p-type material, the electrical neutrality of the materials changes. The p-type material becomes more negative than the n-type. Each electron that diffuses from the n side to the p side makes the p side more negative. Because electric charges of the same type repel, each new electron that tries to diffuse to the p side gets repelled by the extra electrons already on the p side. Eventually a dynamic equilibrium is established between the tendency of charges to diffuse and the repulsive forces that prevent further diffusion.

The force sufficient to halt the diffusion of mobile charge across the pn junction manifests itself as an electric potential difference across the junction. In a typical silicon diode, this potential difference is about 0.7 V at room temperature.

If a battery is applied to the diode, with the negative end of the battery attached to the p-type material, the electric potential barrier across the junction that prevents diffusion becomes even larger and no current flows through the diode. This condition is called reverse bias. Conversely, if the positive terminal of the battery is attached to the p side of the diode, the potential barrier is lowered. If the battery has a voltage greater than the built-in diode potential (about 0.7 V), diffusion occurs and a large current flows through the diode. This condition is called forward bias.

Transistors

The next level of complexity after the diode is the transistor. Bipolar junction transistors (BJTs) are formed from two pn junctions created by layers of p-type and n-type materials arranged in a sandwich structure, either as pnp or npn (see the diagram below). The middle layer is the base, while one outer layer is the emitter and the other is the collector. In typical operation, the base-emitter junction is forward biased, while the collector-base junction is reverse biased. When so biased, small currents that flow through the base region control much larger currents flowing between collector and emitter.

The key to the operation of the BJT is the fact that the base layer is extremely thin, perhaps less than a thousand atoms thick. In the case of an npn transistor, when electrons are removed from the base through an external lead, electrons from the emitter rush in to replace them. Because the base is so thin, the electrons from the emitter often diffuse right through the base and arrive at the collector before combining with holes left in the base. As a consequence, a large flow of electrons can occur between emitter and collector.

In typical operation, an external power supply and a load (component or components providing resistance) are connected across the emitter and collector. Large currents through the load can then be turned on and off using much smaller currents supplied to the base. This is the principle behind amplification of electric signals (see AMPLIFIER).

Field effect transistors (FETs), proposed by U.S. physicist William Shockley (1910–1989) in 1952, are a second important class of transistors. In an FET, a channel of either n-type or p-type material bridges the gap between two heavily doped islands of the same type material (see the diagram on page 1176). These islands are called the source and the drain. By increasing the reverse bias voltage applied to the gate above the channel, the size of the depletion region near the gate can be increased. In effect, the conducting channel becomes narrower, so reducing the ability of the channel to conduct current.

When the gate is in contact with the channel, it must be made of the opposite type of material, and the gate-channel always needs to be reverse biased. Such devices are called junction FETs or JFETs. They operate only as depletion devices. This means that voltages applied to the gate deplete charge carriers in the channel so that conduction can no longer occur between the source and the drain. These devices can switch sections of an integrated circuit on and off.

OPERATION OF A PN-JUNCTION DIODE

Reverse-biased configuration

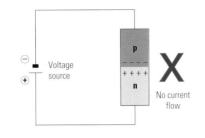

In a pn-junction diode, electrons near the junction diffuse from the n-type semiconductor to the p-type semiconductor, creating an electrical potential difference that resists further diffusion. If a battery is connected with the negative terminal to the p-side, the electrical potential difference is further increased and no current is able to flow through the diode.

Forward-biased configuration

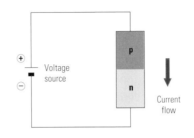

If the battery is connected with the positive terminal to the p-side of the diode, the external voltage opposes the potential difference at the pn junction. If the battery voltage is large enough, it can overcome the potential difference at the junction completely and current may flow through the diode.

One construction frequently used in the design of integrated circuits for calculators and similar devices is formed by the application of a thin layer of silicon dioxide (glass) over the channel. A layer of metal is then placed on top of the glass so that external devices can be connected. This sandwich is called a metal-oxide-semiconductor, and the device is called a MOSFET. Both n-channel and p-channel MOSFETs (n-MOS and p-MOS) can be made, and they are often used together in complementary transistor

NPN BIPOLAR JUNCTION TRANSISTOR

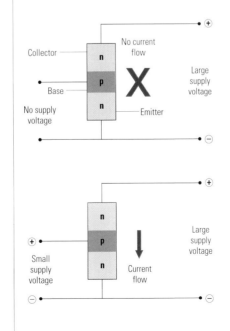

An npn bipolar transistor consists of a thin layer of p-type semiconductor (the base) sandwiched between two layers of n-type semiconductor (the collector and the emitter). When the electrons are removed from the base by the application of a small voltage, electrons in the emitter jump across the boundary to replace them. Some electrons diffuse right through the base to the collector, thus allowing a current to flow around the large voltage circuit. This means the transistor can be used as a switch, allowing current to flow only when a small voltage is applied to the base. (**NB:** The arrows in the diagram show conventional current flow, which is in the opposite direction to electrons flow.)

JUNCTION FIELD EFFECT TRANSISTOR (JFET)

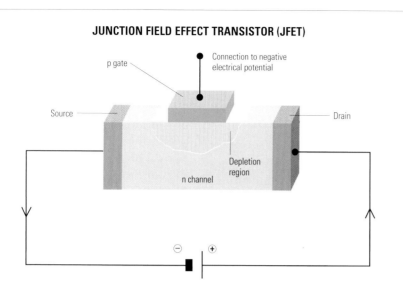

In a junction field effect transistor, electrons are normally able to flow from the source to the drain through a block, or channel, of n-type semiconductor. However, some electrons from the n channel also diffuse into a layer of p-type semiconductor (the p gate) above it, creating a depletion region in which there are no charge carriers. The depletion region can be expanded if the p gate is held at a negative electrical potential. This removes further electrons from the n channel, allowing the transistor to finely control tiny currents to sensitive integrated circuits.

pairs. This technology is called CMOS (complementary metal-oxide-semiconductor). Along with JFETs, CMOS devices can be used to control the current in very sensitive circuitry.

Making wafers

Silicon (Si) is the most common material used in semiconductor devices. Silicon crystalizes into a regular arrangement of atoms identical to the arrangement of carbon atoms in diamond. In this diamond lattice, each silicon atom is surrounded by four nearest neighbors, each sharing one of its valence electrons with another in a covalent bond.

In order for devices to function properly, the silicon lattice must be nearly perfect. As a consequence, it is necessary to chemically purify the raw material, silica (impure silicon dioxide: SiO_2). First the silica is heated with carbon in an electric furnace so that the carbon pulls the oxygen from the silicon (chemists call this step reducing the silicon). Next the silicon is combined with chlorine to produce liquid $SiCl_4$ or $SiHCl_3$. This liquid can be distilled several times to produce an extremely pure substance. Finally, the ultrapure liquid is heated with hydrogen, resulting in hydrochloric acid and polycrystalline ultrapure silicon.

CLEAN ROOMS

To attain air cleanliness of class 100 or lower (less than 100 particles per cubic foot [28,000 cubic centimeters]), special rooms are constructed within which the air is constantly filtered through high-efficiency particulate air (HEPA) filters. These filters consist of a layer of porous microfibers folded accordion fashion so that air is forced though dozens of layers of filter material. In the so-called clean room, air is forced down through HEPA filters in the ceiling. The downward flowing air is immediately collected through holes in a perforated floor. As a result, the air in the room may be completely changed a hundred times each hour.

Especially sensitive processes are conducted in partially enclosed benches with their own filtration systems, which are known as clean hoods. Human workers at manufacturing facilities for semiconductor devices are one of the biggest sources of particle contamination. A person in motion may be responsible for up to 5 million particles per minute from flakes of dead hair and skin, body oils, and clothing. In addition, every human breath exhales water droplets into the air, many of which contain sodium atoms, which are a very serious contaminant to silicon chips.

The only defense against such contamination is to cover workers completely from head to toe: The head is covered with an inner cap to hold hair and an outer cap onto which a body-covering smock is snapped. The face is covered with at least one face mask and the eyes with goggles. Workers breath out through filters to ensure moisture and other particles do not contaminate the room. At least one pair of gloves is worn, and shoes are covered by slippers. Before entering the clean room, workers wearing smocks take an air shower to blow off particles from the smock.

This technician is wearing full clean-room clothing.

A CLOSER LOOK

The next step in the preparation of the silicon is to melt polycrystalline silicon and let it recrystallize into a giant, single crystal. This is done by slowly spinning a small "seed" crystal of silicon at the top of a crucible of molten silicon held just above the melting temperature. The seed crystal is slowly raised as it turns. Molten silicon freezes to the seed, forming an extension of the perfect crystal. The resulting single-crystal cylinders of silicon are 4–6 in (10–15 cm) in diameter and 3–6 ft (0.9–1.8 m) long.

The silicon produced in this process is exceptionally pure. Only one atom in every billion of the crystal is an unintended impurity atom. However, often a dopant (impurity) such as boron is deliberately added to the melt to create a p-type or n-type semiconductor base material.

The last step before actual fabrication of the device begins is to slice the silicon ingot into thin circular wafers using a diamond-edged saw. These wafers are then mechanically polished to a mirror finish. Finally, a combined chemical-mechanical polish is used to make the surface flawless.

Keeping it clean

Semiconductor device fabrication is vulnerable to many types of contamination, including particles and bacteria. Because feature sizes are often so small, a single dust particle that falls on a wafer undergoing processing can ruin the device being made. In a typical city, the air can be filled with over 5 million particles per cubic foot (28,000 cubic centimeters). To ensure a reasonable yield of working semiconductor devices from a wafer that may contain 300 copies of a circuit, the air must be filtered to a level that contains fewer than 100 such particles.

The number of particles in a volume defines the class of the area. An area with no more than 100 particles larger than 0.5 micrometers (millionths of a meter) per cubic foot is a class 100 area. A class 10 area is one in which particles are no larger than 0.3 micrometers (see the box on page 1176).

Fabricating a device

Devices are created on wafers of semiconductor material by a succession of steps often repeated many times. Not all steps are included in every device, and the order may change depending on the desired outcome. The first stage is to grow an oxide layer. This is achieved by heating a silicon wafer to over 2000°F (1100°C) and exposing it to oxygen or superheated steam so that a layer of glassy silicon oxide develops on the exposed surfaces.

After the oxide layer has been grown, the wafer is coated with photoresist—a very thin layer of light-sensitive polymer (see PLASTICS). A patterned layer of film masks some areas of the wafer. The wafer is then exposed to ultraviolet light, which reacts with the unmasked photoresist. The masking film and exposed areas of photoresist are removed and the remaining photoresist is baked hard to give the wafer a patterned protective coating. This coating protects the wafer from acid etches and impurity diffusion.

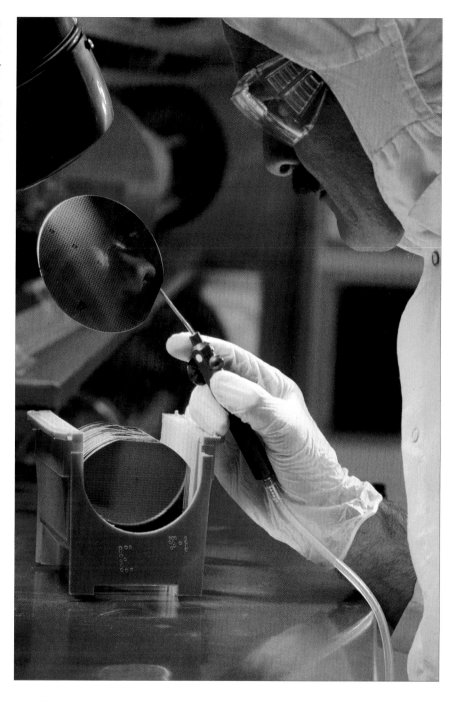

The next stage in the process is chemical etching. Here, solutions of hydrofluoric acid are used to etch away oxide layers in regions not protected by photoresist. After etching has taken place, the wafer is heated to over 1800°F (1000°C) in a furnace, and a gas containing the desired impurity type (for example, arsenic for n-type) is passed over the surface. In areas not protected by silicon dioxide or photoresist, the impurity diffuses into the silicon, creating an island of doped semiconductor.

A semiconductor compound that decomposes at high temperature may then be placed over a wafer in an oven. Individual atoms of the material drift to the wafer surface and join the crystal structure thereby growing more layers of semiconductor on exposed surfaces. This allows complex circuits to be made in three dimensions. Finally, a metal may be evaporated onto the semiconductor to produce areas where contacts are applied (see INTEGRATED CIRCUIT).

A technician examines components on a silicon wafer. The circular wafers are cut from a cylindrical block of pure silicon.

SEMICONDUCTOR LASERS

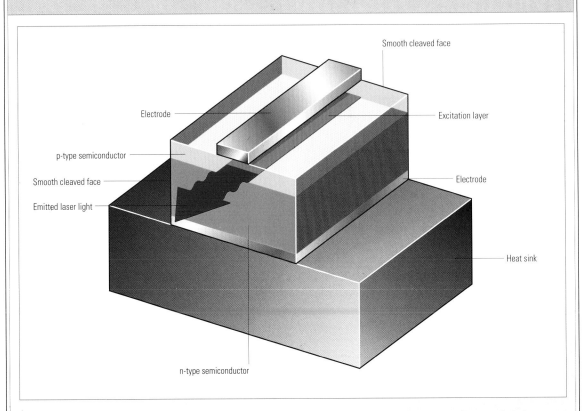

Smooth cleaved face

Electrode

Excitation layer

p-type semiconductor

Smooth cleaved face

Electrode

Emitted laser light

Heat sink

n-type semiconductor

A semiconductor laser produces photons of light from the junction between an n-type and p-type semiconductor.

Semiconductor lasers, also called diode lasers, are the most common form of laser (a beam of coherent light): they are used in compact disc players and for fiber optic communication (see FIBER OPTICS; LASER AND MASER). Semiconductor lasers are efficient, cheap, and small; one type must be viewed through a microscope.

The basic structure of a semiconductor laser is similar to a light-emitting diode. When a light-emitting diode is forward biased, light is emitted at a pn junction when electrons and holes recombine.

A semiconductor laser is a layer of p-doped semiconductor on top of an n-doped substrate that is attached to a heat sink—a substance to which heat energy is dissipated. Photons (light particles) are produced by atoms in a thin active region, or excitation layer, between the p and n regions, when electrons from the n region flow across the junction and recombine with holes in the p region. The thinner this excitation layer is, the smaller the distance the electrons have to travel before recombining with the holes and the better the performance of the laser. The excitation layer is usually made of undoped intrinsic (i) semiconductor, forming a p-i-n layered structure.

The faces of the crystal at each end of the junction are cleaved to produce smooth, shiny surfaces that reflect the photons back and forth within the excitation layer. Collisions between photons and electrons produce more photons, increasing the strength of the laser light until some of the photons escape through one of the cleaved ends of the laser.

A CLOSER LOOK

Types of devices

An increasing array of devices have been made from semiconductors. The oldest and best known are the diodes and transistors that operate in television sets, stereos, and cellular phones. As the size of individual transistors continues to shrink, the number of transistors that can be packed onto single silicon chips increases, allowing the integration of complex circuits onto a single fingertip-sized silicon chip.

Integrated circuits. When many transistors are joined into a circuit on a single chip, the result is known as an integrated circuit. Depending on the number of transistors in the circuit, the integrated circuits are known variously as small scale integration (SSI), medium scale integration (MSI), large scale integration (LSI), and very large scale integration (VLSI). Modern VLSI circuits allow the essential components of a computer to reside on a single chip.

Solar cells. Solar cells may be made of single-crystal germanium, silicon, or gallium arsenide semiconductors. Amorphous silicon (comprising many silicon crystals) can be used; its lower efficiency is offset by the much lower production costs. In solar cells, electrons are separated from the host atom by the energy of incoming light; the energy gained by the electrons may be used to power an external circuit. Solar cells are particularly useful in regions remote from traditional sources of power.

A technician holds a modern amorphous silicon solar cell. Amorphous silicon cells are made from many tiny silicon crystals, unlike the more expensive circular solar cells, which are each made from a single crystal of silicon. These cells can convert light energy into electric current.

They are used to pump water for cattle in remote farmlands and supply electric power for satellites orbiting Earth (see PHOTOCELL; SOLAR POWER).

Light-emitting diodes. Light-emitting diodes (LEDs) emit light when forward biased. In these devices, electrons collide with holes and lose energy, which subsequently escapes as a light photon. Light-emitting diodes are typically made from gallium arsenide semiconductor (see OUTPUT AND DISPLAY DEVICE; TELEVISION AND COMPUTER MONITOR).

Lasers. The creation of small, lightweight, low-power semiconductor lasers has led to a variety of applications. They produce the illumination used to read the information stored on compact discs (see COMPACT DISC). These lasers have made bar code scanners smaller, and they have led to a variety of devices for measuring distance (see SURVEYING).

Charge-coupled devices. Both still photography and filmmaking have been revolutionized by semiconductor technology. Charge-coupled devices (CCDs) are arrays of light-sensitive MOSFETs with segmented gates that pass electric charge from one to another in an electronic cascade. These devices have made video cameras small, lightweight, and inexpensive. Digital still cameras are replacing film cameras in part because they allow the viewer to see the image immediately (see PHOTOGRAPHY; VIDEOGRAPHY).

Particle detectors. Semiconductor materials are also used as particle detectors in high-energy physics experiments. Arrays of reverse-biased semiconductor pn junctions allow very little current to pass through. If ionizing radiation enters the depletion region between the p and n regions, electron-hole pairs are formed. The resulting current signals the presence of radiation (see RADIATION DETECTION).

A. WESTERN

See also: ELECTRON TUBE; PRODUCTION ENGINEERING AND PROCESS CONTROL; RESISTOR, CAPACITOR, AND INDUCTOR.

Further reading:

Sheats, J., and Smith, B. *Microlithography: Science and Technology.* New York: Marcel Dekker, 1998.
Van Zant, P. *Microchip Fabrication: A Practical Guide to Semiconductor Processing.* New York: McGraw-Hill, 1990.

THE FUTURE OF SEMICONDUCTORS

What is in store for semiconductors in the 21st century? Trends will probably involve larger wafers and smaller transistors. Wafers with diameters of over 9 in (23 cm) are likely to become standard, allowing more devices to be created for the same number of processing steps. At the same time, it will probably become possible to manufacture transistors with details smaller than 0.5 micrometers (millionths of a meter), and chips with one million components will be common.

As features continue to shrink, the laws of quantum mechanics (a branch of physics dealing with the behavior of very small particles) will come in to play. Current devices depend on electrons moving in essentially two dimensions. In the 21st century, one-dimensional devices called quantum wires may be used, which will transmit data using waves of electrons (see SPECTROSCOPY).

The future may also see more integration of more mechanical and optical devices on a semiconductor chip. Microsensors will become commonplace, providing a variety of smart appliances for home, medicine, and industry.

Real breakthroughs may occur with the integration of biological components and semiconductors. Semiconductor devices may be able to bridge the gap in damaged nerves. The self-organizing properties of many biological cells may be exploited to produce extraordinarily complex nanodevices that interface with microscopic semiconductor devices (see NANOTECHNOLOGY AND MICROMACHINES).

LOOKING TO THE FUTURE

SEWAGE TREATMENT

Sewage treatment is the removal of waste and cleaning of drainage water before returning it to the environment

Storage tanks and sedimentation pools at a sewage treatment plant in Germany.

CONNECTIONS

● Treated sludge produced in sewage treatment plants may be used to make bricks or **FERTILIZER** or incinerated to generate **ELECTRICITY**.

● Sewage treatment is necessary because raw sewage carries disease-causing organisms that could infect the **WATER SUPPLY**.

Sewage treatment is a part of the water cycle that, like water supply and treatment, has been designed and developed by humans. It involves the collection and cleansing of dirty water, known as sewage, which comes from homes, factories, farms, and commercial buildings. Once it is clean and safe for drinking and bathing, this water can be returned to the natural water supply. Other waste from industry may be classed as hazardous and dealt with separately from the rest of the water sewage system (see HAZARDOUS WASTE).

Most people in the West take sewage treatment for granted, since it has been offered as a community service for the past 100 years or so. In developing countries, sewage is rarely treated and may carry millions of bacteria, viruses, fungi, algae, and protozoans, which are responsible for many diseases affecting humans and livestock. However, newer, less expensive forms of sewage treatment may enable everyone to have access to a clean water supply in the future.

The history of sewage facilities

The Industrial Revolution of the 18th and 19th centuries, with its increase in population (especially in towns) and advances in building technology, eventually led to the development of sewage facilities. Prior to this, people would just throw their wastewater, excrement, and garbage into the streets, or perhaps into nearby streams in the hope that they would carry it away. When the smell became too bad, these drainage channels were covered over and became the first sewers. With population growth and outbreaks of deadly waterborne diseases such as cholera, the untreated sewage became a serious problem.

During the 19th century, engineers began to work on a series of sewer pipes beneath the ground. These led to sewage treatment plants, where the sewage was cleaned up before it was released into the environment. This process of sanitation has been one of the chief contributors to the huge increase in life expectancy the people in developed countries have enjoyed in modern times.

CORE FACTS

■ Sewage is water that contains a mixture of human waste, detergents, and food or industrial material.

■ The sewage system is fed directly by a large pipe called a trunk sewer, which is in turn fed by a network of foul sewers (carrying sewage only) and combined sewers (carrying both sewage and rainwater).

■ There are four main stages of sewage treatment: pretreatment (removal of large debris and grit); primary treatment (separation of sludge and effluent); secondary treatment (degradation of sludge and effluent by microorganisms in two different processes); and tertiary treatment (removal of remaining nutrients, such as phosphates and nitrates and other trace substances).

The sewage system

Sewage contains food materials, human waste, detergents, and various industrial materials. It also includes rainwater from gutters on roofs and roads. It is basically organic in origin and can be broken down by microorganisms. For this reason, it is important for the householder to keep items such as plastics, disposable diapers, and nylon pantyhose out of the system, because they cannot be broken down and often cause blockages. These items should be put into garbage cans for disposal with the rest of the household solid waste.

Pipes from the kitchen and bathroom lead down and out of the house to an underground pipe called a drain. In communities, the drain from each house joins a larger pipe underneath the road called a sewer. Usually the sewer is constructed to follow the contours of the land and run downhill with its flow of sewage. However, in low-lying areas, the sewage may have to be pumped through the system. In many cases the sewage is pumped up to higher ground to allow gravity to move it along. This is done at a location called a lift station.

There are three types of sewers. A surface-water sewer carries rainwater only and leads straight back into the water supply, because rainwater is clean enough not to need treatment. A foul sewer is one that carries only wastewater, and it feeds into the sewage works, often through lift stations. Some areas may use combined sewers, which carry both rainwater and wastewater to the sewage works. The sewers form a network, feeding into a large pipe, which may be up to 16 ft (5 m) in diameter, known as the trunk sewer. This leads to the sewage treatment plant. The system of drains and sewers is known as the sewage system. It is vital that this system be kept in good working order; frequent inspection locates points of blockage or corrosion. Some sewers in the United States and Europe are now very old and prone to cracks and leaks.

How a sewage treatment plant works

Once the sewage reaches the treatment plant, it passes through several different stages before emerging back into the environment. First it passes through a wire screen, which removes large items that would not be broken down and might damage plant equipment, such as plastic, paper, rags, and wood. This material is then used for landfill or destroyed by being ground up or incinerated. On its way to the plant, the sewage also picks up a lot of dirt and stones, known as detritus, from roads and yards. These are removed next by allowing the sewage to flow slowly through a series of channels, where the detritus settles out.

Next the sewage passes to the primary sedimentation tanks, where it separates into two layers. Solids, known as crude sludge, sink to the bottom of the tank, while the liquid portion, known as primary effluent, rises to the top. From there on, the sludge and effluent are treated differently. The sludge is scooped up by electrically driven scrapers and

A worker cleans out large pieces of solid debris from a large trunk sewer in Paris, France.

transferred to a sludge digestion plant. This consists of a series of circular tanks, where microorganisms break down the sludge at a temperature of 95°F (35°C) in an anaerobic atmosphere (one without oxygen). After around 21 days, most of the materials have been converted into harmless products, and they no longer produce unpleasant smells. In addition, this process produces methane gas, which can be used as a fuel to power certain parts of the treatment process. The sludge is then dewatered—made thicker by pressing or spinning it to remove some of its water content. The treated sludge may then be used as fertilizer, or it may be burned in an incinerator to generate electrical power. Sludge can even be shaped into blocks and heated, which turns it into a rocklike material that can be used in certain types of

BIOCHEMICAL OXYGEN DEMAND

The biochemical oxygen demand (BOD) of sewage is the amount of oxygen used by aerobic microorganisms to break down organic matter. A high BOD measurement indicates a large number of microorganisms, which suggests that the water is heavily polluted; if this water were discharged into the environment without being treated, the microorganisms acting on it in the wild would decrease the amount of oxygen available for other aquatic animal and plant life.

It is possible to calculate the BOD of a sample of water by measuring the decrease in dissolved oxygen content that occurs after leaving it in the dark at 68°F (20°C) for five days.

A CLOSER LOOK

A diagram of a modern sewage plant. Waste from homes and industry are treated at sites like these. The sludge produced by plants can be used as fertilizer, incinerated to generate power, or simply dumped in the ocean.

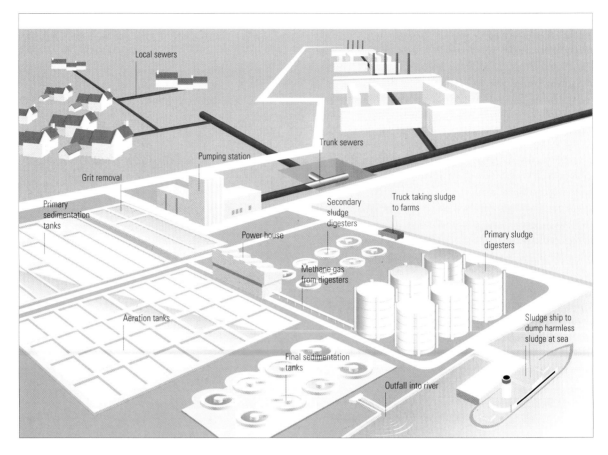

Local sewers

Trunk sewers

Pumping station

Grit removal

Primary sedimentation tanks

Secondary sludge digesters

Truck taking sludge to farms

Power house

Primary sludge digesters

Methane gas from digesters

Aeration tanks

Sludge ship to dump harmless sludge at sea

Final sedimentation tanks

Outfall into river

construction projects. Combined with clay and slate, it can be made into biobricks, which have been used, for example, by the Washington Suburban Sanitary Commission to construct a complete building.

The primary effluent goes through a different process. It is transferred into a secondary treatment plant, which is a series of tanks in which it will rapidly be broken down by microorganisms in the presence of oxygen (an aerobic atmosphere). The effluent may be sprayed onto gravel, upon which microorganisms (called zoogleas) can be grown in a thin film, getting their oxygen from the gaps between the tiny stones. Alternatively, the effluent may go through an activated sludge process, in which

it is mixed with a sludge that is rich in microorganisms and stirred inside an aeration tank through which air is bubbled. (This process is described as activated because the microorganisms used in it can be used again.) Both processes are similar to the microbial breakdown of sewage that would happen in nature, but they occur at a much quicker rate.

As well as degrading organic matter, the microorganisms used in the secondary process may also kill pathogens (disease-causing organisms), which might otherwise cause food poisoning (from, for example, the bacterium *Escherichia coli*) or diseases such as cholera (from the bacterium *Vibrio cholerae*) and dysentery (from the *Shigella* group of bacteria).

After this treatment, the effluent then goes into a final sedimentation tank, where it again separates out from the sludge. By this stage, the liquid may be clean enough to be drained back into the river. However, sometimes it undergoes what is known as tertiary treatment, where it is treated with disinfectants such as chlorine, and phosphates and nitrates are removed. These chemicals, which come from detergents and fertilizers that find their way into sewage, can have a bad effect on the water supply by acting as nutrients for unwanted organisms such as algae. If the algae grow too fast (known as an algal bloom), they use up the oxygen needed by other organisms in the river or sea, upsetting the ecology of the water. Sometimes the effluent is also treated with ultraviolet (UV) light to destroy viruses.

Tertiary treatment is expensive, but cheaper alternatives are being developed. For example, some plant species, such as water hyacinth and duckweed, efficiently absorb phosphates and nitrates through

SEPTIC TANKS

Some isolated houses may not be connected to a sewage system, in which case their waste may run into a disposal unit called a septic tank, where it is held for a short period of time. The septic tank is made of steel, plastic, or concrete and is buried in the ground. The sewage settles in the tank, making a sludge layer on the bottom, which is broken down by anaerobic bacteria (organisms that do not need oxygen). The liquid effluent above is broken down by aerobic (oxygen-needing) bacteria to produce methane gas. When the sludge layer becomes too thick, it has to be pumped out or it will block the flow of sewage from the house.

Once separated from the sludge, the effluent is carried away from the tank in a perforated pipe below the surface of the soil, which distributes it throughout an area called the absorption, or drain, field. It is important that this water is prevented from seeping back into the supply of drinking water, because it may not be completely free of disease-causing organisms.

A CLOSER LOOK

their roots. If the effluent is fed into a holding pond containing these plants, the amounts of pollutants can rapidly be reduced to safe levels. The plants can also be harvested and used as compost for gardens or in animal feed.

Alternative treatment systems

There are alternatives to conventional sewage treatment, and one of the most successful is reed-bed technology. This system takes advantage of natural processes in a similar way to the conventional system, but also uses a variety of wetland plants to remove substances from the water.

Untreated sewage is first screened and then placed in a collecting pit with cut stems from reed plants. The hollow stems provide good drainage and aeration so that microbial breakdown of organic matter can begin. The effluent from the collecting pit then passes through a gravel bed, which is planted with reeds. The roots of the plants are colonized with bacteria, which further break down the waste in the effluent. Then the effluent flows through a pond populated with reeds and other plant species, such as irises, and these digest even more waste.

The effluent then cascades in a waterfall to a lower level, which allows further aeration and exposure to sunlight, which kills viruses. Finally, the cleansed effluent passes along a channel bordered by willow trees, which provide tertiary treatment by absorbing excess phosphates and nitrates through their roots. The effluent can then be discharged into a river, in which any trace pollutants are diluted.

The politics of sewage

Sewage systems and sewage treatment are costly, and most developing countries cannot afford them. Not only does the system of pipes and sewers have to be constructed and maintained, the plant itself is expensive to build and has to be run by highly trained people. Another problem is that conventional sewerage is quite costly in terms of water used. Flushing toilets can take up to a third of the average family's daily water supply. In the early days of sewerage, this was not an issue, but with an ever-expanding population, water has become a precious resource. However, there are now low-flush toilets that use less volume, and even dry toilets, which compost solid waste. In addition, manufacturers are now more conscious of the amount of water that appliances such as washing machines put into the sewage system and are designing models that are more efficient.

S. ALDRIDGE

See also: ENVIRONMENTAL ENGINEERING; FERTILIZER; POLLUTION AND ITS CONTROL; WASTE DISPOSAL, RECYCLING, AND COMPOSTING; WATER RESOURCES TECHNOLOGY; WATER SUPPLY AND TREATMENT.

Further reading:

Biological Waste Treatment. Edited by L. Grady, G. Gaigger, and H. Lim. 2nd edition. New York: Marcel Dekker, 1999.

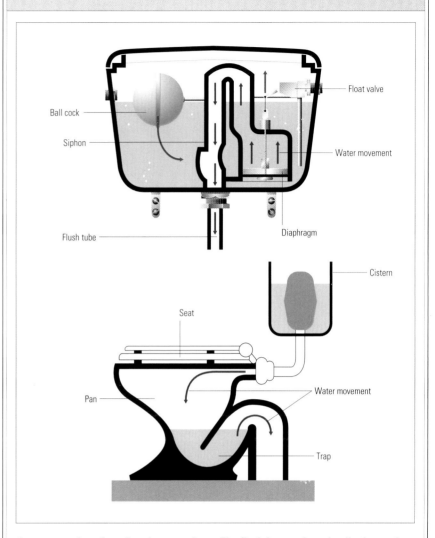

THE FLUSH TOILET

A cross-section of a toilet cistern and pan. The flush lever raises the diaphragm in the cistern, which causes water to be pushed into the pan by atmospheric pressure. The contents of the pan are pushed through the trap by the incoming water.

Ancient flush toilets have been discovered in the Indus Valley, Pakistan, that date from 2500 B.C.E. The modern version of the flush toilet was invented by Sir John Harington (1561–1612), an English Elizabethan courtier. It is commonly believed that he made this invention in 1591 while he was banished from the court for translating a lewd poem. Soon after, however, a flush toilet was installed in Queen Elizabeth's palace outside London.

The use of the flush toilet, as a means of disposing of human waste, was not widespread until large-scale sewage systems were built. A modern toilet consists of a ceramic bowl and a cistern. The cistern contains a pipe system called a siphon, which uses atmospheric pressure to move water from the cistern to the bowl. Pulling the chain or lever forces the water into the siphon and down the flush tube into the bowl. Once the cistern empties, it refills using a floating ball cock, which closes the intake valve once the water has reached a certain level. The flushed water leaves the toilet through a pipe joined to a drain.

A CLOSER LOOK

Cheremisinoff, N. *Biotechnology for Waste and Wastewater Treatment*. Westwood, New Jersey: Noyes Publications, 1996.
Ecological Engineering for Wastewater Treatment. Edited by C. Etnier. Boca Raton: CRC Press, 1993.

SHIP AND BOAT

Ships and boats are built for specific functions but share basic principles of design, construction, and operation

The rectangular frame on this outrigger canoe from Bali, Indonesia, helps to stabilize the craft, allowing it to carry a heavier load more safely.

CONNECTIONS

● Ships and boats use **RADAR** to detect their own positions and the positions of other nearby vessels.

● The chemical consistency and quality of **PAINT AND SURFACE COATING** is extremely important on ships, which are prone to **CORROSION**.

With approximately three-quarters of Earth covered by water, ships and boats have, since early times, played a vital part in making travel and trade possible between continents and island groups. Many boats dating from ancient times still survive today because of their simple designs and their use of plentiful materials and basic construction tools.

Skin or bark canoes made with thin sheets of material stretched over a wooden framework were very popular with native American peoples for transportation and for ferrying goods. The dugout canoe fulfilled a similar function, but it was made in a different way: a wooden log was hollowed out to leave a rigid craft of great strength. Dugout canoes are still used for long voyages between the many groups of islands in the South Pacific.

Simpler than dugouts or skin canoes is the raft, which consists of a series of logs lashed or nailed together to form a flat, rectangular platform. Driven and steered by paddles, the main advantage of the raft is its inherent buoyancy—there is no hollow space that can fill with water and cause the craft to sink. The shape of rafts, however, makes them difficult to propel through water, and they have had most success in places where they are carried by river or ocean currents. Because they lack the canoe's capability for fast and efficient direction changes, rafts are less able to negotiate rapids and are vulnerable to offshore reefs and rocks. However, they are still thought to have been used for epic transoceanic voyages by migrating peoples of the distant past.

Why ships float

Throughout history, the development of ships to carry substantial cargoes over long distances depended on two key advances: the harnessing of wind power with sails, and the developing of hulls (ships' bodies) with sufficient buoyancy to carry heavy loads. Hull development involved the physical principles that govern how objects float in water.

Greek scientist Archimedes (c.287–212 B.C.E.) first realized that an object that is wholly or partly immersed in a fluid experiences an upthrust (upward force) that is equal to the weight of the fluid it displaces. This means that when a boat floats on the surface of the water, the weight of the water displaced by the volume of the boat below the surface

CORE FACTS

■ The hull shape of a ship is directionally stable if a definite external force or action is needed to change the ship's course.

■ Adding a large underwater bulb at the bow provides additional buoyancy and creates a secondary wave that partially cancels out the bow wave, allowing the ship to go faster.

■ When a ship reaches its designed maximum speed, no increase in engine power will be sufficient to push the hull over its own bow wave.

■ Ships can be made to roll less in rough seas by gyro-controlled fins that project below the waterline.

is equal to the upward force exerted on the boat, which enables it to float. This force is also equal to the weight of the boat.

When a boat carries a heavier load, its weight increases, which means that it sinks farther into the water. The boat sinks until its volume below the surface of the water is great enough to displace a weight of water equivalent to the increased weight of the entire boat and its load. The freeboard (the height of the boat's sides above the water surface) decreases, and it is this that finally limits the amount of extra load that can be carried before the whole boat sinks below the surface.

The buoyancy of an object is the difference between the weight of the water it displaces and its own weight, and this is determined by the object's density (the amount of matter compared to size). In the case of the raft, its buoyancy depends on the density of the particular wood used in its construction, which limits the load that can be carried. The only way in which larger loads can be carried on a raft is to make the raft larger, which will increase its buoyancy but will also make it less maneuverable and more difficult to steer in confined waters.

Boats with hollow hulls can be made more buoyant by increasing the weight of the material used to build the boat and its volume, so that it displaces as large a volume of water as possible without sinking. This was originally achieved by fixing rows of extra planks, joined carvel (edge-to-edge) fashion to the tops of the sides of a dugout, which increased its volume and thus its buoyancy and its carrying capacity.

As boatbuilding progressed, the dugout part of the hull gradually shrank to a central framing piece running down its length on the bottom. This was called the keel. The rest of the boat was clinker-built, which meant that overlapping planks were fastened to a series of framing pieces that defined the shape of the hull and held it together. These same basic principles were used for building ships and boats of all sizes, from rowboats to oceangoing merchant vessels that were driven by sails.

Stability and loading

As well as having buoyancy, a ship has to be stable in the way that it floats in the water. The stability of a hull is determined by the position of its center of gravity in relation to its center of buoyancy, which is the center of gravity of the water displaced by the hull (see HYDRODYNAMICS AND HYDROSTATICS). If the center of gravity is lower than the center of buoyancy, the hull will be inherently stable. If caused to heel over (tilt) by the action of wind or waves, the upthrust of the water through the center of buoyancy and the downthrust of the weight of the hull through the center of gravity will act to return the hull to its normal attitude (position) in the water.

If, through overloading or poor design, the center of gravity is higher than the center of buoyancy, then any tendency of the hull to heel over will cause the force of the water and the hull's own weight to increase the angle of heel. The hull will be unstable

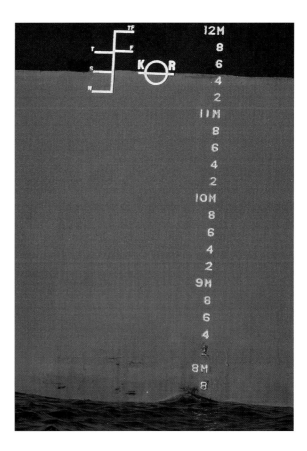

The original Plimsoll mark (the circle with a line through it) shows the level of water at which a ship is fully laden. The load line system on this ship shows how different types of water affect this maximum level: TF stands for tropical freshwater, F for freshwater, T for tropical saltwater, S for saltwater (summer), and W for saltwater (winter). The scale shows the distance to the keel in meters.

and the slightest initial tilt will cause the ship to capsize. For this reason, regulations limiting overloading were formulated in the 19th century.

The crucial measure of any ship is the depth to which its load causes it to sink down into the water. The Plimsoll mark—a line painted on the ship's side that shows the limit to which it can safely sink—was introduced in 1876 by English reformer Samuel Plimsoll (1824–1898) in response to sea tragedies due to overloading ships. Since the limit varies with the density of the water, which is in turn governed by locality and the seasons, the single Plimsoll mark has since been replaced by a series of different lines that take these variables into account.

Shape and steerability

Most engineering designs have to balance different requirements, and this is particularly true of the design of ships and boats. To provide maximum space

---

TONNAGE

The size of ships is expressed in terms of the amount of cargo space they have, with one ton equivalent to 100 cubic feet (2.83 m³). Gross tonnage includes all spaces below the decks and all permanently closed-in spaces above the decks, including for exempted space, which is the space needed for crew accommodation and for working the ship, such as the galley and wheelhouse.

Net register tonnage is the actual load space of the ship, which is equal to the gross tonnage less the exempted space. The tonnage of warships, however, is expressed as displacement tonnage, which is the weight of water displaced by the ship (see MARINE ENGINEERING; WARSHIP).

A CLOSER LOOK

The long shape of this U.S. military sealift ship allows it to move quickly through the water, while providing enough space for troops and cargo. The large bulb at the bow provides additional buoyancy.

the ship heeled over, the bottom of the hull on the side toward which the ship was leaning was more or less horizontal. This provided maximum buoyancy and prevented the heel from increasing. To further improve stability, the sides of the hull were given a tumble home—an inward tilt at the top that reduced the overhang when the vessel was heeling.

In modern motor-driven ships, steering stability is controlled and classified in a different way. A hull shape is said to be directionally stable if a definite external force or action is needed to change the ship's course. This stability is created by concentrating more of the hull area toward the stern (rear of the ship). If a ship has a tendency to wander off course without intervention from any external factor, such as tide, then the hull is considered to be directionally unstable. Although a directionally stable hull will involve less work by the steering gear to maintain a straight course over long distances, a directionally unstable hull tends to be much more maneuverable, which can be vitally important in confined waters.

Bows and sterns

The bow (front of the ship) is in many ways the most vital part of the hull, since it determines the way in which the ship moves through the water. The sharper the bow, the less the water resistance, but also the less the buoyancy at the extreme forward end. Consequently, when the action of a swell causes the ship to pitch (rock forward and backward), a finely profiled bow tends to plunge more deeply into oncoming waves than a broader bow. This effect can be lessened by making the lines of the bow flare out to either side so that the cross-section of the bow increases quickly as it pitches downward. This will reduce the severity of the pitching action.

Water resistance operates in a different way at the stern, especially on cargo ships or boats that do not plane (skim across the surface of the water) at higher speeds. As the ship passes through the water, it produces a vacuum at the stern. Water rushes in to fill the void, which holds back the progress of the vessel. In practice, this means that any hull form has a maximum speed, which is independent of wind strength or even of engine power. As speed increases, the hull creates its own standing wave, with a peak at the bow, a trough halfway down the length of the hull, and another peak at the stern. When the ship reaches this maximum speed, no increase in engine power will be sufficient to push the hull over the mounting bow wave, unless the design of the hull allows it to plane. Since this maximum speed is proportional to the square root of the length of the hull, this serves as another design factor in favor of long shapes over the wide shapes that maximize cargo capacity.

Although the maximum speed of the hull is fixed for a given length, several other factors govern the amount of engine power needed to achieve this speed. Two of the most important factors are resistance caused by eddies (currents that run contrary to the main flow of water) and friction between the hull surface and the water. Eddies are created by the

for carrying cargo, a hull should be short and broad, but this shape creates a lot of resistance, thus requiring more energy to move the boat through the water. A long, narrow hull moves more quickly through the water but provides less space for the cargo. Designers are therefore continually attempting to balance the two design types to come up with one that combines maximum load space with fast and economical motion through the water.

The sailing ship greatly influenced hull shape. With the invention of fore-and-aft sails, as opposed to square rigging, ships were able to sail close enough to the wind direction to make good passage against unfavorable winds (see SAILING). To do this, the sails had to transform a predominantly sideways force on the hull into a forward movement through the water, while preventing the hull from simply being blown sideways. A deeper keel was introduced to give the ship enough grip on the water to stop sideways drift, which allowed the wind pressure on the sails to drive the ship forward. However, unless the wind was blowing from behind the ship, wind pressure on the sails still caused the hull to lean to one side or the other. Designers therefore shaped the bottom of the hull so that the contours on either side of the keel were angled slightly upward. This meant that when brackets that support the propeller shaft and by the rudder structure. The resistance these cause can be reduced by streamlining them as closely as possible to an efficient airfoil shape and by minimizing their angle of attack to the water that flows past the hull. Friction, or drag, is more difficult to reduce for large vessels. One solution is to use a painted steel hull, which will slip more easily through the water. However, this is often hard to justify because of the additional costs associated with painting. For smaller boats, or where performance is all-important, fiberglass hulls can produce useful reductions in surface friction, but their use is limited by available molds to smaller fishing and pleasure craft, or to military minesweepers, where a nonmetallic hull is an additional advantage when dealing with magnetic mines.

In recent years, designers have been able to gain additional speed by adapting the shape of the hull. One way of doing this is to add a large underwater bulb at the bow, which provides additional buoyancy and creates a secondary wave that partially cancels out the standing wave created by the ship's motion. This means that the bow wave, which is the factor that limits maximum speed, will be maximized at a slightly higher speed.

Heavy seas

In stormy weather, the sea's own wave motion has a powerful effect on even the largest and heaviest hulls. As successive waves move past the hull, they cause the ship to roll (sway from side to side) and pitch (rock forward and backward), and these two different movements have different effects. Because the beam (width) of a hull is so much less than the length, the rolling movement happens more quickly than the pitching movement. This became a much greater problem for ship stability when steam power replaced sail and the stabilizing influence of the pressure of wind on the sails was lost.

One roll-damping measure that designers tried was the introduction of bilge keels, which were long, narrow projections that extended along the underwater length of the hull, where the side curves to form the hull bottom. These fixed structures helped to dampen the roll tendency, but more positive counteraction demanded an active system of stabilizers. Some modern stabilizers use internal tanks filled with water, in which the water is deliberately displaced from side to side to counteract the motion of the ship. Others use retractable fins, which are fitted outside the hull and are operated by gyroscopes. The fins create a force that counteracts the rolling motion (see GYROSCOPE).

Particularly rough seas with long and deep wave motions impose extra strains on large hulls. When the center of a long hull is supported on a wave crest, with both bow and stern over deep troughs, it experiences a strain called hogging. When the wave motion moves past the hull, the bow and stern may be raised on wave crests with the center of the hull relatively unsupported. This condition is called sagging. The combination of hogging and sagging creates

MULTIHULLS

This catamaran (twin-hulled) ferry has good stability when traveling at high speed.

Multihulls combine high speed with good load capacity. Developed originally from the outrigger canoes of the Pacific, they have two or three long, narrow hulls supporting the main body of the boat. Twin hulls are now often used for major ships such as high-speed ferries. Buoyancy is maximized by the hulls' being placed side by side. Because buoyancy is proportional to the volume of water displaced, but speed increases with overall length, these long, deep, and narrow hulls allow for high speed as well as sufficient upward thrust to carry a lot of weight well clear of the water. Many multihulled boats have a broad bridge, a deck for engines, and extensive cargo and passenger accommodation.

A CLOSER LOOK

powerful and often damaging forces on the hull structure, which, because many modern hulls are still made with strong transverse frames but relatively little longitudinal reinforcement, can be a major problem. Recent designs, however, put more weight into longitudinal framing and reduce the thickness of the hull plating—and therefore the weight of the hull—to reduce some of the strain.

D. OWEN

See also: AERODYNAMICS; BOATBUILDING AND SHIPBUILDING; HYDROFOIL; POWERBOAT; SHIP AND BOAT, HISTORY OF.

Further reading:
Chappelle, H., and Wilson, J. *Boatbuilding: A Complete Handbook of Wooden Boat Construction.* New York: W. W. Norton and Co., 1994.
Larsson, L., and Eliasson, R. *Principles of Yacht Design.* Camden, Maine: International Maritime Publishing, 1994.
Rawson, K., and Tupper, E. *Basic Ship Theory, Volume 2.* New York: Addison-Wesley Publishing Company, 1994.
Ship Construction Sketches and Notes. Edited by P. Young. Boston: Butterworth-Heinemann, 1997.

SHIP AND BOAT, HISTORY OF

The Egyptian galley in this painting shows a supportive thick rope truss—invented by the Egyptians—running down the center of the boat. The Egyptians also invented woven cloth sails c.3200 B.C.E.

CONNECTIONS

● **MARITIME COMMUNICATIONS** make use of the satellite-based Global Postioning System (GPS).

●Boatbuilding methods improved as **WOOD AND WOODWORKING** tools and techniques developed.

In order to live, humans must have a source of water. Because of this, prehistoric peoples all over the world settled along rivers, lakes, and streams. Generally nomadic in search of game to hunt and eat, early people would often have found bodies of water in their paths. Many would have waded through the water or looked for another route, but once in a while someone would have grabbed a floating log. Perhaps a few logs were lashed together at some point to carry a child or transport supplies across the water. Little by little, the art of boatbuilding took hold. From these humble beginnings came sailing ships, powerful warships, and enormous ocean liners and aircraft carriers, which are practically floating cities in themselves.

The earliest boats

Archaeologists have found pictures of boats that were drawn or painted some 6000 years ago. However, people were probably using simple rafts made of logs or reeds thousands of years before that. Gradually people noticed that hollow logs floated better than solid ones, and they began hollowing them out to build dugout canoes. These little boats were extremely useful and very easy to construct. Dugout canoes were particularly important in areas such as Polynesia, where they were used extensively to travel around the Pacific Islands, and they are still used today (see the box on page 1189). However, dugouts have their limitations. First, trees can only grow so big, and second, a hollow structure may not hold its shape if the material is not strong enough to support its size and weight.

In 1886, an enormous Stone Age dugout dating from before 3000 B.C.E. was unearthed in the town of Brigg, England. Named after the town in which it was found, the Brigg boat was 48 feet (14.6 m) long and more than 4 feet (1.2 m) wide. It had wooden crosspieces that were wedged between the sides to provide extra strength. Rawhide thongs were threaded through holes in the sides of the boat, then stretched across the width of the boat in order to pull the sides tight against the crosspieces.

One way to increase the stability of a dugout canoe was to lash two or more of them together. However, a more common method was to attach a wooden float a few feet out to one side—a construction called an outrigger.

CORE FACTS

- Traditional boatbuilding materials include wood, reeds, and animal skins.
- The designs of ships and boats have been driven by the needs of exploration, competition, commerce, and war.
- Steamboats freed transportation over water from the uncertainties of winds and currents.
- Modern electronic technology has provided valuable aids to navigation and safety.

The ancient mariners

The early civilizations of the Mediterranean and the Middle East were built on trade and conquest. These involved travel over water, along coastlines, among islands, and up and down rivers. Many of these ancient peoples were known for their seafaring expertise. They built long, narrow boats called galleys, which had banks of oars on each side.

The Egyptians invented woven cloth for sails around 3200 B.C.E. A few hundred years later, they learned to build boats with planks of wood. No longer limited to logs or to bundles of reeds, they could now make larger boats, with more variety in their shapes. The Egyptians also invented the truss, which was a thick rope tied from the bow (the front) of the boat to the stern (the back). It was supported down the middle of the boat by a row of vertical supports. The truss prevented the ends of the boat from hogging (drooping) as it rode over a wave.

The Phoenicians were famous sailors, launching themselves from their thin strip of territory—in what is now Lebanon—to take to the sea. They were probably the first people to take their boats deliberately out of sight of land, and they went as far north as England. In around 600 B.C.E., Phoenician sailors made a three-year voyage around the continent of Africa, which is briefly described in *The History of the Persian War* by Greek historian Herodotus (c.484–c.430 B.C.E.).

Phoenician shipbuilders were famous for their fighting vessels, which were long, nimble ships with pointed hulls. These hulls were shaped to cut through the water effectively (see SHIP AND BOAT), and they could also be used as battering rams in war situations. The galleys were propelled by oars, arranged in either two or three banks. Galleys with two banks of oars were called biremes, and those with three banks of oars were called triremes. The galleys also had sails, which were used for auxiliary power in rough seas.

The Vikings

The Vikings were seafaring adventurers from medieval Scandinavia. Accomplished sailors, they used wooden ships with one square sail that was rigged on a central mast. Similar to the ships of the ancient Mediterranean civilizations (the Egyptians and the Phoenicians), the Viking ships were built with planks. Where the Mediterranean ships, however, used carvel planking—planks laid edge-to-edge that were attached to the ribs of the ship—the Viking ships used clinker building techniques, in which the planks overlapped. While carvel planking made for a much sturdier craft, the clinker technique allowed a watertight ship to be built with much thinner and lighter planks.

By around 800 C.E., Vikings were regularly raiding the coasts of western Europe and the British Isles. According to Icelandic sagas, in the 10th century outlaw Erik the Red (940–1010), who was the son of a Norse chieftain, sailed to Greenland to look for a safe haven. His son, Norse explorer Leif Eriksson

BOATS FROM ANOTHER TIME

A Welsh fisherman carries a wicker coracle upstream.

In many places around the world, people still use very similar types of boats to the ones their ancestors used thousands of years before. Polynesian dugouts and outriggers are among such boats. On Lake Titicaca in Peru, craft called balsas, which are canoes made from bundles of buoyant reeds lashed together, have been used since ancient times. Each balsa lasts only a few months, because the reeds start to rot and the boat disintegrates.

Many types of traditional boats are still made of animal hides that are stretched over a light wooden framework. The Irish curragh is a long, narrow boat that has been used for fishing and transportation between islands for many centuries. Light enough to be carried to and from the beach, it is also sufficiently sturdy to hold together in choppy surf. The coracle remains a familiar sight in parts of England and Wales. This tiny circular boat—usually used for fishing— can be piloted downriver by one person. On the return upstream, the boat is carried back by the same person.

Traditional sailing vessels still seen today include the graceful Chinese junk, which is rigged with lugsails. Believed to be a Chinese invention, lugsails hang from supports that cross the mast at an angle. Junks often carry sampans—small boats common in China—as dinghies. The lateen-rigged Arab dhow is also a traditional style of sailboat. It has been used since ancient times for trade along the coasts of India and East Africa.

HISTORY OF TECHNOLOGY

(c.1000 C.E.), sailed west from Greenland to reach the coast of present-day Canada. He called the new land Vinland because of the grape vines he found. In this way, the Vikings—in the form of Eriksson and 35 companions—were the first Europeans to go to the New World, although the colony, Vinland, lasted only three years. The stories in literature are substantiated by the discovery of a Native American arrowhead in a Viking graveyard in Greenland, and of a Viking spindle in Newfoundland.

THOR HEYERDAHL

Thor Heyerdahl is pictured here with his crew on the bow of his reed boat, Ra, *in Safi, Morocco, in 1969.*

Norwegian ethnologist Thor Heyerdahl (1914–) spent decades reproducing the boating techniques of ancient civilizations. A proponent of the diffusionist school of anthropology, Heyerdahl set out to prove that cultural similarities such as the pyramids found in both Egypt and South America could have been the result of ancient travel and migration between far-flung regions of the world.

Many experts scoffed at Heyerdahl's theories, arguing from linguistic and other evidence that the similarities were coincidental or the independent development of similar solutions to similar needs. Undeterred, Heyerdahl organized the *Kon-Tiki* expedition in 1947, during which he sailed a balsa-wood raft from Peru across 4300 miles (6900 km) of ocean to show that early South Americans could have reached the Pacific Islands. His 1969 *Ra* expeditions in reed boats (see the picture above) were an attempt to demonstrate that ancient Egyptians could have sailed across to the New World.

PEOPLE

Discovery and colonization
Between the 13th and the 15th centuries C.E., while the Renaissance was beginning in Europe, the major seafaring powers were England, France, Spain, and Portugal. These nations developed various trade routes in an attempt to find undiscovered riches.

Sailing ships had greatly improved over the centuries. They usually had three masts: a mainmast in the middle, a foremast in front, and a mizzenmast behind. They were square-rigged, with multiple sails hanging from yards (long poles that support the head of the sail) at right angles to the mast. These yards allowed the ship to be controlled over a wide range of conditions at sea. A rudder governed by a wheel provided more precise steering.

The larger size of these ships not only made them more stable in the water, but also made room for passengers, a larger crew, supplies, and traded or stolen goods. Significant variations included the Spanish galleon with its large, elaborate stern castle (a protected space at the rear of the boat) that contained the officers' living quarters, and the Portuguese caravel, a 15th-century ship with broad bows, high narrow poop deck, and usually three masts with triangular sails called lateens or both square and lateen sails. Square sails depend on wind blowing them from behind; lateens could be angled to catch wind from the side as well as from behind. With ships like these, Renaissance explorers could engage in long voyages, including trips around the world.

Of course, the world these explorers were contemplating was much smaller than today's world. Most notably, they had no idea of the existence of the American continents, not being familiar with the Icelandic voyages there. They expected that if they sailed west, they would find a sea route to Asia without having to undertake the long and troublesome eastward circuit around Africa. Portuguese navigator Vasco da Gama (1460–1524) was the first European to complete this arduous eastward trip, which he undertook in 1497–1498.

Still intent on their goal of a western route to Asia, explorers continued to search for a northwest passage around the Americas. They found Nova Scotia, Newfoundland, and Canada—and valuable fishing grounds—but no way through the cold and icy region to the north. In 1519, Portuguese navigator Ferdinand Magellan (c.1480–c.1521) tried going the other way instead, looking for a passage around South America. With five ships and 234 men, the expedition passed through what would later be known as the Straits of Magellan, near the tip of South America, into the calm open waters they named the Pacific. Although Magellan was killed in a battle in the Philippines, what was left of his fleet—18 men and one ship—pressed on to complete the first circumnavigation of the world in 1522.

The age of sail

Over the next few centuries, changes to sailing ships were gradual. Hulls were made stronger and stability was increased by removing the top-heavy castles (protected shelters) in the bow and stern. The ships grew larger and remained slow. Ships called East Indiamen, built by British and Dutch East India companies, which were built to ply the lucrative trade routes, carried guns to defend against frequent attacks by pirates.

One side-effect of improvements in sailing ships and exploration during the 13th to the 15th century was the large-scale importation of human cargo to the New World. Early European colonists established valuable sugar plantations in the West Indies and South America. The colonists looked to western Africa for workers, and large ships containing hundreds of captives began traveling regularly between Africa and the Americas.

A revolution in sailing vessels occurred in connection with the political upheavals of the late 1700s—particularly the Revolutionary War (1775–1783). As speed became an increasingly important factor in battles between American and British forces, small, fast sailing ships called Baltimore clippers played a crucial role in the American war effort.

In 1832, the British government canceled the monopoly over the China tea trade that was held by the British East India Company. It then became a highly competitive race to see which ship would arrive in various ports first with the season's tea supply. In New York in 1845, American naval architect John W. Griffiths (1809–1882) designed a ship called the *Rainbow*, which was based upon the old Baltimore clippers. The *Rainbow* was the first of the Yankee clippers, which were nimble ships that carried many layers of sails. The Yankee clippers rode low in the water with a bow that was built to slice through the waves. Clipper ships gained their speed at the

expense of strength, durability, and stability. Captains generally supervised the loading of cargo into their ships personally, in order to make sure that the balance was right and would not jeopardize the ship's stability too much. Even so, corrections often

The Pride of Baltimore II— *a modern replication of a Baltimore clipper—races in the waters off Annapolis, Maryland, in 1995.*

UNDER CONSTRUCTION

Wooden ships are built by constructing a framework and then nailing planks to this skeleton. Smaller wooden craft, however, may be built using shell construction, in which the hull is molded to a template and internal framing added for strength. When iron ships were first developed, builders used skeleton construction just as they had previously done for wooden ships. Rivets were used on the metal plates instead of nails.

Modern ships are put together in huge shipyards, with welding having replaced rivets since World War II (1939–1945). Much of the process is now automated. Often large sections of the ship are built at other locations, and the sections are assembled at the shipyard. As soon as the empty shell is watertight, the ship is placed in a dock, where the additional outer sections are fitted.

A CLOSER LOOK

had to be made during the journey itself by moving around heavy chains lying on the deck.

The dominance of the clipper ship ended in the 1860s, when railroad lines were completed across the United States. At about the same time, the opening of the Suez Canal in northeastern Egypt gave steamships the advantage by creating a quick passage to China. Great sailing vessels such as tall ships (a sailing vessel with at least two masts) continued to be built for use when speed was less important than the ability to economize by using wind instead of fuel. Tall ships could carry large loads of cargo, and their increased stability allowed them to remain under sail in high winds that would have toppled the less stable clipper ships. Today, some of these beautiful ships are still afloat—gracing exhibitions and races, being used for recreational touring, and providing training opportunities for sea cadets.

Steam and iron

A major problem with sailing ships is their inability to sail against the wind and current. This problem was lessened somewhat by the improved design of ships and sails. While Viking longships could sail only a few degrees against the wind, modern sailing yachts can move at angles up to 45 degrees into the wind. However, if the intended destination is directly upwind, the modern sailboat still has to do a lot of

CRUISING THE WATERS

The Queen Elizabeth II *was the first liner built to combine the tasks of transatlantic liner and cruise ship.*

One of the largest passenger liners ever built was the *Queen Elizabeth*. Originally launched in 1938 and used as a troopship during World War II, it entered the regular transatlantic service of the Cunard line in 1946. The ship was 1,031 feet (314 m) long, 118.5 feet (36 m) wide, and weighed 89,600 tons (81,000 tons).

The ship retired in 1968 and was sold to a university. Unfortunately, it burned and sank in January 1972 while it was being refitted in Hong Kong.

The *Queen Elizabeth* was succeeded by the *Queen Elizabeth II*, which was launched in 1967 and made its maiden voyage in 1969. This was the first liner built to combine the tasks of transatlantic passenger liner and holiday cruise ship. During the summer months the ship makes up to a dozen or so direct crossings of the Atlantic as a passenger liner, and for the rest of the year it is a cruise liner. The ship had the additional role of operating as a fast troop carrier. During the Falkland Islands operations of 1982 it was used as a fast troopship to ferry a brigade 8000 miles (12,875 km) nonstop to the fighting front.

The ship's flexibility is partly due to advances in the materials used in its structure, particularly to the development of nickel-chrome steel with its ability to resist heat. This reduced the number of boilers needed to deliver steam to the turbines in the engine room from 12 in the *Queen Elizabeth* to 3 in the *Queen Elizabeth II*. Other improvements include a refined hull design, light alloy deck, and smaller draught (the depth the ship reaches below water).

HISTORY OF TECHNOLOGY

This image shows the Confederate ironclad **Merrimac** *(left) and the Union's iron* **Monitor** *(center) in battle on March 9, 1862.*

tacking—switching back and forth at an angle—to make any progress (see SAILING).

When the steam engine was invented by English blacksmith Thomas Newcomen (1663–1729) in 1705, it was very quickly seen as a potential solution to the problem of sailing against wind and current. But early experiments were not very successful. In 1783, French marquis Claude de Jouffroy d'Abbans (1751–1832) used a two–cylinder steam engine, with one cylinder driving a pull–paddle wheel and one cylinder driving a push–paddle wheel. His ship *Pyroscaphe*, launched on the Saône River in France, was the first steam-powered vessel to travel upstream. The first regular steamboat service was set up in 1790, on the Delaware River between Philadelphia and Trenton, but it failed because of competition with established stagecoach services over the same route.

A more efficient steam engine, designed by Scottish engineer James Watt (1736–1819), was adapted by his countryman, engineer William Symington (1763–1831), to power a steamboat called the *Charlotte Dundas* in 1802, on the Forth and Clyde Canal in Scotland. In the United States this was followed by steamboat services on the Hudson River with U.S. engineer Robert Fulton's (1765–1815) *Clermont* and in the Atlantic Ocean and on the Delaware River with U.S engineer John Stevens' (1749–1838) steamboat *Phoenix*.

In the early 19th century, iron began replacing wood in ships' hulls. Although these metal hulls were light, inexpensive, and strong, decades passed before they were fully accepted in the tradition-conscious maritime world. It was the American Civil War (1861–1865) that turned the tide. Artillery shells were designed that could penetrate even the hulls of wooden ships with metal armor, called ironclads.

The all-iron Union ship *Monitor*, which became famous for its evenly matched battle with the ironclad Confederate ship *Merrimac*, also illustrated another development in naval warfare—the replacement of the fixed broadside guns that protruded from ships' hulls with the revolving gun turret (see WARSHIP).

Atlantic crossings

As the American economy grew, trade and travel across the Atlantic became routine. This led to the development of a new way of organizing merchant shipping called packet service. Previously, ships had sailed whenever they were full, when the weather looked good, or at the whim of the owner or captain. With packet service, sailings took place on a regular

---

ABOVE AND BELOW

Hydrofoils and hovercraft are vessels that travel just above the water. Hydrofoils have underwater wings that provide lift when the craft is traveling at high speeds, just as the wings of an airplane do (see FLIGHT, PRINCIPLES OF). Hovercraft propel themselves on top of a cushion of compressed air. The hydrofoil is not likely to be used for shipping cargo, because it requires a great deal of power for its weight. However, both the hydrofoil and the hovercraft are fast and give a smooth ride, so they are well suited to ferrying passengers (see HOVERCRAFT; HYDROFOIL). Large hovercraft are also used as military landing craft.

Submarines, used extensively since World War I (1914–1918) for military operations and research, have been proposed as a way of making shipping more efficient. Submarines are able to travel out of reach of the storms and wind that lash the surface, and by crossing under polar ice, they can drastically cut the distance between some ports. State-of-the-art submarines usually run on relatively inexpensive nuclear power (see SUBMARINE).

A CLOSER LOOK

ANCHORS

Crewmen clean the starboard anchor on the USS Iowa *in 1985.*

Boats do not have brakes, but sometimes they do need to be held in one place, whether overnight in port or for a few hours' fishing. For this purpose, they use anchors, which are attached to the boat by a rope or anchor cable and thrown or dropped overboard. The first anchors were simply large rocks, or baskets or sacks full of smaller stones. Today, anchors come in many shapes and sizes, and they are generally made of iron or steel.

The classic anchor is called a fisherman's anchor or yachtman's anchor and is used mainly with wooden boats. Metal ships generally carry a stockless anchor, which does not have a crosspiece. The anchors of large ships are so heavy that they must be raised and lowered using winches. Yachts and other small craft carry a much lighter anchor that is shaped to dig into the mud of the seabed as the craft pulls on it. Varieties of these lighter anchors include the plow anchor, the mushroom anchor (named for its shape), and the grapnel, which has multiple hooks.

A CLOSER LOOK

schedule, and accommodation was set up for passengers. In 1818, the Black Ball Line became the first to institute packet service, and this was soon copied by other shipping firms. Competitive pressure to stay on schedule and reduce crossing times as much as possible was very intense—ships often sailed all night and pressed ahead regardless of bad weather and dangerous sea conditions.

In 1838, the British paddle wheeler *Sirius* became the first vessel to cross the Atlantic under steampower alone, edging out the American *Great Western* in an 18-day race for the much-coveted honor. Two years later, the British Cunard line started a regular transatlantic passenger and mail service by steamship. The competition for fastest crossing continued, and a prize called the Blue Riband of the Atlantic was introduced. From 1909, the Blue Riband was held for 20 years by Cunard's *Mauretania*. The *Mauretania*'s sister ship, the *Lusitania*, was sunk by a German torpedo during World War I

(1914–1918), killing almost 1200 people, including 128 Americans. Following this, "remember the *Lusitania*" became a rallying cry, which served to increase support throughout the United States for entering the war effort.

After the *Mauretania*, the Blue Riband passed back and forth among the German liners *Bremen* and *Europa*, the Italian *Rex*, and the French *Normandie*. The competition may have contributed to the tragedy of the *Titanic*, which sank in 1912 after operating at full speed into an area known to harbor icebergs (see the box on page 1195). Cunard's luxurious *Queen Mary* held the prize from 1938 until 1952, when it was won by the *United States*, the fastest liner ever. Today, the Blue Riband is history—anyone wanting to cross the Atlantic quickly goes by airplane. Cunard's *Queen Elizabeth II* is now the only passenger liner still making transatlantic trips (see the box on page 1192).

New engines, new fuels

Paddle steamers were the fastest long-distance ships until 1868, when the *Paris* became the first winning ship driven by a screw propeller. Another major improvement in steamship technology occurred around 1900 when smaller, lighter, and simpler steam turbines replaced the older steam engine designs (see STEAM TURBINE).

All 19th-century steamships ran on coal. But in the 1890s, German engineer Rudolf Diesel (1858–1913) built a new type of engine that was fueled with a heavy oil subsequently named diesel fuel. Diesel engines are much smaller, lighter, and more efficient than steam turbines, and they do not need to wait for steam to build up before powering the ship. The first diesel-powered ships went into regular service in 1910.

After about 1930, most steamships ran on oil rather than coal. The name of a ship often revealed what kind of engine it had: if the ship's name started with *SS* it was a steamship, whereas *MS* stood for a motor ship, or diesel (not to be confused with *HMS*, a British designation for Her— or His—Majesty's Ship).

Fishing boats

Fishing boats have also undergone changes as technology has improved, though advances in fishing boat design are also the result of commercial needs. Until the mid-20th century, fishing boats were largely of local design, with different types found even in adjacent fishing ports.

Fishing boat designs changed as fishermen started to move farther afield for their catches. Vessels became larger, processing and factory trawlers were introduced, and the designs of vessels became standardized. The designs of different fishing boats are now determined largely by the fishing methods for which they are intended rather than their place of origin. Steel is the most common construction material for fishing boats, while smaller vessels are increasingly being made of fiberglass.

The modern age

While airplanes have largely replaced passenger liners on routine long-distance trips, most cargo still crosses the oceans on ships. These include huge oil tankers and other ships that are designed to carry a single commodity in bulk. General cargo ships were at one time fairly inefficient because of the different shapes and sizes of boxes and barrels that had to be loaded and unloaded by hand. Today, containerized shipping has become the most common practice, where cargo is shipped in standard-sized containers that are loaded before the ship's arrival. This greatly reduces the amount of time the ship must spend in the harbor. Ships' hulls are divided by racks into standard-sized cells, called holds, for maximum efficiency in stowage. Cranes and other heavy cargo-maneuvering equipment can also be optimized to fit the containers (see OILTANKER AND BULK CARRIER).

One of the important features that distinguishes modern ships from their predecessors is the use of electronic aids for navigation and safety. Earlier mariners relied on simple instruments such as the compass, chronometer, and sextant, which was used for astronomical sightings. Today, automatic pilots are governed by gyroscopes, which can detect any change in direction (see GYROSCOPE). The exact position of a ship can be determined from signals received from the satellite-based Global Positioning System, and electronic logs are kept to track speed and direction (see SATELLITE).

Modern technology also helps pilots avoid collisions with ships, icebergs, and other obstacles. With radar and sonar, radio and sound waves are sent out, and their reflections or return signals are analyzed to detect anything that might be in their path (see RADAR). *Radar* stands for *radio detecting and ranging*. The speed of the detected object can be assessed using the Doppler radar effect, in which signals from an oncoming object are observed to increase in frequency, while signals from a receding object decrease in frequency. *Sonar* stands for *sound navigation ranging*; sonar uses sound waves to locate the position of distant objects (see ACOUSTICS AND SOUND). Commonly used underwater, sonar was developed during World War II (1939–1945) for locating enemy submarines; it is still in widespread use.

S. CALVO

See also: AIRCRAFT CARRIER; BOATBUILDING AND SHIPBUILDING; DEEP-SEA AND DIVING TECHNOLOGY; FERRY; FISHING INDUSTRY; LIGHTHOUSE AND LIGHTSHIP; MARINE ENGINEERING; MERCHANT SHIPS; NAVIGATION; PORT AND HARBOR FACILITIES; POWERBOAT; PROPELLER; RUDDER.

Further reading:

Bolster, J. *Black Jacks: African American Seamen in the Age of Sail.* Cambridge, Massachusetts: Harvard University Press, 1997.
Cahill, R. *Disasters at Sea: Titanic to Exxon Valdez.* New York: American Merchant Marine Museum Foundation, 1991.
Hourani, G. *Arab Seafaring in the Indian Ocean in Ancient and Early Medieval Times.* Princeton: Princeton University Press, 1995.
Ships and Shipwrecks of the Americas: A History Based on Underwater Archaeology. Edited by G. Bass. New York: Thames and Hudson, 1996.
Woodman, R. *The History of the Ship: The Comprehensive Story of Seafaring from the Earliest Times to the Present Day.* New York: Lyons Press, 1997.

SHIPWRECKS

A rusty shipwreck rests on the coast of American Samoa in the Pacific Ocean.

On many coasts, such as the outer banks of North Carolina or islands in the Pacific Ocean, shifting sandbars, unpredictable currents, and stormy weather often make the going rough for seafarers. Sometimes the rusting skeleton of a wrecked ship becomes revealed by changing tides. The Mediterranean Sea, which cargo-laden vessels have traversed for thousands of years, hides all kinds of wreckage debris, from graceful vases to rubber boots.

Until the invention of radio, an ocean voyage meant losing contact with the rest of the world for long periods of time. Caught in a bad storm, a ship could easily sink and disappear without a trace. Technology sometimes brings a false sense of security and is often overcome by the forces of nature. The ocean liner *Titanic* was thought to be unsinkable, so it did not even carry a full complement of lifeboats. When the ship hit an iceberg on its maiden voyage in 1912, it sank, and some 1500 people died. Better communications and tracking systems have made it easier to find ships in distress, but rescue efforts must often contend with the same hazardous weather conditions that caused the problem in the first place. Although coast guard stations operate ships, planes, and helicopters that save many lives, the rescue craft cannot always reach the scene of the accident in time to prevent fatalities.

In some cases, a ship runs into mechanical or other difficulties that leave it stranded but in no immediate danger of sinking. Salvage tugs, which are stationed at ports all over the world, then come into play. These sturdy boats are fitted for ocean travel and carry pumps to put out fires and siphon out flooded ships. They are also supplied with apparatus to perform repairs such as underwater cutting and welding. Finally, if necessary, they can tow the damaged ship to safety.

A CLOSER LOOK

SIEGE WARFARE

Siege warfare was a method of conquering fortified garrisons using special weapons and tactics

Medieval battering rams had iron heads of varying design. The rams were either swung from a support or carried by a team of soldiers.

Movies often show scenes in which attackers attempt to scale the formidable walls of a medieval castle or an ancient city. In reality, conquering garrisons (fortified places where troops were permanently stationed) sometimes took years, and the standoffs were called sieges. From the time of earliest civilization in the Middle East and China until about the 14th century (when the invention of guns revolutionized warfare), laying siege to a fortress or garrisoned town was an essential military skill (see LAND WARFARE). The techniques for doing so, called siege warfare, changed remarkably little throughout that time.

The ideal location for a besieged garrison was on high ground so that defenders could rain missiles on the attackers struggling to climb up. Castle architects created obstacles such as walls that sloped outward, and moats (ditches around the walls that were usually filled with water). Parapets (protective walls at the top edge of a fortress wall) and thin window slits in the walls enabled defenders to rain down arrows, spears, stones, fire, and boiling water, oil, or pitch on their enemies. Walls sometimes had bastions (projections) from which defenders could fire even when attackers were right under the defenders' wall. Defenders stockpiled supplies inside their fort and an internal water source was essential. The defenders also tried to destroy or poison sources of food and water the attackers might use outside the garrison (see also FORTIFICATION AND DEFENSE).

WEAPONS AND TACTICS

The least wasteful method of taking a besieged city (both in lives and weapons) was to starve the defenders into submission. However, it required patience

and discipline for the besieging army to wait for many months or even years. Sometimes the army needed to try to end the siege quickly. As in other types of warfare, the determination and spirit of the opposing forces were vital factors. Another relatively easy way to win a siege was to enter the fort secretly by collaborating with traitors inside, which happened surprisingly often. If it came to a battle, a variety of weapons were used.

Battering rams

The weakest parts of a defensive wall were its wooden gates, so from the earliest times, long and heavy wooden beams, called battering rams, were used to break them. Battering rams were usually hung from a frame on wheels and swung repeatedly against a wall or gate by groups of soldiers. The frame was often covered by a wicker or wooden roof, which was itself covered by layers of leather, sand, and felt to protect the attacking soldiers from missiles and fire. The battering end of the beam was usually a piece of metal shaped like a ram's head (hence the name) or a spike. Hooks or spears were frequently attached to the end of battering rams to loosen stones in fortress walls to enable invaders to break through. The Romans had all-iron battering rams. Some medieval European battering rams were rotated mechanically to drill into walls.

Siege towers

Climbing garrison walls with the help of ladders (a technique called escalation) was usually unsuccessful unless carried out by surprise, because the climbers were exposed to continuous fire. One solution was to build wooden towers on wheels, known as belfries, which were the same height as the walls. These towers had several stories packed with soldiers who fired arrows from behind cover to drive the defenders from the walls. The lowest story usually had a battering ram, and the top carried a hinged bridge used by a storming party to cross to the top of the wall. Fresh animal hides were hung over the outside of the tower to protect the wood against fire. The Romans had armored siege towers with elevators to bring assault teams up to the top of the wall quickly.

CORE FACTS

■ Forts could sometimes be conquered with very little fighting by starving out defenders or by taking advantage of treachery within.

■ Specialized siege weapons included battering rams, siege towers, and projectile-throwing machines.

■ Soldiers sometimes tunneled beneath fortress walls and collapsed them. After the invention of gunpowder, explosive devices were used to achieve the same aim.

Roofed or wheeled galleries were also used to protect the soldiers as they built causeways over the moat so that they could pull towers up to the wall.

Mining

A highly effective method of destroying a garrison involved digging under the walls, supporting the foundations with wood, and then setting the supports on fire, causing the walls to collapse. From around 1300 C.E. in Europe, and probably earlier in China, gunpowder was sometimes used to blow up these supporting posts or even the walls themselves.

Soldiers also dug trenches outside the walls to protect themselves from heavy fire as they advanced. Narrow zigzag trenches, known as saps, were dug quickly (by soldiers called sappers) from main trenches toward the moat, where the sappers would build bridges for other soldiers to cross.

Catapults

Many different types of mechanical artillery were used in siege warfare. Catapult-type machines, used in classical Mediterranean civilizations and in China, derived their power from twisted cords made of elastic material such as sinew or hair. One end of a lever was inserted between the cords, and the other end, on which a projectile was placed, was drawn back and fastened with a hook. The tension in the cord was increased by twisting it. When the hook was released, the elasticity of the twisted cord jerked the lever up, hurling the projectile up and forward. Catapults were rarely accurate or strong enough to destroy walls or clear parapets of defenders. They were most effective when used from inside garrisons to cripple machines outside or to break up charging soldiers. Catapults also fired incendiaries.

Ballistas

A ballista was a type of catapult that hurled arrows or spears. A windlass (a simple wooden winch) was used to draw the projectiles back against the tension of a twisted cord; when released, the projectiles flew forward. Ballistas could be fired before they were fully drawn back, which meant their range could be crudely controlled. In the Middle Ages (5th to 13th century C.E.), ballistas in the form of crossbows were used, with the elasticity of the huge bow providing their power (see BOW AND ARROW).

Trebuchets

The trebuchet was invented in late medieval Europe. It worked like a seesaw. One end of a lever held a heavy weight, and a projectile was placed in a cup at the other end or, for greater range, in a sling. The end with the projectile was winched down then let go; the weight caused the lever to fly up and send the projectile on its way. Trebuchets were more powerful than twisted-cord weapons such as catapults and ballistas and could do considerable damage to the walls of a castle. They were also fairly accurate and powerful enough to be used some distance away from the fortifications under attack.

History enthusiasts dressed as Roman legionnaires load a catapult during the reenactment of a battle.

Gunpowder

Gunpowder was invented in China in the 10th century C.E. and used by the Chinese in warfare from the 12th century on (see EXPLOSIVE). Guns and cannons were integrated into European warfare in the 15th century, making the destruction of castle walls and enemy troops far easier. In response, defenders built thicker walls and used guns and cannon themselves. Towers for artillery and trenches for infantry were used by attackers to move slowly across ground defended by sweeping gunfire.

M. COBERLY

See also: ARMOR; BOMB, SHELL, AND GRENADE; HAND WEAPONS; ROCKETRY.

Further reading:
Dargie, R. *Castle under Siege.* Hove, England: Wayland Publishers, 1998.
Diehl, D. *Sieges: Castles at War.* Dallas: Taylor Publishing, 1999.
Gravett, C. *Medieval Siege Warfare.* Oxford, England: Osprey Publishing, 1990.
Parker, G. *The Cambridge Illustrated History of Warfare.* New York: Cambridge University Press, 1995.

MASADA: ROMAN SIEGE WARFARE

After the Roman Empire put down the first Jewish revolt in 70 C.E., the remaining rebels fled to fortresses in the desert, which were all eventually taken by siege. The last of these, Masada, stood on a mountain plateau 1300 ft (400 m) above the Dead Sea, which enabled it to hold out for three or four years.

Around 10,000 Roman troops camped around the base of the mountain, which was held by around 1000 defenders. The Romans built a wall completely around the mountain to prevent the rebels from slipping out. They then constructed a remarkable 3-mile (4.8-km) earthen ramp up one side of the plateau. When the ramp was complete, the Romans brought siege engines and troops up it to destroy and enter one of Masada's gates. Most of the defenders, anticipating torture and death, killed themselves before the Romans broke through.

HISTORY OF TECHNOLOGY

SKYSCRAPER

Skyscrapers are tall buildings that use modern building techniques

This aerial photograph taken above Lake Michigan in 1997 shows the many skyscrapers in downtown Chicago.

CONNECTIONS

● A **CRANE** is an essential piece of **CONSTRUCTION AND EARTHMOVING MACHINERY**: it can lift building materials to the top of a skyscraper.

● The **COMPOSITE** of steel and concrete used to build skyscrapers is often used to make **SUSPENSION BRIDGES**.

The development of the high-rise building began in the United States in the late 19th century. Architects were beginning to discover the limitations of traditional building techniques, and the tallest buildings were four or five storys high. Buildings relied solely on the idea of the load-bearing wall—the barrier between the inside and outside of the building that also transmitted the building's weight to the ground (see BUILDING TECHNIQUES, TRADITIONAL). The taller and heavier the building became, the thicker these walls had to be to support the weight. Because people still had to travel up and down by the stairs, taller buildings were also impractical.

However, there was growing social and economic pressure for taller buildings. New York and Chicago were becoming overcrowded, and, with the formation of large corporations, individual companies wanted to house all their employees in one building. This need, along with a growing understanding of the impression a company's building could make on its customers, drove the invention of the skyscraper.

The birth of the skyscraper

The development of the first real high-rise buildings relied on two inventions. The first of these was Elisha Graves Otis's (1811–1861) safety elevator, used in a cast-iron building on Broadway, New York, in 1857 and in the same city's seven-story Equitable Building in 1870 (see ELEVATOR). Although the first buildings with elevators dwarfed their neighbors, they were built using traditional techniques.

The second crucial invention was mass-produced structural steel. U.S. architect William Le Baron Jenney (1832–1907) was the first to realize that a steel frame, rather than masonry in the walls themselves, could be used to carry the building's weight to the ground—an idea he first introduced on a small scale in the Home Insurance Building in Chicago in 1884. This structure used steel columns to support the weight, surrounded with a thin curtain wall that served only as a casing to keep out the weather.

Early skyscrapers disguised their structures behind traditional facades, but from the early 1900s, architects started to recognize the freedom the new building techniques gave them. A key building often called the first skyscraper was New York's 792-ft (241-m) Woolworth Building, built from 1910 to 1913, which pioneered many important construction methods, including the principle of using deep foundation piles, and solved many of the problems of supplying services to the upper storys.

Construction of skyscrapers

Changes in engineering and materials during the 20th century have given rise to many skyscraper construction techniques, but today, four principle construction methods are widely in use.

Core wall construction. The simplest form of skyscraper construction relies on the principle of the cantilever (see STRUCTURES). The center of the building is a hollow tube made of reinforced concrete (see CEMENT AND CONCRETE). With its solid walls, the box is very rigid. Cantilever beams are anchored in the core wall, and are made of prestressed concrete, which increases the weight they can support.

The cantilevers are extended from the core in every direction, resulting in a cylindrical or polygonal building. A lightweight concrete floor is laid on top of the cantilevers, and, when necessary, steel structural columns transfer weight down the outer ends of the cantilevers to the ground, adding to the building's stability. An exterior curtain wall, usually made of glass, is suspended from the floors.

Core wall construction is a popular method of construction for small skyscrapers. It essentially creates a traditional building turned inside out, so the floors are outside the load-bearing wall. This allows the floors to be large open spaces, while the core can act as a useful conduit for elevators, stairwells, and utilities. However, there is still an upper limit to the height of building a core wall can support, so for buildings above 20 storys, other techniques are used.

CORE FACTS

■ The most important element of skyscraper design is the use of a load-bearing frame that is independent of the building's walls.

■ Skyscrapers use a variety of strong building materials, including steel, concrete, and glass.

■ Different methods of construction are used for building skyscrapers of different heights.

■ The tallest skyscrapers are built from several skyscraper frames joined together.

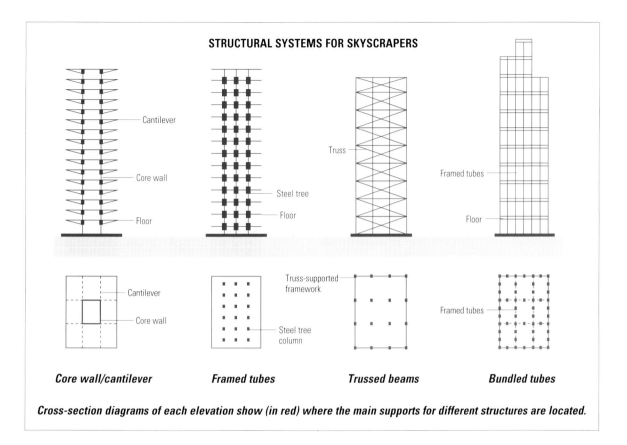

STRUCTURAL SYSTEMS FOR SKYSCRAPERS

Cantilever

Core wall

Floor

Steel tree

Floor

Truss

Framed tubes

Floor

Cantilever

Core wall

Truss-supported framework

Steel tree column

Framed tubes

Core wall/cantilever   **Framed tubes**   **Trussed beams**   **Bundled tubes**

Cross-section diagrams of each elevation show (in red) where the main supports for different structures are located.

Framed tube construction. The framed tube method is based on steel components called trees. The trees are stacked, then linked together to form a framework of beams and columns that run close to the perimeter of the building, and are anchored to the ground by deep piles. Steel beams are fixed to the trees, crisscrossing the building and supporting corrugated metal floors overlaid with concrete. The outsides of the trees support a glass curtain wall.

With a framed tube building, it is the network of columns formed by the trees that supports the structure. Because the tube is a flexible structure, it bends slightly in the wind, making it more resistant to sudden winds than a completely rigid building—the forces created by expansion and compression of opposite sides of the tube act to right the building. This construction method has particular advantages because it is not subject to the usual height limitations. To build a higher or heavier building, it is simply necessary to increase the number or width of the load-bearing columns. The only restrictions concern the positioning of the building's windows.

Trussed beams. To get around the problem of the increasing number of columns required for taller buildings, the main forces in the building can be transferred to trusses—long, diagonal beams arranged in an X across each wall. Since these transmit most of the building's weight to the ground, they must be well anchored. A horizontal and vertical steel framework extends from the trusses to make the building's walls, and this supports the beams and curtain wall just as in a framed tube building.

Bundled tubes. Today, the tallest buildings in the world use bundled tube construction. As its name suggests, this method involves building with a series of framed tubes arranged alongside and on top of each other. Bundled tubes are very stable, and since weight is transmitted down the internal frames, the number of columns on each frame can be reduced. It is because each layer of tubes provides a stable platform on which further layers can rest that the Sears Tower in Chicago has its tiered appearance, and the Petronas Twin Towers in Kuala Lumpur are tapered.

G. SPARROW

See also: BUILDING TECHNIQUES, MODERN; CIVIL ENGINEERING; FOUNDATION; INSULATION.

Further reading:
Gooderham, M. *A Building Goes Up: The Making of a Skyscraper.* Toronto: HarperCollins, 1998.
Powell, R. *Rethinking the Skyscraper.* New York: Whitney Library of Design, 1999.
Sabbagh, K. *Skyscraper.* New York: Viking, 1990.

REACH FOR THE SKY

Until recently, the skyscraper was an American phenomenon, but it has become a symbol of economic prosperity in many countries. Some of the world's tallest buildings are the 1483-ft (452-m) Petronas Twin Towers in Malaysia, but the race for the title of world's tallest building is on.

The sudden economic slowdown of the late 1990s has put many of Southeast Asia's promising projects in doubt. At the turn of the century, the most likely contender for the tallest building was the 1508-ft (460-m) World Financial Center in the heart of the financial district of Shanghai, China. The 94-story building is scheduled for completion in 2001.

HISTORY OF TECHNOLOGY

SLAUGHTERHOUSE

The purpose of a slaughterhouse is to kill animals and prepare their carcasses for meat processing

Slaughterhouse workers drain the blood from hog carcasses at a slaughterhouse in Dubuque, Iowa.

A modern slaughterhouse is a specialized processing plant for the rapid, efficient, and hygienic slaughter of livestock. It processes the products of the livestock-farming industry (animals) into raw materials for the food-processing industry (meat and meat products). Other materials for use in nonfood industries are also obtained; for example, bones are used in the preparation of plant fertilizers.

Most slaughterhouses are highly mechanized production-line operations, which can quickly handle many animals (see PRODUCTION ENGINEERING AND PROCESS CONTROL). In standard cattle slaughterhouses, around 250 cattle are killed per hour. The highest degree of automation is achieved with poultry because of their small size.

Preparing livestock
Animals are starved and given only water for several hours before slaughter, which makes their carcasses easier to process. Since stress makes livestock difficult to handle, and can even affect meat quality, animals awaiting slaughter are usually held in as spacious conditions as possible. Space requirements for holding livestock vary from country to country.

Preslaughter stunning
Before slaughter, animals are stunned unconscious to reduce their stress and pain. Large animals are restrained in a rack or pen and stunned by one of various methods. An electric shock may be applied to the head, a bolt may be shot into the brain, or animals may be anesthetized by exposure to carbon dioxide gas. Poultry are nearly always stunned by electric shock. This is achieved by suspending them by their legs from an overhead conveyor, which moves the birds so that their heads pass through an electrified basin of water (see CONVEYOR).

Slaughter
Stunned animals are killed by severing the large blood vessels in the throat while they are suspended upside down from a conveyor. This is usually done by hand with a knife, although poultry are often killed with a mechanized rotary blade. Animals are then hung to bleed, and the blood is collected for making certain foods and for use in other industries.

Dressing the carcass
The bled carcasses move on the conveyor system to the next stage. For most livestock, this will be skinning, either by hand or by machine. Skins are retained for leather manufacture (see LEATHER). Pigs and poultry are not usually skinned, however. Pigs are scalded in hot water to loosen their hairs, which are then removed by mechanical scouring. Poultry go through similar mechanized processes in order to remove feathers.

Carcasses are then beheaded, and poultry also have their feet removed. The next stage is evisceration (removal of the internal organs). This is done by hand, except for poultry, which may be gutted by a specialized machine. The organs, called offal, will either be used for food production or removed for disposal. The carcasses of large animals are then split down the spine into two halves. The final stage is chilling, which is done in a large cooling room or, in the case of poultry, in cold-water tanks. Chilled carcasses can then be shipped (under cooled conditions) to butchers, processors, or packing plants (see FOOD PRESERVATION; REFRIGERATION).

Slaughterhouse standards
All slaughterhouses in the United States must conform to certain legal requirements, which define standards for animal welfare, hygiene, and carcass quality. Most countries have similar standards. Frequent inspections ensure that standards are met; in the United States these are organized by the U.S. Department of Agriculture. These may include veterinary examination of animals before slaughter, inspection of all aspects of the production line, and inspection of dressed carcasses (see VETERINARY MEDICINE). Certain specialist meat markets may require additional standards to be met, such as adherence to Jewish and Islamic religious dietary laws or to organic marketing standards (see ORGANIC FARMING AND SUSTAINABLE AGRICULTURE).

T. ALLMAN

See also: FOOD PRESERVATION; FOOD TECHNOLOGY; LIVESTOCK FARMING.

Further reading:
Romans, J., *et al. The Meat We Eat.* Danville, Illinois: Interstate Publishers, 1994.

CONNECTIONS

● Some **ADHESIVES** were traditionally made of animal products.

● Animal products are used by some companies in the manufacture of **COSMETICS AND PERFUMES**.

SNOW AND ICE TRAVEL

Traveling on or through snow and ice is made possible by a number of different technologies

Humans did not evolve to travel on ice or snow and, consequently, they need artificial extensions to feet and sometimes hands to get around on those surfaces. That has not stopped them from developing efficient modes of transportation in these harsh, cold, and often dangerous conditions.

Remaining on top of soft snow is similar to staying afloat on water. The basic technique involves spreading the weight of the body over a wide surface. (Feet have too small a surface area for the weight to do this, so people walking in snow will sink into it.) The most common devices for spreading weight are skis or sleds. The best way to move on snow and ice is to slide over them. This happens as the pressure of the body's weight melts the snow or ice, creating a film of water that presents little friction.

When body weight is concentrated on a small area, as when skates or runners are used, the increased pressure causes more melting. With even less friction, high speeds can be achieved. In addition, falling down on ice is much less dangerous than falling onto rocks, because bodies tend to slide when they hit the ground.

Snowshoes

Solid wooden snowshoes were used by prehistoric humans from the ice age on (SEE PREHISTORIC TECHNOLOGY). The open-frame design used today was invented by native North Americans for hunting and trapping during winter. Today snowshoes are used mainly for recreation and by infantry troops trained in alpine warfare.

Modern snowshoe frames are ovals made of bent wood or aluminum, partly filled in by rawhide lacing or by pieces of solid fabric attached by nylon cord. Rawhide lacing is highly resistant to cutting and breaking in temperatures below freezing (32°F; 0°C), but nylon cord is stronger in warmer temperatures when the cords become wet. Bindings of various kinds hold the walker's toes to the snowshoe, while the rest of the foot is free to rise with each step. Serrated metal or spikes on the bottom help to grip in steep, slippery terrain, and a ski pole or ice ax can be used for balance.

Snowshoes come in several sizes and shapes. A larger, heavier person needs a larger snowshoe to stay on top of soft snow. The front of the snowshoe should be bent upward for easier walking in soft

CORE FACTS

- People stay on top of soft snow by spreading their weight over broad surfaces, such as snowshoes, skis, or flat sleds.
- People travel faster on hard snow or ice by concentrating their weight on small surfaces, such as runners or blades.
- It is important to match snowshoe, ski, or skate with body type and level of skill, as well as with the type of competition or activity and the snow conditions.
- Motorized snowmobiles are used for practical travel, and skiing, skating, snowshoeing, and sledding have become sports.

CONNECTIONS

- Modern snow and ice **SPORTS EQUIPMENT** has been developed using a number of different technologies to ensure the user is safe and can make the most of their chosen sport.

Snowshoes stand in a snowbank in Anchorage, Alaska, during a dogsled event.

powdery snow, but it should be flat for ascending slopes of compacted snow. Snowshoes that are too long or too wide can be very uncomfortable and inefficient to walk in.

Skis

Skis have been used for travel in northern European countries since prehistoric times. Before modern sport skiing, people often used one pole, or no poles, to free their hands for hunting, fighting, or carrying things. Nowadays, two poles are commonly used to help with balance and turning while traveling at high speed down very steep slopes.

Skis must be matched to each individual's size and skill level, and also to the type of skiing he or she is doing. Because long skis are more difficult to turn, beginners start with skis that are shorter than their own height and gradually become able to handle longer ones. Cross-country skis, for traveling mainly in a straight line, are longer than skis for slalom and giant slalom, which involve constant turning.

However, longer skis are more stable than short ones, so they are also useful to downhill racers who want to go very fast without turning much. The hourglass shape of most skis (narrower in the center, wider at the tip and the tail—called the sidecut) also helps skis turn. Skis for slalom and giant slalom have pronounced sidecuts, while cross-country skis have little or none. Jumping skis are longer, wider, and heavier than downhill skis and are designed for speed and stability.

Skis are built with a slight arch, called the camber. When the skier's weight—or a propulsive kick—presses the arch down, the ski's bottom surface grips the snow, preventing backward sliding. When the arch rises away from the snow, the tip and tail of the ski glide faster. Downhill skis tend to be especially resistant to bending in order to go fast, while cross-country skis are built to grip the snow when the skier kicks strongly, and also to glide when simply supporting the body. Skiing on hard snow requires stiffer skis than skiing on soft powder.

Skis have wood or foam cores with layers of fiberglass woven around them. The bottoms are made of hard plastic to withstand wear from rocks and other surfaces. Most skis are also waxed regularly to reduce friction against the snow. However, different waxes reduce friction at different temperatures: a wax designed for $-20\,°F$ ($-29\,°C$) will actually produce more friction if the temperature rises to $0\,°F$ ($-18\,°C$), obliging skiers to stop and apply a different wax. Cross-country skiers use friction-producing waxes on the arches of their skis to make them grip harder when pushed down by a propulsive kick. Some cross-country skis are also made with irregularities in the middle of the ski, called fish scales, to produce a frictional force without waxing.

Ski boots for downhill racing are made from plastic, which transmits even small movements of the

DAMPING VIBRATIONS IN SKIS

Because skiing has become a major international sport, the technology behind the different types of skiing has accelerated dramatically. Recently ski manufacturers have developed several high-tech methods of damping vibrations in skis, allowing beginners to have better control of their skis on bumpy terrain and experts to ski faster without losing control. An electronic method formerly classified by the U.S. Department of Defense absorbs vibrations and dissipates the energy as heat and light through a red lamp that glows on the ski. Another method inserts magnets into the layers of material in the ski. As vibrations start to move the layers apart, magnetic attraction draws them back together. A simpler method is to place rubber pads on the bindings of the skis to absorb vibrations.

A CLOSER LOOK

skier's legs and feet to the skis, giving greater control. The high, stiff boots also prevent ankle and leg injuries, give greater insulation than leather, last longer, and have standard bindings that are safer. Cross-country skiers use leather boots because of their comfort and flexibility when walking.

A number of variations on skiing have been invented. A skier can sit on a skibob, which is like a bicycle with skis instead of wheels, and glide downhill. Hang-gliders sometimes work up speed to take off by racing downhill on skis. Very short, wide skis—called skiboards—are ridden downhill in plastic boots. The popular snowboards are used to race or to do acrobatics (in leather boots), as on surfboards or skateboards.

Ice skates

The earliest skates, dating from prehistoric times, were bones ground to produce flat bottoms and tied under shoes. The wearer propelled themselves along with sharp poles. Skates made of wood or steel, tied to street shoes, were used for everyday travel in Holland and elsewhere for sport until the 20th century. Today, steel blades, screwed onto leather boots, are used for racing, ice hockey, and artistic and acrobatic figure skating and ice dancing.

As with skis, different types of skates are used for different competitions. Blades for racing are long, straight, and flat, and blades for figures (such as tracing figure eights) are almost as flat, to achieve long, steady glides. By contrast, freestyle dancing, pairs dancing, ice dancing, and hockey use short blades, curved slightly from back to front, to aid in making quick turns. Freestyle blades cannot be too short, however, because they must support landings from jumps. Racing and hockey blades are thinner than figure-skating blades to allow for greater speeds. Skates used in figure skating all have small, sharp projections at the fronts of their blades called toe picks or toe racks. These are used mainly in jumping, pivoting, spinning, and other tricks. Blades for the acrobatic freestyle skating have especially long toe picks, while others have shorter ones to avoid tripping. Freestyle boots are stiffer than others and give greater control. Each blade has two edges, with a tiny hollow between them; hockey blades have especially deep hollows to help the blades sink into the ice in stopping and turning.

Sleds

Sleds, pulled by humans as well as by dogs, have been used from ancient times to carry loads (see the box on page 1204). Traditional Native American sleds were made of driftwood, with runners reinforced by bone. In Europe and Asia, sleds and sleighs were wood or metal, and eventually had metal runners. Sleighs pulled by horses or reindeer are still used by Arctic people today. In the 20th century, as mechanized vehicles replaced them, sleds have chiefly become a recreational mode of transport.

Two exciting international competitions have developed in which sleds race down curving, icy tunnels at speeds of up to 90 mph (145 km/h): bobsledding and luge, a small sled that is ridden in the supine position. Bobsleds are long metal sleds with hoods in front. They carry two or four riders, who sit facing forward. The bobsled has two sets of runners: the front ones are steered by the driver, the back ones are fixed. Weight shifting by the team members also helps to steer. Luges are flat wooden sleds with a single set of metal runners. They carry one or two riders, who lie back most of the time to avoid being slowed by air friction. The driver steers by pushing against the runners with his or her feet, and also by the riders shifting their weight around.

Snowmobiles

Snowmobiles are gasoline-engine vehicles propelled by a rubber track and steered by handlebars attached to two short skis on the front. The more powerful

ENVIRONMENTAL DAMAGE CAUSED BY SNOWMOBILES

A snowmobile jumps off a small slope on Mount Bailey in Oregon.

Any winter sport may disturb wilderness areas, but the explosion in the numbers of snowmobiles used in recent years has created special problems. Snowmobiles often frighten deer, elk, and moose, driving them from winter grounds or disrupting their mating behavior. Some irresponsible snowmobilers even chase animals for what they consider as sport.

Snowmobilers sometimes frighten livestock, cut wire fences, injure seedling trees, or damage structures on ranches that are covered by snow. Because snowmobiles are not limited to roads, it is difficult to monitor them, and cases of vandalism or theft from ranches or from empty summer cabins have occurred.

The loud engine noise of snowmobiles is sometimes offensive to the people who live or spend holidays in wilderness areas. A few states in the United States have set specific sound levels for snowmobiles and have prohibited snowmobiling on farms and newly replanted lumbering areas. U.S. National Parks limit snowmobiles to certain trails in certain areas, but U.S. National Forests welcome snowmobiling, preferring instead to educate the public on how to act in a responsible way.

WIDER IMPACT

The Yamal, *a nuclear-powered Russian icebreaker, makes its way to the North Pole.*

snowmobiles can go over 80 mph (130 km/h). They are popular for winter recreational use because they can carry people quickly into isolated wilderness areas, and they also have the appeal of power acceleration and high speeds. In snowy country, snowmobiles have replaced skis and snowshoes for rural law enforcement personnel, outdoor research, rescue, surveying, repair and maintenance work, and military exercises. Inuits and Laplanders (the Arctic people of America and Europe, respectively) use snowmobiles to herd reindeer. Snowmobiles have almost completely replaced sleds.

Snowplows and icebreakers

Sometimes travel is not possible unless snow and ice are removed from the path of the vehicle. The simplest snowplows are trucks or tractors with heavy blades attached in front to push the snow out of the way. More specialized snowblowers, some small enough to be used by a single person walking along, break up the snow and blow it up and out to the side.

Icebreakers are ships with steel-reinforced, wedgelike bows. They ride up on sea ice, cracking it with the weight of the ship, or ram it until it breaks. Icebreakers lead other ships through sea ice, as well as rescuing stranded ships and people. Russia, Canada, and the United States maintain large fleets of icebreakers, some powered by nuclear reactors.

M. COBERLY

See also: ANIMAL TRANSPORT; HORSE-DRAWN TRANSPORT; PREHISTORIC TECHNOLOGY.

Further reading:

Milton, S. *Skate: One Hundred Years of Figure Skating.* North Pomfret: Trafalgar Square, 1996.
Scott, A. *Tracks across Alaska: A Dog Sled Journey.* New York: The Atlantic Monthly Press, 1990.
Walter, C. *The Complete Idiot's Guide to Skiing.* New York: Alpha Books, 1997.
Zives, J. *Back-Country Skier: Your Complete Guide to Ski Touring.* Champaign, Illinois: Human Kinetics, 1999.

DOGSLEDS

No longer an everyday means of transportation in the north, dogsledding has become a sport. Dogsled races are held frequently in the parts of North America that have high snowfall every year.

One of the great appeals of dogsledding is the close bond between driver and dogs, who work as a team. Sled dogs think for themselves, sense danger humans may be unaware of (such as shifting sea ice), and often find their way when the driver is lost. Traditionally, Native American sled dog teams were not treated as pets and could become dangerous when they were hungry. Just like a wild pack, the team usually had an alpha male and female at the top of a strict hierarchy, which was maintained by fighting. Nowadays, dogs are better fed, and fighting is discouraged. A modern dog team considers the human driver as the alpha leader.

Modern dogsleds are made of wood with hard plastic runners and nylon, rather than rawhide, lines. The driver stands on the back of the sled, holding handlebars; a steel claw, pressed into the snow by the driver, acts as a brake. There are two methods of harnessing dog teams in North America. The old Inuit way, still widely used in Canada, attaches each dog individually to the front of the sled, so the team fans out. This works well in country without trees or narrow trails. The long lines give the dogs freedom to avoid obstacles and insecure footing, but they are more likely to become tangled. The dogs are guided by voice command and by a whip, which is cracked in the air on the side opposite to the direction they are supposed to turn.

The other method, used more in Alaska and other parts of the United States, harnesses the dogs in pairs by short lines on each side of a central line. Control is entirely by voice. The lead dog has great importance in this system, and dogs in other parts of the line also have special roles. For example, the pair nearest the sled—called the wheel dogs—are usually the biggest and strongest dogs and may carry most of the sled's weight on difficult turns.

A CLOSER LOOK

SOFTWARE AND PROGRAMMING

Software programs are the instructions that control the operation of computers

Today software is a huge business, with hundreds of different products available on DVDs, CD-ROMs, or floppy diskettes in stores across the world. But before the 1980s, most software was written by a programmer for a specific computer to do a specific task. Even today, the computer systems of large companies use custom-written software, and almost all companies employ at least a small staff to manage the company's computers and software (see COMPUTER).

Software may be categorized in a number of ways. One of the most basic is whether it is systems software or applications software. Systems software includes programs that manage the computer's memory, keep its file system organized, and control peripheral devices such as printers, modems, disk drives, and monitors (see TELEVISION AND COMPUTER MONITOR). Operating systems such as Unix, MSDOS, or Windows are systems software and perform all these tasks. Internet browsers and databases are also classified as systems software, since they also interface with the hard disk or peripheral devices.

Applications software includes programs that can be used for specific tasks other than running the computer itself. Common applications include word processing, spreadsheets, payroll or personal finance packages, and games.

Specifying actions

Regardless of what a computer program does, its basic function is the same: to provide a list of specific instructions and the order and conditions in which they are to be performed. The list of steps in a food recipe is analogous to a simple software program. For example, to make a batch of muffins, a selection of dry ingredients, such as flour and sugar, and moist ingredients, such as milk and eggs, are required. These ingredients are analogous to the data that a user would input into a computer program. The recipe, much like a computer program, describes how to process these items one step at a time, according to various conditions.

Programmers often use a notation system called pseudocode to simplify their program and allow them to plan its production more easily. Pseudocode is a way to break down the task of program into individual logical steps, before translating the steps into any particular computer language. If the muffin recipe were written in pseudocode, it might look something like this:

CORE FACTS

- Computer programs are ordered lists of specific actions to be performed by a computer.
- Computer languages provide a bridge between a description of the desired action and the binary code that computers can understand.
- Structured and object-oriented programming are ways to improve software writing and maintainability and to encourage reuse.
- Ada Lovelace, the daughter of poet Lord Byron, assisted the inventor of the first computer, Charles Babbage, and is often considered to be the first programmer.

CONNECTIONS

- **PATTERN RECOGNITION** and **VOICE RECOGNITION AND SYNTHESIS** software can give a computer **ARTIFICIAL INTELLIGENCE,** allowing it to do some of the tasks performed by the human brain.

TRANSACTION PROCESSING

Software has radically altered how businesses and their customers handle money.

The concept of the transaction is central to business computing, just as it is to business in general. Examples of transactions include booking an airline reservation, buying or selling a share of stock, or withdrawing money from an automatic teller machine (ATM). Transaction processing systems require a database that is consulted to determine whether the transaction is possible, and upon which the transaction is performed and recorded. However, the physical location of the transaction may be far from the database itself.

For example, an ATM network includes many terminals. They all connect to the network's central computer, which in turn communicates with all the banks served by the network. For each transaction, the network computer connects to the bank specified in the coding on the user's card. When the user enters a desired transaction, such as a withdrawal, first the request is checked against business rules such as the maximum allowable amount that may be withdrawn at an ATM. If the request is acceptable, the withdrawal amount is then checked against the user's account balance.

In transaction processing, it is necessary to guard against simultaneous occurrences to prevent errors. Suppose a joint savings account contains $100, and one account holder goes to an ATM to withdraw that amount. At about the same time, before that withdrawal is recorded in the database, the other account holder attempts to make a withdrawal. Allowing this to happen would be a problem for the bank, so when the first transaction on an account begins, that account is locked to prevent others from accessing it until the transaction process is completed.

WIDER IMPACT

1. Mix dry ingredients.
2. Mix moist ingredients.
3. Add moist ingredients to dry ingredients.
4. Mix until well blended.
5. Spoon into muffin tin.
6. If muffin pan is glass then set oven to 325°F, else set oven to 350°F.
7. Bake for 30 minutes.
8. Remove from oven.

There are a few important things to notice about this list of steps. First, the steps must be performed in the right order. If the ingredients were baked before being mixed, muffins would not be the result. In a computer program, if the steps are not performed in the right order, the program would crash and fail to perform the task it is designed to do.

The fourth step—*mix until well blended*—is a type of statement that in computer programming is called a "do loop." This specifies that an action be performed until a particular set of conditions is achieved. Similarly, in calling for baking temperatures suitable for different types of pans in the sixth step, a conditional statement is used: *if* a particular condition exists, *then* do something; *else* do something different. As with a recipe, the results of a computer program should be reproducible. Given the same ingredients (or data) and the same conditions, the same result should always be achieved.

Computer languages

Pseudocode is easy to write, but unfortunately computers do not understand it. In fact, at the most basic level, computers only understand the binary code of ones and zeros. For each type of computer processor, particular combinations of binary code translate into specific low-level operations such as switching a circuit on and off or moving a piece of data into a memory register. These codes are called the computer's instruction set, or its machine language. Often these numeric instructions are given short alphanumeric names, making an assembler language. This language is easier for humans to understand. A program called an assembler can translate a program written in assembler language into the machine language the computer can understand.

However, this process soon became too slow as programs became more powerful. Therefore, in the 1950s higher-level languages were developed for faster and simpler programming. These languages are much easier to work with, because each of their statements represents several steps of machine or assembler language. In addition, the statements are more like English, or at least resemble familiar arithmetic or algebraic expressions. This makes the logic of a program easier to follow. Typical statements in higher-level languages include "PRINT NAME, ADDRESS," "NET=GROSS−WITHHOLDING," and "DO WHILE x<10." The exact form of the statements depends on the particular language, each having its own syntax.

An advantage of higher-level languages is that a programmer can learn one and use it on a number of different computers, as long as a compiler program is available. The compiler is similar to an assembler in that it is a type of software that takes the source code written in the higher-level language and translates it into the machine language suitable for the specific type of computer. For commonly used languages, compilers have been developed for most popular types of computers.

Computer programmers usually know several higher-level languages, because each is suitable for different types of applications. One of the earliest computer languages was FORTRAN. Short for *for-*

mula translation, this language was designed for numeric applications and quickly became an essential tool for scientists and engineers. As computers became more common in business, a need arose for a language that handled strings of characters, such as names and addresses, more efficiently. The result was the Common Business Oriented Language, or COBOL. Many other languages were developed, some for special purposes and others to fix perceived problems in existing languages. While many languages are no longer in use, FORTRAN and COBOL are still used today. Other higher-level languages commonly in use today are BASIC (Beginner's All-Purpose Symbolic Instruction Code); Pascal; and C, C+, and C++—a group of powerful languages that grew up along with the Unix operating system.

In the infancy of computing, hardware was large and expensive and memory was at a premium. Programmers would spend long hours making each line of code as efficient as possible. But the price of hardware has come down, and the amount of accessible memory and hard disk capacity increased exponentially at the same time as computers began to be used in almost every field of activity. Machine efficiency became less important than making the best use of programmers' time. Computer code had to become easier to maintain and reuse.

Software architectures

Early programmers wrote their codes however they seemed most efficient and expedient. They often wrote complex lists of statements that were very difficult for another programmer to follow through.

The result was referred to as "spaghetti code"—programs that were almost impossible to maintain or develop, particularly once the original programmer had moved on.

A schoolgirl takes a computer programming class in Israel.

MARKUP LANGUAGES

The first applications for computers were numerical. Computers are ideal for making complex calculations at high speed, and they are still used extensively for that purpose. But as they became an indispensable part of operations in business, government, and science, it became important to work with text and image documents, as well as new forms of multimedia documents that are unique to computers, such as Web pages and e-mail.

Documents must be readable by the users. They must be viewable on-screen in a number of different software environments and as an easy-to-read hard copy, preferably without cumbersome conversion procedures. A solution to this problem arose in the form of the markup "tags" used to label the parts of a document. So, for example, if a phrase were meant to be the title of the document, it would have the tag <title> before it and the tag </title> after it. Other tags serve to mark paragraph breaks, images, colors, and the size of the type on screen and paper.

An important feature of markup languages is that, unlike traditional programming languages that specify a sequence of well-specified steps, they allow flexibility in processing the tags. Any system intended to work with the documents should be able to interpret a title tag, for example, but one might display the title at the top of a computer screen, while another might print it out in large bold letters.

Standards are important in this environment so that documents can be published with confidence that they will be readable. To this end, markup languages have been developed with standard tag sets. One of the earliest was the Standard Generalized Markup Language, or SGML. An offshoot of SGML, the Hypertext Markup Language, or HTML, has become the most widely used because it is the most common form in which documents are placed on the World Wide Web. Keeping HTML standards up to date is a constant problem because developers of Web browser software are always eager to provide enhanced features requiring new tags. A new markup language, XML or the Extensible Markup Language, may ameliorate this problem by providing a way for a document to include its own tag definitions that the interpreting software can use, or it can refer to a specialized set of tags in specific situations.

A CLOSER LOOK

ADA LOVELACE

Ada Lovelace is considered by many to have been the first computer programmer.

Ada Lovelace (1815–1852) was the daughter of the famous English poet Lord Byron (1788–1824), by a marriage that broke up only a few weeks after she was born. Ada's mother, Annabella Milbanke, perhaps understandably disillusioned about poets, discouraged her daughter's own poetic inclinations and brought her up to be a mathematician, an unusual occupation for a woman of her day. In 1834, Ada met English inventor Charles Babbage (1792–1871), who was working on plans for a calculating engine that is now regarded as the first computer. She was among the first people to take his work seriously.

While married to the Earl of Lovelace and raising their children, Ada undertook a translation of a French article about Babbage's ideas, adding voluminous notes that are today the most extensive record of the dawn of computing. They included her predictions about using computers for non-mathematical uses such as graphics and music. These ideas would not come to fruition for almost 150 years. Her suggestions to Babbage about using his machine to solve mathematical problems to do with hydrodynamics are considered to be the first computer program. In 1979, a programming language developed for the U.S. Department of Defense was named Ada in her honor.

PEOPLE

Structured programming improved the situation by arranging code into modules with defined start and end points. A module can be debugged separately to ensure that it is working properly, and it can be reused in any number of programs.

As more software applications were distributed across many interconnected computers, client-server programming became important to help users share information. Information is held in a repository called a server, with server software responsible for managing requests for data. These requests are made by client software on each user's computer. The Internet is a set of protocols by which servers anywhere in the world can respond to client software such as Web browsers (see INTERNET).

Modern software

Since the late 1980s, object-oriented programming has changed the way many software systems have been designed. Instead of structuring a program in terms of the procedures the entire system must perform, object-oriented programs are a collection of encapsulated objects (self-contained packets of code), each with its own predefined set of actions. The data contained in an object can be transmitted to or modified by other objects through methods that are specific to each object. Programming is done by creating objects that send messages to one another to cooperatively accomplish tasks after an input from a user has occurred. Computer programs that operate by waiting for and responding to such signals are called event-driven. This type of programming has become very important because of the prevalence of graphical user interfaces (GUIs) and other devices that take input at human speeds.

With the rise of the Internet, software languages that can be used on all types of computers have been developed (see the box on page 1207). Java is the most widely used of these new languages. Unlike other languages, Java does not have to be compiled into machine language. Instead, a Java application is run by another piece of software called the Java Virtual Machine (JVM). As the name suggests, the JVM interprets the program, doing the job of the computer chip. All modern Web browsers include the JVM. This means that small Java applications—applets—can be transferred to and from all types of computers and run without having to convert or recompile them into the machine language of each type of computer.

S. CALVO

See also: COMPUTER GRAPHICS; CONTROL SYSTEMS AND CONTROL THEORY; DIGITAL SIGNALS AND SYSTEMS; ELECTRONICS; INFORMATION THEORY.

Further reading:
Campbell-Kelly, M., and Aspray, W. *Computer: A History of the Information Machine.* New York: HarperCollins, 1996.
Hafner, K. *Where Wizards Stay Up Late: The Origins of the Internet.* New York: Simon and Schuster, 1996.

SOIL SCIENCE

The study and management of soil is essential to ensure appropriate land use, especially for agriculture

Healthy, productive soil has been of paramount importance to human prosperity since the dawn of agriculture. Knowledge of soil management is vital to enhance its quality for successful farming. The soil must also be considered in any activity that involves changing the use of land, including forestry, construction, mining industries, and drainage. Furthermore, such human activities are increasingly affecting the biology, chemistry, and physical structure of soils, often damaging or depleting them. Pedology (soil science) is therefore a very significant field of study and practice.

The nature of soil

Soil is the natural covering of much of the world's land surface. It is a matrix of mineral particles of varying sizes (clay particles being the smallest; sand, the largest), combined with organic matter (both living and dead), water, and air, in varying proportions. Soil is formed by the interactions of climate, parent material (usually a type of rock), and soil organisms. Therefore, soil is very much a dynamic substance, not an inert medium.

Soil surveys—the starting point

Knowing the characteristics of soil in a certain area is necessary for all applications of soil science. This information is usually obtained by surveys. The soil layers, called horizons, can be mapped by digging a small pit to a depth of around 3 ft (1 m). The top layer, the O-horizon, is made up of dead and decaying organic material (humus). The topsoil is termed the A-horizon, the subsoil is called the B-horizon, and the lowest, the C-horizon, is generally a layer of partially weathered parent material.

Digging many pits over a large area is rarely feasible, and so surveyors usually sample most of the study area with a specialized tool called an auger. This is a corkscrew-like tool that removes a sample of soil from a certain depth. An alternative tool is the soil probe. This is a tubular tool designed to extract a core showing the soil horizons. Taking samples from different sites allows the variation of soils to be represented on a map of the area. Soil maps can be very useful when considering land-use options, especially when combined with aerial photographs and observations of rock outcrops, vegetation, and drainage.

A researcher with the U.S. Department of Agriculture checks the ability of soil types to absorb water. He is using a computer to enhance images of the soils' structures.

Agricultural soil requirements

Soil must provide crop roots with water, oxygen, nutrients, and support. A good agricultural soil therefore contains particles of varying size that create many pores—spaces for the retention and movement of air and water—when mixed together. Soil should also contain a suitable balance of nutrients (generally only available to plants when dissolved in soil water to form the soil solution). Land can be rated to indicate its ability to sustain crops. This rating takes the climate and relief of the land into account as well as the quality of the soil.

All but the best land will usually need improvement of the soil to create good harvests, and then careful management if yields are to be sustained year after year. The most important improvement is the addition of nutrients using fertilizer. Tillage, the physical treatment of soil, is also an important practice and must be appropriate for the soil conditions. The management of soil water levels may also be necessary to create high crop yields (see IRRIGATION AND LAND DRAINAGE).

Soil damage and degradation

There are many ways in which soils can become degraded. The physical structure can be damaged; the soil chemistry can be altered; and the ecology of soil organisms can be unbalanced. Due to the interdependence of soil components, all parts of a damaged soil are usually affected eventually, as are rivers, wildlife, and farmland.

CORE FACTS

- Soils are dynamic and complex, and their health is crucial to agricultural food production.
- Knowledge of soils is the basis for many important decisions about the sustainable use of land.
- Soils are increasingly becoming damaged or eroded, and the need for soil conservation is growing.

CONNECTIONS

● Knowledge of the condition of soil on **ARABLE** farms can play an important part in **PRECISION FARMING**.

● Excessive use of **FERTILIZERS** and **PESTICIDES AND HERBICIDES**, and contamination from **POLLUTION**, can all dramatically alter the chemistry of soil.

This Canadian hillside has been badly affected by soil erosion due to overgrazing by farm animals.

Soil structure can be damaged by a number of factors. Repeated tilling or the passage of heavy machinery can compact the soil, reducing the pore space between particles and thus affecting the ability of water, gases, and plant roots to penetrate. Specialist treatments such as chisel plowing can help to break up compacted land (see PLOW). Depletion of the soil's humus layer can also harm soil structure; this depletion is an inevitable result of continuous farming as plants are removed rather than allowed to rot. Chemical fertilizers provide the plants with nutrients but do nothing to build humus or enhance soil structure. Therefore, practices that add organic material to the soil, such as spreading manure and mulch (a type of compost), are important to maintain the long-term quality of agricultural land. Crop rotation can also help (see ORGANIC FARMING AND SUSTAINABLE AGRICULTURE).

The biology and chemical composition of soil can both be dramatically altered by pollution and overuse of synthetic pesticides. Overfertilization with certain nutrients can also affect the soil. Similarly, plowing unused crops such as straw into the soil introduces a sudden input of carbon, stimulating the activity of certain microorganisms that use nitrogen in the soil as they decompose the straw; this can deplete soil nitrogen and hinder plant growth.

Preventing contamination is always preferable to attempting to repair polluted soil. Repair is usually a time-consuming and expensive operation, often with an uncertain chance of success. Repair treatments will vary according to the nature of the contamination. For example, a soil polluted with toxic levels of heavy metals can be sown with resilient plant varieties (such as clover), which will take up the metals; the plants can then be harvested and burned. Repeating this process several times can reduce contaminant concentrations to an acceptable level for the growth of other plants.

Soil erosion

Erosion is the removal of soil, chiefly by the action of water or wind. It is a natural process, balanced by soil formation, but human activities tend to accelerate the rate of erosion, which can lead to a decline in soil depth and reduced agricultural productivity. Removed material can cause sedimentation that obstructs and clouds watercourses. If unchecked, rapid erosion can turn farmland into wasteland. This was most famously illustrated in the 1930s by the dust bowls in the previously fertile prairies. Soil erosion is a significant global environmental problem, which threatens food supplies in many areas; it is estimated that as much as half the world's farmland is being degraded, especially in the developing world.

Practices that accelerate erosion include excessive tilling, overgrazing, and deforestation. Certain soils are more erosion-prone than others. For instance, steep slopes are liable to water erosion, especially if vegetation has been removed. Erosion can be stabilized by building terraces to channel water runoff and replanting forests. If erosion is left to continue unchecked, the area becomes a desert.

T. ALLMAN

See also: AGRICULTURAL SCIENCE; FORESTRY; FOUNDATION; HORTICULTURE.

Further reading:
Foth, H. *Fundamentals of Soil Science.* 8th edition. New York: John Wiley & Sons, 1990.

SOIL CLASSIFICATION

Classifying soil helps when comparing soil from different areas. Soil characteristics vary in three ways—from site to site, from the surface down, and with time. Classification (also called taxonomy) is therefore a complex procedure.

The first major advance in scientific soil taxonomy was made in the late 19th century by Russian soil scientist Vasily Dukochaev (1846–1903). He grouped soils into three classes, such as podsol (wet, acid soils), according to the factors presumed to have influenced the soil's development. Dukochaev divided these three classes into many soil types. This taxonomy has since been updated.

There are various modern taxonomic systems. The U.S. Department of Agriculture system has also been applied widely outside the United States and has similarities with the systems of many other countries. It divides soils into 12 groups called orders according to criteria such as external structure and texture. Orders are subdivided into other groupings (order, suborder, great group, subgroup, family, and series), each describing a more restricted range of soil types. The smallest classification unit is the series, describing a characteristic soil profile; each is usually named after the location where it was first identified, although individual soils grouped in the same series may be widely dispersed. More than 16,000 series have been recognized in the United States alone.

A CLOSER LOOK

SOLAR POWER

Solar power is the collection, concentration, conversion, and application of the Sun's energy for human purposes

This parabolic reflector at Odeillo Font-Romeu solar power station in the eastern Pyrenees, France, concentrates the Sun's rays onto a dark-coated furnace at its focus. As a result, thermal power of 1000 kilowatts is produced.

Each day, the Sun showers Earth with more solar energy than the total amount of energy the planet's inhabitants would consume in 27 years. Only a small portion of this energy needs to be tapped into to replace the use of other limited, environmentally damaging energy resources (see ENERGY RESOURCES). However, the amount of sunlight available varies over Earth's surface. It depends on geographical location, time of day, season, and clouds. For example, the southwestern United States receives almost twice as much sunlight as other U.S. regions. Other parts of the world with high solar intensities include nations close to the tropics.

The idea of harnessing the Sun's energy to serve human needs is as old as humanity itself: even the earliest human living spaces took advantage of the Sun's heating power in the winter. Today's solar power systems use either solar cells or some form of solar heat collector to generate electricity and heat homes and other buildings.

CORE FACTS

- Each day Earth receives more than enough energy from the Sun to fuel all of humanity's industrial, agricultural, and domestic activities.
- The most efficient solar electric cells are used to power satellites and space stations.
- Highly concentrated sunlight can power electric generators or detoxify soil and water.

Using the Sun to generate electricity

In 1839, French physicist Antoine-César Becquerel (1788–1878) first discovered that certain materials produce small amounts of electric current when exposed to light. This phenomenon, called the photovoltaic effect, remained a curiosity until 1954, when several scientists at U.S. telecommunications company Bell Laboratories developed the first photovoltaic device, which helped to provide a practical way of generating electric power from the Sun.

The first crystalline silicon photovoltaic (or solar) cell had a conversion efficiency of about 4 percent, but by the late 20th century, the world record solar cell conversion efficiency was just over 32 percent—still substantially less than the theoretical maximum of just over 50 percent. Because the solar energy resource is free, solar electricity costs cannot be compared to costs of other energy technologies (see POWER STATION). But more efficient solar cells mean more electricity is produced per square foot of surface area. The most efficient cells power satellites and space stations (see SATELLITE; SPACE STATION).

The direct current (DC) electricity made by solar cells can be used directly to power DC equipment, such as that found on satellites, or it can be stored in batteries. An inverter that converts DC electricity to alternating current (AC) makes solar electricity suitable for appliances, but it also increases system costs.

Many developing countries are looking to solar cells as a way of avoiding the cost and environmental damage of generating plants and power distribution

CONNECTIONS

● **GEOTHERMAL ENERGY, WAVE POWER, WATER POWER,** and **WIND POWER** are other alternative **ENERGY RESOURCES**.

● Solar cells are designed to convert **LIGHT** to **ELECTRICITY**.

PARABOLIC TROUGH-TYPE SOLAR COLLECTOR

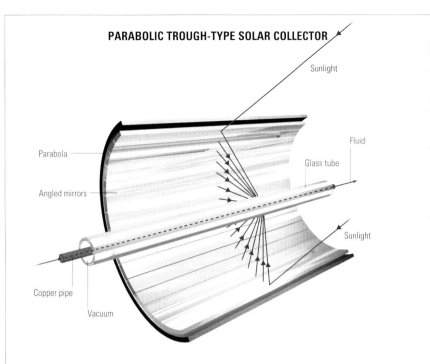

Sunlight

Fluid

Glass tube

Parabola

Angled mirrors

Sunlight

Copper pipe

Vacuum

Sunlight reaching the collector is reflected by mirrors onto the vacuum-filled glass tube. The copper pipe within the tube absorbs the heat radiation that crosses the vacuum. Like most metals, copper will lose a lot of heat by conduction but very little by radiation. Therefore, copper conducts heat to the fluid moving through the pipe but does not radiate much heat back across the vacuum.

Using the Sun's heat

Anyone who has ever climbed into a vehicle parked in the sun with the windows closed will appreciate how well thermal solar collectors work. The flat-plate solar collector uses this phenomenon: a closed space exposed to sunlight collects heat, which is used to warm up domestic and industrial water, to heat or cool indoor air, to desalinate water, or to produce salt. Flat-plate collectors are large, flat boxes with one or more glass covers. Inside these boxes, dark-colored metal plates absorb the Sun's heat that passes through the glass. Air or a liquid, such as water, flows through tubes and is warmed by the heat in the plates. If the collector system uses pumps or fans to move heated air or water, it is called an active system. If natural ventilation and design features transport the heat without additional energy input, the system is passive. Solar homes and buildings with this type of heating often use solar collectors, to heat indoor air, while natural daylight can replace or supplement electric lighting (see HEATING SYSTEMS; BUILDING TECHNIQUES, TRADITIONAL). Commercial buildings can reduce heating costs by using a solar ventilation system to preheat air by as much as 54°F (30°C) before it is drawn into the heating system.

Other ways to use the Sun's energy

Several recent inventions promise to reduce our consumption of fossil fuels and reduce the cost of performing certain activities. For example, electrochromic "smart" windows have been developed that have a film that can become dark or transparent in response to a small electric charge. Computerized sensors trigger changes in the film to increase or reduce solar gain in commercial buildings. A small solar cell in each window can provide the electricity to control the sensors and film.

The Sun's energy can also be used to destroy contaminants in soil, air, and water. One approach uses the Sun to activate a catalyst that removes unwanted contaminants, such as human waste and industrial chemicals, in a process called photocatalytic oxidation. Another system uses sunlight concentrated up to 1000 times its normal intensity to destroy polluting substances and microorganisms in soil.

Highly concentrated sunlight can also be used in a solar furnaces to make advanced materials for the electronics, automotive, aerospace, and defense industries. A series of mirrors creates an intense, focused beam of sunlight concentrated up to 50,000 times its normal intensity. The largest solar furnace, in Odeillo, France, can generate a beam of light with a temperature of over 7000° F (3800° C).

P. WEIS-TAYLOR

See also: ENERGY RESOURCES, PHOTOCELL; SEMICONDUCTOR AND SEMICONDUCTOR DEVICE.

Further reading:

Tapping into the Sun: Today's Applications of Photovoltaic Technology. Washington, D.C.: U.S. Department of Energy, 1995.

lines. Today, solar generating systems with batteries can provide light for social and work activities without the costs and pollution of using fossil fuels to produce the necessary power. Solar electricity can also power refrigeration for vaccine storage at health clinics, drive water pumps and filtration systems, and power radios and telephones in rural areas to reduce the reliance on commercial power from fossil fuels.

The Sun's heat can also be harnessed to make electricity. Solar thermal generating systems capture and concentrate the Sun's energy to run steam generators that produce electricity. In this system, a receiver absorbs concentrated sunlight and converts it into heat, usually in the form of a heated working fluid. The hot fluid moves to a steam generator or engine where its energy is used to make electricity. The cooled fluid then recirculates to the collector.

Parabolic trough-type solar systems use mirrored troughs to focus the Sun's energy onto a receiver tube filled with fluid located at the trough's focal point (see the diagram above). The hot fluid then turns a turbine, which operates a generator to produce electricity. These systems can be very powerful: one parabolic trough plant in California produces 160 MW of electricity, meeting the needs of more than 350,000 people. Dish systems use parabolic mirrors to focus solar energy onto a receiver pipe mounted above the dish at the focal point.

Receiver stations use thousands of tracking mirrors (heliostats) to reflect solar energy onto a receiver on top of a tower. This receiver uses fluid to transfer heat to a conventional generator, such as a steam turbine system, which generates electricity.

SOLVENT, INDUSTRIAL

Liquids that are used to dissolve other substances are called solvents and are used widely in industrial applications

A solvent is a substance—usually a liquid—that is used to dissolve another substance. The resulting mixture is called a solution and is homogeneous, which means its composition is uniform throughout. By contrast, a mixture that contains regions that are richer in one component and other regions that are richer in another component is called a heterogeneous mixture. Any substance that is of uniform chemical composition and physical state is called a phase. Homogeneous mixtures are therefore single phase, while heterogeneous mixtures are multiphase.

Ionic and molecular solutions

The most familiar solvent—and arguably the most versatile—is water. Solutions of salt (sodium chloride, NaCl) and sugar (sucrose, $C_{12}H_{22}O_{11}$) are familiar from everyday life and illustrate two typical types of solutions: ionic and molecular. In both cases, the resulting mixture is called a solution and is one continuous phase, or state of matter. The major component of a solution is the solvent—in this case water—and the minor component is called the solute—in this case salt or sugar. Although the solute may seem to have disappeared in the solvent, in reality it has broken down into tiny particles that are spread through the solvent.

Ionic solutions. Salt dissolves in water to form an ionic solution. When it does, it splits into sodium ions (Na^+) and chloride ions (Cl^-). Because water is a polar molecule (it has regions of positive and negative charge), there is an electrostatic attraction between the positive sodium ions and the negative portions of the water molecules (see ELECTRICITY AND MAGNETISM). Hence, water molecules gather around the positive ions and form a barrier that discourages the positive sodium ions from reforming salt crystals with the negative chloride ions. The sodium ions are said to be solvated by the solvent molecules, or, in the special case of water, hydrated by the water molecules. The chloride ions are also hydrated. In this case, the negatively charged chloride ions are attracted to the positively charged portions of the water molecules.

A cleanup worker demonstrates the cleaning ability of chemical solvent PES-51 on an oil-soaked cloth following the **Exxon Valdez** *oil spill off the coast of Alaska in 1989.*

Molecular solutions. Sugar dissolving in water is an example of a molecular solution. Unlike salt, sucrose remains in molecular form when it dissolves. In this case, hydration of the sucrose molecules is favored because both water and sucrose contain oxygen-hydrogen bonds (O–H bonds), in which the hydrogen atom carries a slight positive charge and the oxygen atom carries a slight negative charge. Hence, hydrogen atoms in water molecules are attracted to oxygen atoms in sucrose molecules, and oxygen atoms in water molecules are attracted to sucrose hydrogen atoms. This type of attraction, called hydrogen bonding, plays an important role in solutions where the solvent and the solute contain hydrogen atoms that are bonded to atoms of electronegative elements (those that attract electrons and leave the hydrogen atom with a partial positive charge) such as oxygen, nitrogen, and chlorine.

Solubility and the choice of solvent

The solubility of a solute in a solvent is usually given as the number of grams of the solute that can dissolve in a liter of solvent. It is possible to predict whether two substances will form a solution—in general, substances with similar chemical properties are likely to form a solution, those with very different properties are not. The most important of these chemical properties is polarity, which is the tendency of a chemical compound to be either ionic or covalent. Put simply, an ionic compound consists of electrically charged particles (ions) and is highly polar; a covalent compound consists of molecules that have no overall charge, but may have areas of positive and negative charge—in which case the compound can be moderately polar—or have essentially no variations in charge throughout the molecules and be nonpolar. Heavy molecules, including polymers,

---

CORE FACTS

- A solvent—usually a liquid—is a substance that dissolves solids, liquids, and gases to form solutions.
- The material that becomes dissolved in a solvent is called the solute.
- The solubility of a solute in a solvent is defined as the maximum concentration of that solute that will dissolve in a given solvent.
- Solubility depends on the chemical natures of both the solute and the solvent, and on the conditions of temperature and pressure.

CONNECTIONS

- Solvents are used in making **PAINT AND SURFACE COATINGS**.

- Many solvents are products of the **ORGANIC CHEMICAL INDUSTRY** or of **OIL REFINING**.

tend to dissolve with great difficulty. Ionic compounds in which the ions are very strongly bonded tend to be sparingly soluble at best.

Polar solvents, including water, some alcohols, and organic acids such as acetic acid (CH_3COOH), will dissolve ionic solutes and other polar molecules. Nonpolar solvents, including benzene (C_6H_6), hexane (C_6H_{14}), and carbon tetrachloride (CCl_4), dissolve nonpolar compounds. Iodine, which is nonpolar, dissolves in hydrocarbons, but not in water. Salt, which is ionic, will not dissolve in benzene, but it is readily soluble in water.

The most familiar solutions are solid-in-liquid solutions. In general, the solubility of a solid in a liquid increases with temperature. Gases can also form solutions in suitable solvents, although gases become less soluble with increasing temperature as they overcome the attractive forces of the solvent molecules and escape the solution. Solid solutions can occur when two materials solidify together without forming separate regions of varying compositions. Alloys such as brass and bronze are solid solutions.

Properties and uses of solvents

Solvents are used in a wide range of applications, such as in the manufacture of chemicals and pharmaceuticals, for cleaning, and as paint thinners. There are several properties that determine the choice of solvent for a given application.

Solubility. The types of materials that are soluble in a given solvent determine the solvent's suitability for a particular purpose. A dry-cleaning solvent must dissolve dirt and grease well while having no effect on clothing fabrics and dyes. A solvent that is used to purify the product of a chemical reaction must dissolve that product well while leaving the impurities in solid form so that they can be filtered off.

Volatility. The volatility (tendency to evaporate) of a solvent is related to its boiling point. A mixture of low- and high-boiling solvents is used in the manufacture of paints. The low-boiling components evaporate quickly, making the paint film dry to the touch in a short time, while the high-boiling components keep the film liquid long enough for the brush marks to level out. Solvents with very high boiling points called plasticizers are added to some plastics to make them more flexible. Flexible paints are needed to provide a long-lasting coat for structures that need to bend.

Odor. Solvents often have strong odors, which is a consequence of their volatility. A solvent's odor is not critical if the solvent is to be used in a sealed system, such as a dry-cleaning machine. However, a solvent with a weak or inoffensive odor is preferred for applications involving closer human contact, such as paint formulations.

Toxicity and flammability. Some solvents are toxic (poisonous) and can be dangerous if inhaled. There is a trend toward replacing toxic solvents such as benzene with water or alcohols, which are less harmful both to manufacturers and to end-users of solvents.

Similarly, some solvents are highly flammable. For example, paint stripper and white spirit are two commonly used solvents. These liquids must be stored away from heat in child-proof containers.

S. ALDRIDGE

See also: ADHESIVE; CHEMICAL INDUSTRY, INORGANIC; COLORANTS AND PIGMENTS; PLASTICS; POLLUTION AND ITS CONTROL.

Further reading:

Callahan, M., and Green, B. *Hazardous Solvent Source Reduction.* New York: McGraw-Hill, 1995.
Emsley, J. *The Consumer's Good Chemical Guide.* New York: W. H. Freeman, 1994.
Herrera, C. *Evaluation of Solvents and Methods of Extraction.* Austin: Texas Department of Transportation, Research and Technology Transfer Office, 1996.

SOLVENTS AND THE ENVIRONMENT

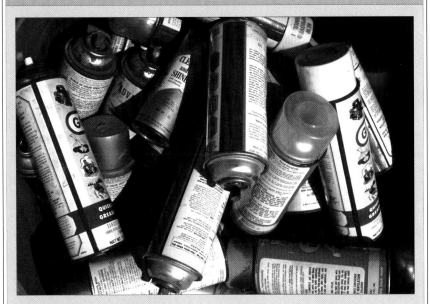

Empty aerosol cans wait for safe disposal at a gas station in Los Angeles.

Many solvents have adverse effects on human health or on the environment. Benzene, which was once used widely for dry cleaning and in the chemical industry, is now known to contribute to cancer and its use has been restricted. There are also concerns about the solvents used in home-improvement products, such as paints and adhesives. Although many of these products have been reformulated to use water in place of much of the solvent, good ventilation is still essential when these products are used.

In the 1940s, when chlorofluorocarbons (CFCs) were developed, they were hailed as wonderchemicals—they are relatively inert, nontoxic, and cheap. They were used as refrigerants and as propellants for aerosols, in which they dissolved the active substance and provided the pressure for the spray. It is now known that CFCs decompose very slowly in the atmosphere. When they reach the stratosphere, they react with the layer of ozone that protects Earth from the Sun's ultraviolet (UV) light. Extensive use of CFCs has led to the depletion of the stratospheric ozone layer and to an increase in the incidence of skin cancer caused by UV light (see POLLUTION AND ITS CONTROL). The production and use of CFCs is now strictly limited, and many countries are phasing them out altogether.

WIDER IMPACT

SOUND RECORDING AND REPRODUCTION

Recorded sound has become a huge industry, fostering the spread of musical styles worldwide

A mixing desk at a modern recording studio includes fader switches that control the volume of each separate track of sound.

The ability to record music, the human voice, and other sounds has vastly increased the variety of music and information to which people are exposed. Before the advent of sound recording, orchestral music was heard only by the privileged few. Most people only ever heard performances by local musicians or by the occasional wandering minstrel. However, by the early 20th century, even before radios had become common, phonograph records began to allow wider distribution of the work of singers and musicians, and the concept of popular music arose. Today, recorded music, with its changing fashions, is the focus of a huge industry.

Capturing sound

The phonograph was the first recording technology. In its earliest versions, the vibrations of the sound waves were used to move a needle that cut a wiggling groove in the record (see ACOUSTICS AND SOUND; WAVE MOTION). The record was played back by drawing a needle over the groove to make the needle vibrate in the same way as when it cut the groove, which would generate some approximation of the original sound waves (see the box on page 1219).

The development of technology to convert sound waves into electrical signals and back again paved the way for all modern communication systems, including telephony, broadcasting, and electrical sound recording (see RADIO RECEIVER; TELEPHONY AND TELEGRAPHY; WIRELESS COMMUNICATION).

In modern sound recording, the sound waves are converted to electrical signals using one or more microphones. One of the most common microphone types is the dynamic or moving coil microphone, in which the sound waves vibrate a wire coil within a magnetic field to generate a varying electrical current (see ELECTRICITY AND MAGNETISM; MICROPHONE AND LOUDSPEAKER).

The frequency (speed of oscillation) of the electrical signal represents the pitch of the sound, and the amplitude (size of oscillation) of the signal corresponds to the sound's volume. Even for a single instrument, the shape of the signal is generally quite complex and comprises many different waveforms overlaid on top of one another.

Regardless of how the resulting electrical signal is processed and recorded, the final step in playback is to convert the signal back to sound waves using one or more loudspeakers. Loudspeakers—which are often just called speakers—are, in effect, microphones that work in reverse. The electrical signals run through a coil in a magnetic field. This causes the coil to vibrate, and the stiff paper or plastic cone of the speaker then vibrates as a result, and this reproduces the sound waves.

CORE FACTS

- Sound recording began in the late 1870s when Thomas Alva Edison invented the acoustic phonograph.
- Modern recording systems convert sound waves into electrical signals, which are recorded in a number of ways for later conversion back into sound waves.
- In digital recording, the sound wave is encoded by a series of numbers and then decoded at playback.
- The goal of sound recording is to reproduce the sound of the original performance as closely as possible.

CONNECTIONS

- By the early 1990s, **COMPACT DISCS** had become the most popular sound recording media.

- Systems of **ELECTRIC MOTORS** and **GEARS** are used to turn phonograph turntables, compact discs, and the reels of magnetic tapes.

Despite the popularity of CDs, many disc jockeys still prefer to use vinyl records because of the degree of hands-on control these allow when mixing together the music of two separate records. This disc jockey is using two phonographs and a mixing desk to play continuous dance music to a young crowd in Venezuela.

Cutting a record

Phonograph record production begins with a blank master disc made of aluminum covered with black lacquer. The disc is placed on a cutting lathe—a machine with a turntable and a bridge holding the cutting needle. The electrical signal representing the sound is fed into the cutting lathe, causing the needle to vibrate from side to side. Meanwhile, the needle moves very slowly along the bridge as the turntable rotates beneath it. The result is a spiral groove three miles long, with the marks within it corresponding to the shape of the sound waves.

When the master disc has been cut, a thin layer of metal is applied and then peeled off. This creates a reverse image of the disc called a negative. The negative is used as a stamper to produce more records. Stampers must be made for each side of the master disc, and they are placed in a record-making press. The record is pressed from a disc of vinyl, about half the diameter of the finished record but thicker. The disc is warmed to soften the vinyl, then it is placed in the press. Hot steam melts the vinyl so that it flows into all the grooves, and then cold water hardens the record so that it can be removed (see PLASTICS).

Phonograph formats

The phonograph (or record player) reproduces the sound stored on a record by turning the record on a turntable, running a needle (stylus) in the groove, and processing the resulting sound caused by the vibration of the stylus through an amplifier and loudspeaker (see AMPLIFIER).

The earliest standard for turntable speeds was 78 revolutions per minute (rpm). These thick phenolic (plastic made with the compound phenol) records were 10 in (25 cm) in diameter and could contain about four minutes of music on each side. Initially, no

good way could be found to make longer-playing records. More music could be fitted in a groove by recording more slowly or by making the grooves smaller, but both these options were difficult to achieve using the stiff phenolic discs. Another option was to make the discs much larger, but this was also impractical because the big discs were hard to handle and the material shattered easily.

In the 1940s, vinyl discs were developed that were easier to work with. These could be cut with microgrooves to produce long-playing records that were 12 in (30.5 cm) in diameter and that ran at 33⅓ rpm. Albums began to be manufactured, with each disc running about 20 minutes per side. The 78 rpm records that held one song per side were replaced by 45 rpm singles—small vinyl microgroove records that could be produced more economically.

Parts of a phonograph

The essential components of a phonograph are the turntable, which turns the record; the motor that drives the turntable; and the tonearm, which contains the stylus and also, in modern record players, the system for transforming the vibrations of the stylus into electrical signals.

Turntable. The turntable of a record player must run at a very steady speed, or the sound will be distorted. Irregularities in the turntable's speed result in audible changes in pitch and speed called wow. Faster variations in speed, called flutter, are too slight to hear directly, but manifest themselves as a general reduction in the clarity of the sound produced. Another turntable problem is rumble—a low-pitched hum from the motor.

Motor. There are several different types of turntable motors. The least expensive, and the most prone to causing wow and flutter, is the induction motor. The synchronous motor is more expensive, but it runs very evenly. High-end turntables use servomotors, which continuously measure the rotational speed and adjust it as necessary. The turntable may be connected to the motor by a belt drive or a rim drive, in which the motor turns a rubber wheel pressed against the turntable from underneath. In direct-drive turntables, the motor drives the turntable directly, without an intervening belt or wheel. Direct-drive turntables are often used by disc jockeys, because their smaller number of moving parts makes them more durable and the drive is very smooth (see ELECTRIC MOTOR AND GENERATOR; MECHANICAL TRANSMISSION).

Tonearm. The job of the turntable is to rotate the record under the tonearm. On a modern phonograph, the tonearm is where the transformation of the wiggling shape of the record's grooves into electrical signals takes place. The part that contacts the record is the stylus. The steel needles that were used in the past were found to flatten over time and damage the grooves. The stylus is now usually made of a tiny cone of diamond or sapphire.

The stylus is held in a cartridge, in which the vibrations from the stylus cause a magnet to be

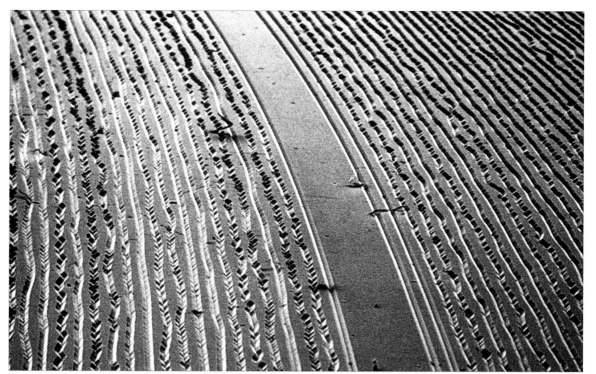

A scanning electron microscope reveals the series of microgrooves on the surface of a vinyl record. The smooth area in the middle is the silent interval between two sections of recording (magnified x 40, approximately).

moved near two coils of conducting wire or vice versa, in order to generate electrical currents corresponding to the right and left stereo signals. The cartridge must respond to a wide range of frequencies, and the response should be flat, meaning that it is equally strong for all frequencies.

The tonearm itself is the long, thin beam that holds the cartridge over the record. The tonearm usually includes a spring or magnet to compensate for the arm's tendency to skate inward. The shape of the tonearm may be straight or curved in the shape of an S or J. These shapes adjust the distribution of the tonearm's mass so that its movement does not reinforce any distortions arising from record warp (slight curves in the surface of the record). The mass of the tonearm is also important, because it should be just heavy enough to keep the stylus in the groove without wearing it down. Any additional mass will lead to excess wear of both the stylus and the record. The angle of the tonearm and cartridge system is designed to minimize tracking error as the tonearm pivots inward from the outer edge of the disc.

Magnetic tape

In addition to recording sounds in grooves, sound vibrations can be represented by the orientation of magnetic particles on a strip of tape. Magnetic tape consists of a thin plastic base covered with an emulsion of metal or metal oxide particles 20–30 millionths of an inch long. Each of these particles behaves like a tiny magnet and has a north and south pole (see MAGNET). Initially, the poles of these particles are randomly oriented lengthwise, but the particles can be given the same orientation by subjecting them to an external magnetic field. When sound is being recorded on a magnetic tape, the tape is run past a head that contains a small electromagnet. The magnetic field in the head changes in

response to the electrical signal coming from a microphone or other source, creating new alignments on the tape.

To play the tape, it is also run past a head. This time the magnetic particles on the tape create a current in the coil of a conducting wire in the head (sometimes this is the coil of the electromagnet used for recording). The current, which varies in the same way as the original sound signal, is then passed along to the amplifier and loudspeakers. A separate erase head uses an alternating current to jumble the mag-

---

NOISE REDUCTION

Magnetic tape recordings are often plagued with a high-pitched hiss, produced as the tape passes over the head. While loud music masks the hiss, it becomes more obvious during soft passages. American scientist Ray Dolby (1933–) developed several processes to reduce tape hiss. In the original Dolby noise-reduction process, loud passages are recorded as normal, but soft passages are amplified in the high frequencies. When the recording is played back on Dolby equipment, again the loud sections are left unchanged, but the soft passages are reduced to their original level, with the high-frequency amplification removed. This reduces the level of hiss; technically this is called increasing the signal-to-noise ratio (see INFORMATION THEORY). If the playback equipment is not Dolby-compatible, the high frequencies remain excessively amplified, resulting in a shrill sound. A later Dolby process, HX Pro, records with fewer high-frequency losses and without any encoding of the signal. Because it requires no decoding, HX Pro can therefore be used to improve the sound quality on all tape decks.

In a system made by audio equipment manufacturer dbx, which is designed for dynamic range expansion (increasing the difference between loud and quiet sections of a recording), noise reduction is a beneficial side effect. The process is not frequency-dependent and it eliminates tape hiss, but dbx recordings must be played on dbx equipment for a high-quality sound. The process not suited for solo pieces, because it works by compressing and expanding sound, and the effects of this can be heard as variations in the silences between the notes of the solo.

A CLOSER LOOK

Sound recording has introduced people to different styles of music from all over the world. Here, the flute song of a Mauritanian man is recorded on magnetic tape.

netic particles so that they are again in random orientations lengthwise (see MAGNETIC STORAGE MEDIA).

Magnetic tape is now most frequently packaged in small plastic cassettes. Unlike the larger reel-to-reel tapes, which are used mainly in professional studios, cassettes can simply be popped into the recorder without having to thread the tape through the head. The compact size has also allowed for the development of dashboard systems and the personal cassette player, which can be easily carried or worn during activities such as working or exercising.

Standard audio cassette tape, which is 0.15 in (38 mm) wide, has four tracks (separate channels of music). Two tracks are required to reproduce stereophonic (or stereo) sound, and the cassette can contain one stereo recording on each of its sides.

Magnetic tapes up to 2 in (5 cm) wide are used in professional recording studios because they can accommodate 16 tracks or more. Using multitrack recording techniques, individual musicians or groups of musicians can be recorded separately, and then the tracks can be combined with a mixing board to achieve a balanced sound. In some cases, recordings are made to sound as if musicians are performing together when they have in fact never even met. Using tape, it is also possible to record many takes

of a performance, after which a tape editor pieces together, or splices, the best sections. Because of these capabilities, tape is traditionally used to create the master from which other recording media, such as vinyl discs and compact discs, are produced.

Unlike vinyl discs, which can be quickly reproduced by stamping, a tape must be run through tape heads in order to be copied. However, this does not have to happen at normal speeds. Cassettes are manufactured using banks of tape recorders hooked together. They are speeded up so that making a cassette with a normal running time of an hour and a half takes just over a minute. Sound quality suffers slightly in this process, and for this reason some audio enthusiasts avoid commercially recorded cassettes. Another potential drawback of cassettes is their fixed size: cassettes that provide 120 minutes of running time must use even thinner tape. Thin tapes are prone not only to breakage but also to print-through—this is when sounds recorded on one side of the tape are heard as a faint echo on the other.

The major advantage of magnetic tape systems for the consumer is that anyone can record sounds using a home tape recorder, which can both record and play tapes. While the ability to make recordings is desirable to home users, it is considered a threat by those working in the music business who are concerned about unauthorized reproduction of copyrighted material. However, during the 1970s and 1980s, when inexpensive cassette recorders became widely available, the sales of recorded music continued their consistent growth in most markets.

Digital recording

Phonograph records and most audio tapes are made with analog recording techniques. This means that the grooves in a record, or the magnetic particles on the tape, are made to contain information resembling that of the original sound wave so that, for example, the needle in the disc-cutting lathe moves farther for a louder sound. Looking closely at a record's groove, you will see jagged and smooth sections: in some sections the wiggles are closer together and in others they are farther apart. This is essentially an image of the sound waves recorded when the disc was made.

With digital audio systems, it is the instructions to reproduce the music that are stored, rather than the music itself. Digital recording starts just like analog, with the conversion of sound waves to a corresponding electrical signal. This signal is then fed into an analog-to-digital converter (ADC). The ADC measures, or samples, the voltage at fixed intervals, usually 44,000 times per second. The output of the ADC is also electrical voltage, but for each interval, the voltage is represented as 16 binary (0 or 1) digits. As in a computer, binary numbers can be used to represent any quantity. Here, they represent the level of input at each sampling interval, so that a series of numbers defines the shape of the sound wave. The sound can be played back using a digital-to-analog converter (DAC), which decodes the binary numbers (see DIGITAL SIGNALS AND SYSTEMS).

Digital audio can be reproduced more cleanly, because electronic equipment can easily pass along a series of numbers. In binary systems, there are only two signal levels to worry about. With analog systems, the waveforms may be distorted at each step in the system. Digital information can be processed by computers, which can easily combine, modify, and reproduce sounds, and even transmit them over the Internet (see the box on page 1220).

Compact discs

By the early 1990s, compact discs, or CDs, had become the most popular digital recording medium. CDs have a diameter of 4.7 in (12 cm) and are made using a master cut with a laser, then mass-produced by pressing. The discs have a nonreflective interior covered with a reflective surface. A strong laser, driven by the digital output of the ADC sampling 44,000 times per second, cuts tiny holes, or pits, in the master disc where the nonreflective layer shows. The reflective areas between the pits are called lands. The length of each pit represents a 16-digit binary number, or channel code. Information stored in channel codes includes the output of the ADC, and also error-correcting codes that can fix flaws introduced in manufacture or playback (see COMPACT DISC).

In a CD player, a laser beam that is less powerful than the one used for cutting the master shines on the disc. As the disc rotates at hundreds of revolutions per minute, the intensity of reflected light changes, depending on whether the laser beam strikes a pit or a land. The reflected light is directed toward a photodiode, an electronic sensor that measures light level (see PHOTOCELL). A microcomputer determines the channel codes from the electrical output of the photodiode and reproduces the sound signal. During this process the output is held briefly in a buffer (temporary storage unit), so that error-correcting codes can be checked (see COMPUTER).

CDs have replaced phonograph records in the mass market because they have many advantages. As well as excellent sound reproduction and error-correcting capability, the small size of CDs makes them easier to carry and store than phonograph records. CDs can also be played in cars and portable stereos; records cannot. Their tiny pits, which are less than one thousandth the size of the period at the end of this sentence, allow them to store 75 minutes worth of sounds using only one side of the small disc. Unlike the groove of a record, which can be slowly worn out by the stylus, the pattern of pits and lands on a CD are read by light and are never actually touched; a transparent plastic coating protects the disc from most accidental scratches. There is also no magnetic field to slowly decay, as in the case of a magnetic tape. This means that, unlike tapes and records, CDs should not deteriorate with use.

Digital audio tapes

Digital information can also be stored on magnetic tape; magnetic tapes were once the most common method of storing computer data. On digital audio

Using studio multitracking technology, the vocals are often recorded after the other musicians have recorded their parts.

tapes (DATs), the magnetic particle positions do not define an analog representation of the sound signal, but instead encode a series of binary numbers representing the sound signal. DATs are capable of achieving sound quality as high as that of a CD, and they are often used in recording studios. Introduced onto the consumer market in 1987, DAT recorders are, however, expensive and do not have a high consumer profile. This is in part because of music industry concerns about a potential increase in unauthorized copying of CDs because of the availability of such a high-quality home recording method.

Realistic sound

The goal in recording music has always been to reproduce the sound of the original performance as closely as possible. In a concert hall, sound comes from many directions. The performers are spread out across a stage, and there are reflections off all the room's surfaces, which affect the final sound.

Re-creating realistic sound, or maintaining fidelity, was difficult to achieve with early monophonic or monaural recordings, in which a single microphone recorded the sound. The high-fidelity, or hi-fi, systems of the 1940s were still monophonic, but increased the frequency range they could faithfully reproduce. In the 1950s, stereo recordings were introduced. In early stereo recordings, microphones on the right and left sides of the performers were used to obtain two separate sound tracks, which were played in a stereo system incorporating a separate amplifier and loudspeaker for each channel. Today, right and left tracks are created in the studio by mixing and editing the multiple tracks that are produced in recording sessions. The result may not bear any resemblance to the musicians' actual seating pattern, if indeed the musicians sat together at all.

Quadraphonic sound, which appeared in the 1970s, was an effort to improve on stereo using four channels of sound, and four speakers, rather than two. This allowed the listener to be surrounded with sound, but recordings made in this format did not have mass appeal. Quadraphonic hi-fi systems failed to become popular, but quadraphonic circuits and full-frequency-range recording were combined to create Dolby Stereo, which produces surround sound for motion pictures. Surround playback was used in home audio and video installations in the 1980s, and music producers began using the technology for recordings. Today, advanced processing made possible by microchip circuitry has created many ways to achieve ambience enhancement and come closer to producing results that are identical to live sound. These include surround-sound systems with up to seven speakers and slight time delays to imitate the acoustic patterns of performance spaces.

Motion-picture sound recording often makes use of tapeless recording, a recent technology that stores digitally coded sound in the random access memory (RAM) of a specially equipped computer. The electronic signals create and coordinate visual, musical, and sound effects to a level of accuracy that was unthinkable before the advent of computers.

S. CALVO

See also: ELECTRONICS; MUSICAL INSTRUMENT; VIDEOGRAPHY.

Further reading:

Alkin, G. *Sound Recording and Reproduction.* Boston: Focal Press, 1996.

THE MP3 CONTROVERSY

The Internet has made it easier to distribute all sorts of information, and music is no exception. The MPEG-3 or MP3 format is a data compression system that has been found to be useful for packing music into conveniently downloaded files while retaining a sound quality acceptable for casual listening. This has infuriated those who make their money by manufacturing and selling recorded media, because they can be neatly bypassed when musicians put their own work out on the Internet. Some artists have established Web sites where music can be purchased by credit card for about a dollar a song. Of course, the unauthorized copying known as pirating is still a concern; many people have put up their own Web sites of duplicated MP3 files, which can be freely downloaded.

When a company called Diamond Multimedia introduced a small portable MP3 player, it had to fight off a music business trade group that attempted to get an injunction against it. The Diamond player includes copy-protection software, but this can be easily bypassed using a program that has been posted on the Internet. With the growing influence of the Internet in marketing and especially its increasing dominance in information exchange, it is likely that the record industry will have to work with rather than against MP3 if it is to survive (see INTERNET).

A CLOSER LOOK

SPACE FLIGHT

Space flight involves moving through space in a craft that is either fixed in orbit or escaping the pull of gravity

A huge amount of energy is necessary to boost any spacecraft beyond the atmosphere of Earth. After this has been accomplished, differing amounts of energy are necessary to reach different destinations. For example, the velocity necessary to reach a low Earth orbit is about 17,500 mph (28,000 km/h), whereas the velocity needed to escape Earth's gravitational pull completely is about 25,000 mph (40,000 km/h).

Huge rockets, such as the Apollo program's Saturn 5, provide a lot of thrust, but they must also overcome their own weight, most of which is due to the propellant they are carrying. This is why launch vehicles have detachable stages. When the fuel in a lower stage is spent, the empty stage separates and falls away, lightening the load and so reducing the amount of propellant that the next stage must carry (see FUELS AND PROPELLANTS; LAUNCH VEHICLE).

In the case of the space shuttle, large solid-propellant rockets boost the shuttle, while its own liquid-propellant rockets burn at the same time. In one minute, the combination has pushed the shuttle past the speed of sound. After two minutes, the solid rockets are spent. At an altitude of 28 miles (45 km), the solid boosters are jettisoned. Six minutes later, the propellants in the shuttle's external tank are nearly exhausted, and the shuttle enters Earth orbit (see ROCKET ENGINE; ROCKETRY).

Orbiting Earth

The altitude of a spacecraft's orbit depends on its purpose. A space shuttle's orbit depends upon the nature of its mission, but generally the craft orbits at altitudes above 150 miles (241 km). There the atmosphere is thin enough to cause only minimal frictional interaction with the craft. During most missions, the shuttle has to change its orbit to accomplish all of its objectives. Spacecraft make such orbit adjustments using small onboard engines or thrusters. To move to a higher orbit, the engines

The space shuttle Endeavour in orbit over San Francisco and the Sierra Nevada. The shuttle is carrying the Spacehab laboratory for studying the effects of weightlessness and an experimental satellite.

must push the spacecraft forward. To move to a lower orbit, they must push the spacecraft backward toward the surface of Earth.

Most orbits are actually elliptical, moving from the closest point to Earth (perigee) to the farthest point away from Earth (apogee). The position and direction of the orbit depend on the spacecraft's mission. For example, polar orbits, which cross over both of the poles of the planet, allow spacecraft to survey almost all of Earth at least once a day. Such orbits are useful for surveying, monitoring parameters such as surface temperature, and watching natural phenomena develop. Geosynchronous orbits are 22,300 miles (35,900 km) high. At this altitude, it takes precisely as long for the spacecraft to complete one orbit as it does for Earth to rotate once. Thus, the spacecraft appears to hover over the same spot on Earth at all times. Such orbits are useful for communications satellites (see SATELLITE). Some spacecraft idle in orbit around Earth waiting for the correct conditions to head for distant destinations.

Docking

Meeting another spacecraft in space is a difficult endeavor. A rendezvous procedure is even more difficult if the two spacecraft are to dock (touch and link up). Knowing where you are in space requires sophisticated navigational tools. This is particularly important when docking. There are many parameters to control in the process of linking two

CORE FACTS

- Huge multistage rockets are used to accelerate craft to the high velocities that are necessary to reach Earth orbit. Leaving the gravitational pull of Earth completely requires even more energy.
- Spaceflights to other planets are timed to coincide with launch windows when the journey time to the planet is at its shortest.
- Collisions with human-made space debris from abandoned launch vehicles and satellites is one of the chief dangers of space flight.
- The weightlessness that astronauts experience in orbit can cause motion sickness, loss of muscle and bone, impaired immune functions, and fluid imbalance.

CONNECTIONS

- The path of an object in orbit is determined by the laws of **MECHANICS**.

- Spacecraft are tracked and controlled by **GROUND STATIONS**.

SLINGSHOT ORBITS

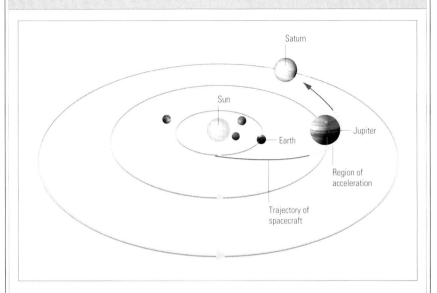

Spacecraft accelerate by using the gravitational pull of planets. For example, NASA's Voyager 2 used the gravitational pull and high orbital speed of Jupiter to increase its speed on its journey to Saturn. This technique is sometimes called a slingshot.

The propellant demands of some missions may exceed the capacity of the spacecraft. To overcome this limitation, the gravity of another body can be used to assist the spacecraft on its way. The gravity-assist or slingshot orbit can help a probe reach targets that would otherwise be essentially inaccessible.

The principle of the slingshot orbit is that some of the energy of the probe in its orbit can be exchanged with the energy of an orbiting body (either a planet orbiting the Sun or a moon orbiting a planet). A probe can increase or decrease its energy as long as the body that slingshots it onto a new trajectory experiences an equal but opposite change, thus satisfying the fundamental physical law of the conservation of energy. Because planets and moons are so much more massive than spacecraft, their speed shifts only minutely compared with the change in speed of the craft.

As an example of the effectiveness of such a technique, when *Voyager 1* encountered Jupiter in 1979, it received a boost of about 36,000 mph (58,000 km/h). Without Jupiter's gravity to assist it, the probe would have needed about 3.20 million lbs (1.45 million kg) of propellant to accomplish the same maneuver. This is significantly more mass than any of the world's launch vehicles can deliver to space. While the tiny probe gained a tremendous increase in its speed, Jupiter slowed in its orbit of the Sun by about one foot (30 cm) per trillion years.

A CLOSER LOOK

spacecraft, including their relative positions, velocities, and orientations. The complexity of the maneuver requires computers to aid pilots or to control automatic systems to bring the spacecraft close together in a safe way.

Navigation

Most spacecraft navigation is accomplished using a variety of techniques in which the spacecraft's radio signal reveals the speed of the craft and its location. Computers on the ground combine this information with a knowledge of the forces acting on the spacecraft, such as gravitational attractions and the action of the propulsion system, to calculate where the spacecraft will be at any time in the future.

Escaping Earth's gravity

Spaceflight to other planets in the Solar System involves a lengthy trip. The relative movement of the planets as they orbit the Sun means that the length of a trip to another planet can vary greatly depending on when the spacecraft leaves Earth. The best times to launch are called launch windows. Launch windows occur when a trajectory from Earth to the target can be the shortest distance while still launching with a minimal expenditure of energy. Launch windows to Mars and Venus, our nearest neighbors, occur every two years or so. These trips take many months, but they are not nearly as long as the flights to the outer planets.

A spacecraft designed to orbit another planet must change its initial trajectory to be captured by the gravity of its target destination. When captured into an orbit, the spacecraft's speed will balance with the gravitational pull of the planet. This is analogous to swinging a tethered ball on a length of string: the string pulls the ball inward (in the same way as gravity pulls craft toward planets), altering a straight trajectory into a circle (see ROTATIONAL MOTION).

The space environment

Spacecraft must be designed to operate in an environment that is very different from that of Earth. In space there is no atmosphere. This means that there is nothing to slow the spacecraft; there is also no protection for instruments and people from heat or radiation. The range of temperatures can span hundreds of degrees (see HEAT, PRINCIPLES OF; ELECTROMAGNETIC RADIATION).

As well as fully functioning satellites, there is now a large amount of space junk—human-made debris—in orbit around Earth. This debris ranges from complete unused satellites and expended launch vehicles to tiny shards of material left behind after explosive tests in orbit. Colliding with such debris, even the tiniest speck, is one of the greatest hazards of spaceflight because orbit speeds are so high. Micrometeoroids (tiny fragments of space rock) provide another hazard, although in low Earth orbit the risk of colliding with debris is far higher than the risk of colliding with natural objects.

Although it is not empty, space is essentially a vacuum environment. The lack of pressure affects both people and machines. While outside Earth's atmosphere, astronauts must always be inside either a pressurized cabin in their spacecraft or a pressurized space suit that provides them with life-support systems (see SPACE SUIT).

Weightlessness (also called freefall, microgravity, or zero gravity) has many adverse effects. Astronauts inside an orbiting spacecraft float and no longer have any sense of up or down. This can create a number of physical problems, especially when weightlessness lasts a long time. Astronauts are subject to a form of motion sickness called space adaptation syndrome (see the box on page 1223), loss of muscle and bone, impaired functioning of the immune system, and, sometimes, fluid imbalances. Another problem that can be caused by weightlessness is that the returning astronauts may be at risk of fainting, because without the downward pull of gravity, blood and other bodily fluids accumulate in the upper part of the body. Interpreting this as an excess of fluid everywhere in its tissues, the body then responds by diminishing the total volume of fluid. Returning astronauts therefore have very low blood volume. To prevent any unpleasant side effects or dangerous losses of fluids, they drink a great deal of liquid prior to returning to a full gravity environment at the end of their missions.

Returning to Earth

If a spacecraft is destined to return to Earth, it must be able to withstand the enormous heat it will generate when it reenters Earth's atmosphere, moving at more than 16,000 mph (26,750 km/h). At this speed, the friction with the atmosphere can heat portions of its surface to more than 3000°F (1667°C). Most reentering spacecraft simply burn up. Sections of some larger spacecraft, such as the derelict *Skylab* space station, do not burn up completely on reentry and survive to crash into the Earth's surface.

Many craft, of course, are designed to survive and land safely, including the aerodynamic space shuttle. A gradual descent and heat shields prevent them from burning up. Shuttle reentry usually begins about 5000 miles (8050 km) from the intended landing site. As the shuttle descends to the denser air, it begins to fly more like a glider, using its aerodynamic control surfaces more and its control rockets less (see GLIDER). The shuttle lands at more than 200 mph (322 km/h) and uses a small parachute to slow its progress across the landing strip (see PARACHUTE).

The future of space flight

Colonizing space around Earth, the Moon, and Mars may be possible in the future. Some scientists hope to make observations from probes sent beyond the Solar System. Even flights to other stars are theoretically possible. However, the distances involved make missions to even the nearest stars impractical using the technology of the foreseeable future. Nonetheless, four spacecraft that were launched many years ago will soon be leaving the Solar System: *Pioneer 10* and *11* and *Voyager 1* and *2* have all completed their primary missions to investigate the outer planets and are now on course for the stars. However, it would take many thousands of years for them to reach other stars, and they are not expected to operate for more than another few decades, so they will eventually drift inertly (see SPACE PROBES).

Spacecraft bound for deep space may one day use engines that produce minute amounts of thrust for long periods of time to power them on their outbound journey from Earth orbit. The ion engine is an example of such an engine. It needs very little propellant and can work for long periods of time.

J. TEMPLE-DENNETT

See also: AERODYNAMICS; LAUNCH SITE; MISSILE; SPACE STATION; SPACE TRAVEL AND TECHNOLOGY.

SPACE ADAPTATION SYNDROME

A training astronaut inside a device used to produce conflicting sensory signals.

One of the biggest health problems for people traveling in space is space adaptation syndrome, also known as space motion sickness. The condition was first experienced by Soviet cosmonaut Gherman Titov (1935–) in 1961. The symptoms include nausea, vomiting, depressed appetite, lethargy, gastrointestinal discomfort, and disorientation. After a few days in space, most individuals adapt to their weightless environment. Some 70 percent of the astronauts who have flown on the space shuttle have suffered from space adaptation syndrome, but all of them recovered after a few days.

Space adaptation syndrome is probably the result of conflicting messages from the body's sensory organs. The human vestibular system measures both rotation and orientation, but the sensors do not work correctly in the absence of gravity. As the brain attempts to sort out the conflict between what it feels and what it sees, it produces the various symptoms of imbalance. Since most people recover from the condition quickly, scientists have tried to devise ways to train astronauts to rely primarily on visual orientation. On most missions, few critical activities are scheduled in the first few days of flight to allow time for the crew to adjust to conditions in space.

A CLOSER LOOK

Further reading:

Brown, C. *Spacecraft Mission Design*. 2nd edition. Reston, Virginia: American Institute of Aeronautics and Astronautics, 1998.
Gurzadian, G. *Theory of Interplanetary Flight*. Amsterdam: Gordon & Breach, 1996.
Suvorov, V. *The First Manned Spaceflight: Russia's Quest for Space*. Commack, New York: Nova Science Publishing, 1997.

SPACE PROBES

A space probe is an uncrewed spacecraft sent to study other parts of the Solar System close up

The Galileo space probe visited Jupiter, the largest planet in the Solar System, in December 1995. The craft dropped a probe capsule equipped with a parachute to study the planet's atmosphere at close quarters. The probe is shown here superimposed on a photo of the planet Jupiter.

Uncrewed space probes provide a number of advantages over crewed space missions. Besides the fact that their use eliminates any risk to human life, it is also much more expensive to launch a craft containing a crew and all the supplies that would be necessary to keep them alive for the enormous duration of an interplanetary journey (see LAUNCH VEHICLE).

A number of other worlds in the Solar System have been explored by space probes, including the Moon, seven of the eight other planets and their many moons, a few comets and asteroids, and even the Sun. Carrying sophisticated instrumentation, space probes approach their targets in several ways. Some early lunar landers were designed to crash-land on the Moon. More sophisticated probes can achieve a soft landing using rockets or parachutes. Others are designed to fly past or orbit their target.

The race to space

Shortly after the first spacecraft were launched in 1957 and 1958, the United States and the Soviet Union were involved in a tense technological contest to explore the Moon. The Soviet lunar program began with the Luna spacecraft series, some of the later versions of which included Lunokhod roving vehicles. The Soviet Zond (probe) program was designed to prepare for piloted lunar missions (although these never became a reality). The U.S. program began with Pioneer, followed by the Ranger, Lunar Orbiter, and Surveyor series.

As the race to land humans on the Moon continued, both the United States and the Soviet Union raised their sights to the nearby planets. Venus was the first target. Ultimately, the United States sent eight probes there, some using the gravitational field of Venus to direct them to other targets. The Soviet Union sent eighteen probes to Venus, but only some of them succeeded in sending back information. Mars proved even more enticing. By 1998, nineteen probes had flown by, orbited, or landed on Mars.

While the Moon, inner planets, and the Martian moons were being explored, other missions set out to study the giant outer planets and their moons, as well as other bodies such as asteroids, comets, and the Sun itself. As spacecraft and instruments became more complex, missions became more ambitious.

CORE FACTS

■ As well as being a safer way of exploring the Solar System, using space probes is much cheaper than sending people into space.

■ Space probes can collect information on other objects in the Solar System by flying past them, going into orbit around them, or landing on their surface.

■ Space probes have been sent to all the other planets of the Solar System, except Pluto. They have also been sent to asteroids, comets, the Moon, and even the Sun.

■ Many space probes have produced a wealth of scientific information. For example, in just one flight, *Voyager 2* has encountered the planets Jupiter, Saturn, Uranus, and Neptune, as well as many of their moons, and was still sending data back to scientists on Earth over twenty years after its launch.

CONNECTIONS

● Many space probes use **SOLAR POWER** to generate electricity.

● Space probes require an **ANTENNA AND TRANSMITTER** for sending and receiving information to and from **GROUND STATIONS** on Earth.

Successful missions

The following list of probes include the world's major efforts to explore the Solar System.

Luna. The first Soviet lunar probes were launched in 1958. *Luna 1*, launched in 1959, missed the Moon. However, its successor, *Luna 2*, became the first human-made object on the Moon later that year. *Luna 3* photographed the far side of the moon in 1959. In 1966, *Luna 9* soft-landed and relayed TV photographs of the lunar surface. In 1970 and 1973, Lunokhod robotic rovers carried by Luna probes investigated the surface.

Pioneer. The Pioneer space probes were the workhorses of the early U.S. space program. Of the five Pioneer lunar probes, only *Pioneer 4* was successful. It flew by the Moon and provided valuable information on radiation levels in space. Pioneer spacecraft were later redesigned to explore beyond the Moon.

Pioneer 10, launched in 1972, was the first probe to operate beyond Mars. It targeted the asteroid belt, Jupiter, and Saturn. Incredibly, *Pioneer 10* is still operating more than 25 years after its launch.

The last two Pioneer craft were named *Pioneer Venus.* They were both launched toward Venus in 1978 (see the box on page 1226).

Ranger. The U.S. Ranger series included nine missions to the Moon in the early 1960s, but only *Ranger 7, 8,* and *9* were entirely successful, taking photos of the lunar surface before hard-landing.

Surveyor. Surveyor, the next U.S. series of lunar probes, was designed to make soft landings. In 1966, *Surveyor 1* successfully soft-landed on the Moon. Five of the seven Surveyor probes succeeded in making detailed investigations of their landing sites and, in some cases, making chemical analyses of the soil.

Lunar Orbiter. The five U.S. Lunar Orbiter missions provided scientists at the National Aeronautics and Space Administration (NASA) with data needed to help select the first landing site for astronauts.

Venera. Sixteen Venera (Venus) space probes were launched by the Soviet Union. *Venera 4* was the first successful one and the Soviet Union's first successful planetary mission. Arriving at Venus in 1967, it released a lander into the corrosive atmosphere. This survived only briefly but sent back observations of an inhospitable world. In December 1970, *Venera 7* became the first space probe to drop a lander that survived to observe the surface of Venus.

Subsequent Venera spacecraft carried landers that sent back data about the atmosphere, climate, and surface of Venus. Probes dropped by *Venera 13* and *14* in 1982 carried robot drills to sample the soil, and equipment to record and transmit color images. A year later, *Venera 15* and *16* made radar surveys of the surface to provide a near-global map of the planet.

Vega. Encouraged by the success of the Venera spacecraft, the Soviet Union organized two more Venus probes. Each carried experiments to study both Venus and Halley's Comet, which was then returning to the inner Solar System. *Vega 1* and *2* reached Venus in 1985. They dropped landers, which in turn dropped their own probes that were buoyed by balloons to keep them floating in the atmosphere for several days.

MISSION SUMMARIES

Launch date	Name	Country	Purpose
1958	Pioneer 0–4	United States	Study the Moon
1959	Luna	Soviet Union	Explore the Moon
1961	Ranger 1–9	United States	Provide close-up images of the Moon
1961	Venera	Soviet Union	Explore Venus
1962	Mariner	United States	Explore Mars, Venus, and Mercury
1962	Mars 1–7	Soviet Union	Study Mars
1965	Zond 3–8	Soviet Union	Explore the Moon
1966	Lunar Orbiter 1–5	United States	Find landing sites for crewed craft
1966	Surveyor 1–7	United States	Land on the Moon
1975	Viking 1, 2	United States	Explore Mars with landers and orbiters
1977	Voyager 1, 2	United States	Explore outer planets
1978	Sun Earth Explorer–3	United States	Study comets
1984	Vega	Soviet Union	Explore Venus and Halley's Comet
1985	Giotto	ESA	Study two comets
1985	Sakigake	Japan	Study Halley's Comet
1985	Suisei	Japan	Study Halley's Comet
1989	Magellan	United States	Map Venus in detail
1990	Ulysses	ESA/United States	Study the Sun
1994	Clementine	United States	Test military technologies
1996	Mars Global Surveyor	United States	Study Martian atmosphere and surface
1996	Mars Pathfinder	United States	Study Martian surface
1998	Deep Space 1	United States	Test high-risk, advanced technologies
1998	Lunar Prospector	United States	Map the Moon's structure
1999	Deep Space 2	United States	Map the Martian surface

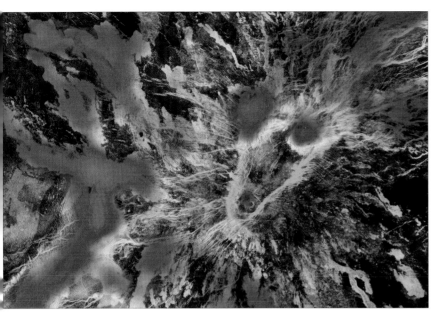

This enhanced color map of an unnamed volcano on Venus was made using radar equipment on the Magellan space probe.

Mariner. The U.S. Mariner probes were designed to explore the planets of the inner Solar System. *Mariner 2* was the first successful planetary mission, encountering Venus in 1962. *Mariner 5* repeated the feat in 1967. In 1965, *Mariner 4* became the first spacecraft to reveal the surface of Mars.

As technology advanced, the Mariner space probes evolved. *Mariner 6* and *7* teamed up on a Mars flyby that provided measurements of surface temperature and images showing the polar ice caps. Placed into orbit around Mars in 1971, *Mariner 9* mapped the planet and provided images of the Martian moons, Deimos and Phobos.

In 1974, *Mariner 10* used the gravitational field of Venus to bend its path and direct it on toward Mercury. This was the first time a single space probe had visited two planets and demonstrated that this slingshot technique worked (see SPACE FLIGHT). *Mariner 10* carried a sunshade and solar panels that could rotate to help keep the temperature down as it flew close to the Sun. During its three flybys of Mercury, the cameras on *Mariner 10* imaged about 40 percent of the planet's surface. One remarkable finding was that Mercury had a metallic core. As of 1999, no other spacecraft had visited Mercury.

Mars. The Soviet Mars program began in 1960; however, a Soviet Mars space probe did not successfully reach Mars until 1972. Both *Mars 2* and *3* deployed landers before entering orbit, but the first apparently crashed, and the *Mars 3* lander succeeded in returning only a few secondsworth of data from the surface. In 1973, *Mars 4*, *5*, *6*, and *7* were launched. *Mars 5* was successful; entering Martian orbit and sending back data about the planet below.

Viking. In 1976, two U.S. Viking spacecraft entered orbit around Mars and each released a lander equipped to study and sample the surface. Among the on-board instruments were a seismometer, cameras, meteorological instruments, a remote-control arm to gather soil samples and a biology laboratory to analyze them (see METEOROLOGICAL INSTRUMENTS; SEISMOGRAPHY). However, these studies did not resolve the long-standing question about whether life exists or has existed on Mars. In total, the Viking landers produced more than 4500 images of the surface. Between them, the Viking orbiters mapped 97 percent of the surface.

Voyager. NASA's Voyager spacecraft were the next probes to study the outer planets. They carried much more sophisticated instruments than their Pioneer predecessors. The two craft were launched in 1977. They took slightly different routes, arriving at Jupiter after 18 months and 22 months, respectively.

Voyager 1 flew by Jupiter in 1979, discovering, among other things, a previously unknown ring. It took closeup pictures of three Jovian moons: Ganymede, Callisto, and Io. Then the craft took advantage of Jupiter's gravity to push it farther on its journey. A year and a half later, it reached Saturn and made measurements of the planet and its environment, including its largest moon, Titan.

Voyager 2 took closeup photographs of the moon Europa before continuing on its grand tour of the outer planets. It encountered Saturn in 1981, Uranus in 1986, and Neptune in 1989, returning images and other important scientific data on the planets, rings, and moons it encountered. Then *Voyager 2*, like its twin, continued on a forever outward journey. Both spacecraft are still sending signals back to Earth.

Sakigake and Suisei. Launched in January 1985, Japan's first interplanetary probe *Sakigake* (pioneer) was one of several spacecraft to study Halley's Comet on its 1986 visit to the inner Solar System. *Suisei* (comet) was launched seven months later.

Giotto. The European Space Agency (ESA) designed *Giotto* to fly past Halley's Comet, sending back information on the comet's tail, nucleus, and its visible head, or coma. Giotto flew past the nucleus at a distance of about 1000 miles (600 km). While its

PIONEER VENUS

Pioneer Venus was one of the many outstandingly successful missions that have sent back to Earth a whole range of information about another planet over a number of years. Although often considered as a single mission, two spacecraft were involved: the *Pioneer Venus Orbiter* and the *Pioneer Venus Multiprobe*. They were launched separately and traveled to Venus independently. The multiprobe contained five entry vehicles. On reaching Venus in December 1978, these were plunged into the atmosphere and sent back scientific data on atmospheric structure and composition.

The *Pioneer Venus Orbiter* was left in a 24-hour elliptical orbit that ranged in altitude from 115 miles (184 km) to 41,000 miles (65,600 km). This sturdy, drum-shaped, spin-stabilized spacecraft weighed 810 lbs (368 kg) and was 8.2 ft (2.5 m) in diameter and 4 ft (1.2 m) long. The orbiter made the first radar maps of the surface of the cloud-covered planet, gathering data for 14 years.

In 1986, Venus was much better situated than Earth for the rare visit of Halley's Comet to the inner Solar System, so the versatile optical instruments of the orbiter were used to obtain the first image of the coma, the visible head of the comet, surrounding the comet as it sped by. The orbiter was also used to provide data about five other passing comets. In 1992, the craft finally burned up in the atmosphere of Venus.

A CLOSER LOOK

camera was damaged in the encounter, all other systems remained operational. The probe encountered a second comet, Grigg-Skjellerup, in 1992.

Magellan. In August 1990, NASA's *Magellan* probe entered orbit around Venus. Using a sophisticated radar system, the spacecraft mapped the cloud-covered planet's surface at far higher resolutions than previous spacecraft, returning more data than all previous planetary missions combined (see RADAR).

Galileo. Launched in 1989, NASA's *Galileo* entered orbit around Jupiter in 1995. It dropped a probe capsule into the atmosphere of the giant planet and for several years conducted a detailed study of the Jovian system. Its findings have suggested that there may be an ocean under the ice crust of Europa.

Ulysses. The joint ESA/NASA *Ulysses* craft is the only probe to have studied the Sun from far outside the plane of Earth's orbit. As it flew "under" the Sun, *Ulysses* also provided the first measurements of emissions from the poles of the Sun.

Clementine. Actually part of a project to test military hardware (see STRATEGIC DEFENSE SYSTEMS), *Clementine's* five imaging sensors accomplished the first multispectral global mapping of the Moon. It took more than 2.5 million pictures while in lunar orbit before heading off to encounter an asteroid.

Mars Global Surveyor. Launched in 1996, *Mars Global Surveyor* provided information about the Martian atmosphere and images of the surface to allow global mapping. This U.S. probe used the novel technique of aerobraking to adjust its orbit. Rather than carrying a heavy load of propellant, it made repeated passes through the tenuous upper atmosphere to allow air resistance to modify its orbit.

Mars Pathfinder. NASA's *Mars Pathfinder* reached Mars in 1997, using a system of air bags to cushion itself at landing. It released a small rover vehicle that returned pictures, weather information, and chemical analyses of rocks and soil.

Lunar Prospector. The U.S. spacecraft *Lunar Prospector* gave compelling evidence for the presence of ice on the Moon, perhaps as much as 6.6 billion tons (6 billion tonnes) of it, from a low-altitude polar orbit. The probe also made measurements of the chemical composition of the surface.

Deep Space 1. NASA's *Deep Space 1* was launched in 1998 to test high-risk, very advanced technologies that will be important for NASA's subsequent space probes. It proved the effectiveness of ion propulsion, paving the way for future highly capable, low-cost missions (see ROCKET ENGINE).

Missions in progress

Because of the long periods of time involved in spaceflight, a number of space probes that have already been launched have yet to reach their targets. A selection of these are listed below:

Cassini / Huygens. NASA's *Cassini* probe began its seven-year journey to Saturn in October 1997. *Cassini's* instruments will image the planet, measure fields and particles, and deploy the ESA *Huygens* probe, which will study the moon Titan.

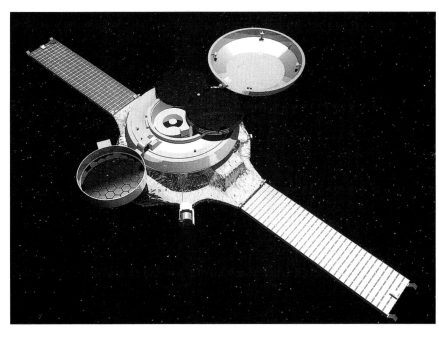

Mars Surveyor '98. As part of a long-term program of exploring Mars, NASA launched *Mars Climate Orbiter* at the end of 1998 and *Mars Polar Lander* at the beginning of 1999. The lander is aimed for the south polar region of Mars. The orbiter is designed to perform detailed studies of the Martian climate.

Stardust. The U.S. probe *Stardust* is designed to reach Comet Wild 2 in 2004. *Stardust* is the first probe to attempt to obtain samples from deep space. Pieces of comet dust will be collected and transported back to Earth for analysis.

Future missions

Space probes are likely to continue to play a major role in space exploration for the foreseeable future. Probes planned for launch in the near future include NASA's low-cost *Genesis* probe, which is designed to collect samples of the solar wind (a stream of particles constantly emitted by the Sun) and return them to Earth. The Comet Nucleus Tour (CONTOUR) is an ambitious NASA mission to fly a space probe past at least three separate comets and analyze the dust flow around each of them.

NASA also has a number of Mars missions planned for Mars for the early part of the 21st century. One of the most exciting ideas proposed is to send a probe to the planet's surface to collect a small piece of rock and return it to Earth for analysis. This would be the first time that material has ever been brought back from another planet, and it is hoped that the findings will shed light on the continuing debate concerning the possibility of life having once existed on Mars.

J. TEMPLE-DENNETT

See also: ROBOTICS; SATELLITE; SPACE TRAVEL AND TECHNOLOGY; UNPILOTED VEHICLES AND AIRCRAFT.

Further reading:

Dudley, M. *An Eye to the Sky*. New York: Maxwell Macmillan International, 1992.

The **Genesis** *space probe is designed to collect particles from the solar wind and return them to Earth for analysis in 2003. Scientists hope that this information will give vital clues about the formation of the Solar System.*

SPACE STATION

A space station is a facility where a crew can live and conduct long-term experiments in space

Following undocking from the space shuttle Atlantis _in September 1996, the Russian space station,_ Mir, _passes over Cook Strait in New Zealand._

Space stations share many characteristics with other piloted spacecraft. They must provide living quarters, provisions, and full life-support systems for their crew, along with the facilities to conduct experiments. However, space stations are designed for longer missions than other craft, such as the U.S. space shuttle. They tend to be larger and more comfortable and usually feature docking facilities to allow for the regular resupply of food, propellant, and other expendable resources and for occasional changes of crew. Small space stations have been built on Earth and launched into orbit by rocket. Larger stations require assembly in space (see LAUNCH VEHICLE; ROCKET ENGINE; ROCKETRY).

Salyut stations

The first space station, the 21-ton (19-tonne) Soviet *Salyut* ("Salute") *1*, was launched on April 19, 1971. Salyuts were launched until 1977, with various unpiloted Soviet spacecraft joining the stations in orbit, some remaining as permanent parts. Soyuz ("Union") craft ferried crews back and forth.

Salyut 6 and 7 were the first space stations to use automatic resupply missions. These two stations had international crews, including astronauts from Cuba, France, India, Vietnam, and Eastern Europe. The Salyut crews set many long-term endurance records, conducted scientific research, and provided the Soviet Union with unique and extensive experience in designing, building, and operating space stations.

Skylab and Mir

The first U.S. space station was *Skylab*, launched on May 14, 1973—two years after the first Salyut. The three three-person crews of *Skylab*, which weighed just under 100 tons (90 tonnes) conducted many scientific experiments, including the first complete view of the Sun with the Apollo telescope mount.

The *Mir* ("Peace") space station evolved from the Salyut stations. Launched on February 20, 1986, with six docking ports, *Mir* became the versatile workhorse of space station science for more than a decade. It housed crews for years without interruption and welcomed astronauts and research projects from the international space science community.

The International Space Station

As *Mir* aged, the next space station—a truly international effort—was planned. The assembly of the International Space Station (ISS), due for completion in 2003, has required an unprecedented number of space missions and construction space walks. Fully assembled, solar panels unfurled, the ISS will be nearly the size of two football fields, and the brightest human-made object in the nighttime sky. Costs are estimated at between $40 billion and $100 billion, making it the most expensive construction ever.

It is estimated that the building of the ISS will involve at least 43 launches, 34 of which will be by space shuttles. The construction schedule involves 144 space walks, totaling 1800 hours. The final orbit of the fully assembled ISS will be 265 miles (425 km)

CONNECTIONS

● Experiments can also be conducted in space using robotic **SATELLITES** and **SPACE PROBES**.

CORE FACTS

- Space stations are designed for much longer missions than other piloted spacecraft.
- Space stations can be built on Earth and launched by rocket or assembled in stages in space.
- Endurance records in space have been set by cosmonauts (the Soviet name for astronauts) in space stations, such as the Salyut series and *Mir*.
- When completed, the International Space Station will be the largest spacecraft ever put into orbit.
- In the future it may be possible to exploit the low gravity inside a space station in order to manufacture chemicals, medicines, and other materials that could not be produced easily on Earth.

high, traveling between 51.6 degrees north and south of the equator. This orbit provides coverage of 85 percent of Earth and 95 percent of the total human population. It will also allow all international ISS partners to reach the space station from their own launch sites (see LAUNCH SITE).

The U.S.-funded, Russian-built *Zarya* ("Dawn" or "Sunrise") control module was the first of 100 ISS components to be launched. It was carried on a Russian Proton rocket from Baikonur, Kazakhstan, on November 20, 1998. Dubbed the space tugboat, its role is to supply propulsion, power, and communications. Shortly after the *Zarya* launch, the *Unity* connecting module—the first U.S.-built component to reach orbit—was carried by space shuttle *Endeavour*. The shuttle crew linked *Unity* and *Zarya* using robotic arm operations and three space walks.

Fully assembled, the ISS interlocking modules will offer pressurized working and living space similar to that inside two 747 jumbo jets (46,000 cubic feet, or 1300 cubic meters). The ISS is a unique opportunity to investigate physical phenomena and industrial production processes in a low-gravity environment (see the box at right), and it will also provide information on how humans respond to long-duration weightlessness (see SPACE FLIGHT).

The nations agreeing to build the ISS were Belgium, Brazil, Great Britain, Canada, Denmark, France, Germany, Italy, Japan, the Netherlands, Norway, Russia, Spain, Sweden, Switzerland, and the United States. Some components were supplied by individual nations: Canada built the 55-ft (17-m) robotic arm used for assembly and maintenance tasks; the Italian Space Agency built the *Leonardo* module, used to carry supplies to and from orbit aboard U.S. space shuttles; Japan built a laboratory with a facility to expose experiments to open space. The nine member nations of the European Space Agency together supplied a data management system and built a pressurized laboratory. The United States led the overall design and development of the station.

Space stations of the future

Although the ISS is expected to have a long life, designers are already thinking about the next space station—perhaps a full-scale space manufacturing facility, perhaps a comfortable habitat with spinning portions that use centripetal acceleration to simulate Earth's gravity (see ROTATIONAL MOTION). It may include a rehabilitation hospital where people can recover from broken limbs or undergo heart surgery in low gravity, or it may be used as a way station to other planets. In theory, a space station could be self-sustaining, with no need for resupplying from Earth. Some designs involve onboard hydroponic farming to produce food and oxygen (see HYDROPONICS). It may be possible to put self-sustaining space stations into orbit around other planets, allowing people to live entirely independently of Earth.

J. TEMPLE-DENNETT

See also: SPACE TRAVEL AND TECHNOLOGY.

Further reading:
Logsdon, J. *Together in Orbit: The Origins of International Participation in the Space Station.* Washington, D.C.: NASA Headquarters, 1998.

An artist's impression of the International Space Station (ISS) over Florida and the Bahamas.

LONG-TERM STUDIES IN SPACE

There are many potential scientific and economic benefits of low-gravity (or microgravity) science and technology. Research plans for space station laboratories range from fundamental studies in microgravity science to assessments of the possibilities of manufacturing chemicals, medicines, and other materials in space.

Eventual production of materials in space requires a detailed understanding of how a microgravity environment affects physical processes. For example, alloys, foams, and polymers may solidify in low gravity without separating or settling. This could allow the production of superalloys with important and valuable new properties (see ALLOY; PLASTICS).

In microgravity science, much can be learned about the behavior of fluids and materials in space that will help insure the safety and success of long-term space missions. Microgravity changes the way in which some familiar processes work, such as combustion (burning), boiling, and the formation of crystals. These altered physical processes must be understood before either long-term spaceflight or space manufacturing can become a reality.

Space manufacturing offers possibilities ranging from making the materials needed to build other space stations (or lunar or planetary outposts) to processing high-quality materials for sale on Earth. For example, near-perfect spheres can result from manufacturing in low gravity. If affordable in large quantities, such spheres would find ready use in laser-optic systems, medical applications, and laboratory standards. Processes that are expensive in gravity-laden facilities might be much less expensive in space, despite the huge launch and retrieval costs. A few private companies are currently funding research into space-based manufacturing, with little success so far.

However, the idea of conducting science on a space station has been criticized by some scientists. Many do not consider the ISS a worthwhile investment and believe that the vast sums of money involved could be better used to fund alternative scientific research on Earth.

WIDER IMPACT

SPACE SUIT

A space suit provides a self-contained, safe, and comfortable environment for a person working in space

An astronaut on a space shuttle mission is able to float in the vicinity of the shuttle wearing an extravehicular mobility unit.

The dangers of working outside the relative safety of a spacecraft, which include exposure to radiation, extreme pressures and temperatures, and micrometeoroids (small, high-speed particles), are reduced to acceptable levels through the wearing of a space suit. A space suit is like a one-person spacecraft. It must provide breathable air and be engineered so that the astronaut is not immobilized by a stiff, ballooning pressure suit. Space suits have been in use since the early 1960s, and designs have evolved as technology has matured and needs have changed. Although many different models exist, this article focuses on the NASA extravehicular mobility unit used on space shuttles in the 1980s and 1990s.

Preparation

Before putting on a space suit, which keeps the body at a pressure well below normal atmospheric pressure to prevent it swelling up in the vacuum of space, astronauts must breathe pure oxygen to flush nitrogen from their blood. This prevents the bends (dysbarism)—the painful, dangerous condition that results from bubbles of nitrogen gas forming in the bloodstream when pressure outside the body drops significantly (see DEEP-SEA AND DIVING TECHNOLOGY).

Parts of the suit

The astronaut wears special liquid-cooled underwear. Because trapped metabolic heat can harm the life-support system of the space suit, part of an astronaut's training includes pacing activities to produce a level of heat output that the suit can handle. The space suit's cooling layer removes heat generated by the astronaut, while the overall design insulates him or her from extreme exterior temperatures, which can range from being deadly cold to extremely hot.

The space suit has an inner layer of rubber to hold in the air that envelops the astronaut's body; a layer of Dracon polyester to maintain the suit's shape and prevent it from overexpanding; and several layers of fireproof fabric, metal, Kevlar, and Teflon to protect against radiation and micrometeoroids. The extravehicular mobility suit consists of several parts that must be joined together. For example, the trousers come apart at the knee and have attached boots. A stiff aluminum torso section connects to the top trouser sections and to the sleeves, which have flexible bellows at both the shoulders and elbows.

The torso section includes a bag of drinking water with a tube leading to the helmet. A urine collection bag is also provided. Gloves with rubber fingertips for extra sensitivity and a one-piece plastic helmet with a detachable visor for protection from meteorite fragments and radiation complete the outfit. Controls mounted on the chest allow the astronaut to adjust a life-support system and operate a two-way radio. A microphone and headphones are built in to a cap worn under the helmet.

Fit is important in a space suit, but some areas are more crucial than others. Helmets, for example, came in one size, but if the astronaut is to manipulate tools efficiently, custom-made gloves are essential.

Life-support system

The life-support system in the backpack of the extravehicular mobility unit includes batteries, oxygen, and water. In modern space suits these will last for over seven hours. The system also contains a ventilator to circulate oxygen to the suit, a refrigeration unit to keep the water cold, and a pump to circulate it through cooling lines in the suit. If exhaled carbon dioxide is left to build up in the suit, it will eventually suffocate the astronaut. There is therefore a container with lithium hydroxide and activated carbon to absorb expended carbon dioxide and unpleasant odors. A ventilator absorbs water vapor exhaled by the astronaut. A back-up system insures that if there is a fault, the astronaut will have enough time to return safely to the spacecraft.

Future of space suits

Although robotics technology increasingly allows astronauts to perform tasks without leaving their spacecraft, space suits are necessary for operations outside the spacecraft and as emergency equipment.

S. CALVO

See also: BODY PROTECTION; SPACE FLIGHT.

Further reading:

Kozloski, L. *U.S. Space Gear: Outfitting the Astronaut.* Washington D.C.: Smithsonian Institution Press, 1994.

CONNECTIONS

● **ERGONOMIC** designs ensure that modern space suits are as comfortable and easy to move about in as possible.

● Much of the International **SPACE STATION** has been assembled in space by astronauts wearing space suits.

SPACE TRAVEL AND TECHNOLOGY

Space technology has let people and robots travel in space, showing major scientific achievement and endeavor

The space age began with the launch of the first satellite, *Sputnik 1*, by the Soviet Union on October 4, 1957. In the decades since then, space flight and satellite launches have become routine, and space probes have visited the farthest reaches of the Solar System. But crewed space flight beyond Earth has not progressed as rapidly as predicted; the farthest a person has traveled is the quarter-million miles (400,000 km) to the Moon. The reason that ambitious plans to put astronauts on other planets have failed has more to do with politics and money than failure of technology. Rapid and unexpected advances in microelectronics have rendered crewed space flight unnecessary on many missions.

Space flight pioneers

The first theories and experiments in space flight came in the late 19th and early 20th centuries, when many young scientists were inspired by science-fiction stories such as those of English author H. G. Wells (1866–1946) and French author Jules Verne (1828–1905). Wells and Verne were in turn inspired by the rapid industrial and scientific progress they saw around them; it seemed as if nothing were impossible (although actually their plans for space flight were completely impractical).

The first person to develop the idea of space flight in a scientific way was Russian schoolteacher Konstantin Tsiolkovsky (1857–1935), who established much of the theory of space flight but never built a practical rocket (see the box on page 1232). In the meantime, other young scientists and engineers were also becoming fascinated with the possibilities of rockets and space travel (see ROCKET ENGINE; ROCKETRY). U.S. rocket pioneer Robert Goddard (1882–1945) launched the first liquid-propelled rocket in 1926, while space flight groups in Germany and the Soviet Union soon began to develop their own rockets. When the Nazis came to power in Germany in 1933, they realized the rocket's potential as a weapon and funded the development of a

This photograph taken from Apollo 7 in 1968 shows a discarded stage of its launch vehicle over the Gulf of California.

series of ever-larger missile vehicles, culminating in the V-2 rocket-powered missile first launched in 1943 (see MISSILE).

At the end of World War II (1939–1945), U.S. and Soviet troops competed to attract the Nazi rocket scientists and put them to work on their own rocket programs, with the aim of developing intercontinental ballistic missiles (ICBMs) that could carry a nuclear warhead halfway around the world (see NUCLEAR WEAPONS). Many of the scientists involved in these programs promoted rockets' possible use as vehicles for putting satellites into space.

Dawn of the space age

In 1954, both the United States and the Soviet Union announced that they would be launching artificial satellites as part of the International Geophysical Year 1957–1958. This was the beginning of the space race, although few realized it at the time. The Soviets kept their plans shrouded in secrecy, and most Western experts did not think the Soviet Union had the capability to launch a satellite. Meanwhile, the U.S. rocket program slowed as it became clear to the politicians who controlled the funds that it was politically inadvisable for the space program to be seen as an overtly military operation. As a result, the Orbiter rocket program, run by German engineer Werner von Braun (1912–1977) and other V-2 rocket scientists, had its resources cut because it was

CORE FACTS

- The space age began in 1957. Development in the early decades was driven by a space race between the United States and the Soviet Union.
- The majority of space missions are unmanned. Manned spacecraft require far more complex and expensive systems than automatic satellites and space probes.
- The space shuttle is the world's first reusable spacecraft. It can launch and repair satellites and act as an orbiting laboratory.
- The Soviet Union pioneered the development of space stations, and Russia is a major partner in the International Space Station.

CONNECTIONS

● All space missions to explore other planets in the Solar System have used unmanned **SPACE PROBES**.

● An understanding of **MATERIALS SCIENCE** and of the properties of **METALS** has been fundamental to space technology.

● Spacecraft are often controlled by Earth-based **GROUND STATIONS**.

A dog named Laika was sent into orbit around Earth aboard the Soviet satellite Sputnik 2 in 1957. Laika's last meal was poisoned to prevent her from dying slowly from starvation.

Animals in space

Putting a person in space quickly became a major challenge between the competing superpowers. The Soviets had a clear advantage because of the power of their launch vehicles, and within a month of the first satellite launch—even before the United States had succeeded in reaching orbit—they launched *Sputnik 2*, a huge 1121-lb (509-kg) satellite carrying scientific instruments and a dog named Laika.

Of course, putting animals or humans into orbit involved more than just launching additional weight, and over the next three years both U.S. and Soviet scientists and engineers conducted a series of test flights (some with animals on board), developing the systems that would allow crewed spaceflight.

Returning to Earth

One of the most fundamental problems facing the developers of crewed space missions was how to return a space capsule to Earth safely. When any object enters Earth's atmosphere at high speed, friction with air molecules generates a lot of heat. This can cause the object to burn up, which is what causes meteors to glow and appear as shooting stars. Some method had to be found to reduce the heat buildup.

It was soon realized that the solution was to construct a heat shield that was designed to burn and break away, carrying heat with it. The first of these ablative heat shields were thick coatings of synthetic resins, tested on *Sputnik 4, 5, 6, 9,* and *10,* which were in fact disguised tests of the Soviet Vostok East spacecraft that would later carry humans into orbit.

Humans in space

Meanwhile, the United States was racing to develop its own crewed spacecraft: the Mercury capsule. The Mercury program was initiated in 1959 by the newly established National Aeronautics and Space Administration (NASA)—the U.S. civilian space agency that had taken over the various efforts of different military and civilian projects. The United States used primates rather than dogs as test subjects for its spaceflights. In January 1961, NASA successfully put a chimpanzee named Ham into space (although not into orbit) and safely returned him to Earth. They then began to make preparations for a crewed suborbital spaceflight.

But once again, the Soviet Union surprised the world by announcing, on April 12, 1961, that Soviet cosmonaut Yuri Gagarin (1934–1968) was on board *Vostok 1* in the middle of a flight making one orbit of Earth. Within a month, NASA stole back the headlines by launching U.S. astronaut Alan Shepard (1923–1998) on a suborbital flight in *Freedom 7.* However, by the time U.S. astronaut John Glenn (1921–) became the first American in orbit (flying for less than six hours) in 1962, the Soviet Union had already kept an astronaut in space for a day and was planning other firsts. These included missions that would put two capsules in orbit alongside each other and launch of Valentina Tereshkova (1937–), who became the first woman in space in 1963.

sponsored by the U.S. military's ICBM arm. Instead, the Vanguard program, which was based on a U.S. Naval Research Laboratory survey rocket, was chosen to produce the U.S. satellite launch vehicle.

Without these political troubles, the Soviet program was free to use its ICBMs as launch vehicles. When the Soviet Union announced the launch of *Sputnik 1,* giving its weight as an astonishingly heavy 184 lb (83.6 kg), the United States realized it had been overtaken in the space race. U.S. scientists hurried to launch a Vanguard rocket in December 1957. The rocket carried a tiny 3¼-lb (1.5-kg) satellite equipped with a transmitter. It rose to just 3 ft (90 cm) before falling back down and exploding. Nevertheless, the satellite survived and began to transmit signals from the burning launchpad. Within days, Project Orbiter was restarted, launching the first U.S. satellite *Explorer 1*—weighing only 31 lb (14 kg)—on January 31, 1958.

KONSTANTIN TSIOLKOVSKY

Russian schoolteacher and scientist Konstantin Tsiolkovsky (1857–1935) has been called the father of the Soviet space program. Although he developed much of the fundamental theory of space flight still in use today, his work went unpublicized for many years, and he never applied his ideas to practical rocketry.

Tsiolkovsky was born in a remote Russian village, and although he had very little formal education, he showed his intelligence and fascination with flight at an early age. While working as a schoolteacher in the 1880s, Tsiolkovsky developed his ideas, proving that a rocket was the only practical propulsion system for spacecraft, and that, in order to escape Earth's gravity, it would have to be liquid-propelled. He calculated Earth's escape velocity and recognized the benefits of the multistage launch vehicle.

Some of these ideas were published by Tsiolkovsky in 1903, but it was not until after the Russian Revolution in 1917 that his efforts were recognized and he was hailed as a pioneer by the Soviet government.

PEOPLE

The conical command module of Apollo 11 *"splashed down" at the end of the historic mission in 1969 that took astronauts to the surface of the Moon. The balloons were used to turn the module right side up, while the inflatable, ring-shaped float increased buoyancy.*

Life-support systems

Any crewed spacecraft has to carry a number of life-support systems in order to keep the astronauts safe. A pressurized capsule and an oxygen supply are critical. The U.S. Gemini capsules were conical and had titanium shells for lightness and strength, while the remainder of the capsule was made of a nickel alloy called Rene-40. Oxygen-supply cylinders could be located inside or outside the capsule. Soviet capsules used a mixture of nitrogen and oxygen to generate a normal air mixture (20 percent oxygen), but early U.S. spacecraft reduced their weight by using a pure oxygen mixture at one-third sea-level pressure. NASA used a special mixture of oxygen and nitrogen in its *Skylab* space station and switched to a normal air mixture in its space shuttle.

Just as important as oxygen supply is absorption of the carbon dioxide that is released when astronauts exhale. In a sealed capsule, the carbon dioxide builds up, with levels easily becoming toxic. Spacecraft therefore incorporate scrubbing mechanisms, which are chemical filters that usually contain lithium hydroxide to absorb the waste gas, and activated charcoal to remove odors and freshen the air.

Although even the first spacecraft had air supplies, many early astronauts wore space suits throughout their flights in case of accidents that might puncture the spacecraft's hull. As well as supplying oxygen in case of an emergency, a spacecraft's pressure suit protects the body from the vacuum in space, in which blood would be boiled by human body heat alone (see SPACE SUIT).

A spacecraft must also shield its crew from the extreme temperatures of space. Most spacecraft are well insulated and equipped with cooling systems that use extremely low temperature fluids to redistribute heat around the spacecraft.

The first space probes

As well as racing to set new milestones in crewed space flight, the United States and the Soviet Union were also competing to explore the inner Solar System with robotic probes. Despite many failures, the Soviets accomplished some impressive firsts, par-

DOCKING IN SPACE

Although some of the Vostok spacecraft came briefly within a few miles of each other in orbit, docking in space did not become a strong goal until NASA and the Soviet Union started planning lunar missions and space stations. The first successful dockings took place between Gemini space capsules and Agena rocket stages. Gemini was fitted with a radio system that communicated with a transponder (a radio set that responds to a specific signal) on the Agena rocket and monitored the distance between the two craft in the same way that radar operates (see RADAR). Other elements of the docking maneuver, such as orientation, had no technical assistance and relied on the skills of the Gemini pilot. Once in position, the Gemini pushed forward, inserting a docking probe into a target device called a drogue on the other spacecraft. As the two parts locked together, clamps clicked into place around them, forming an airtight seal. The technology to rendezvous, dock, and move crew between the joined spacecraft was vital to the success of the Apollo program, in which one craft orbited the Moon while another ferried astronauts to the surface and then back to the orbiter.

The Soviet Union used a similar docking system but developed instruments to automate the entire process. This has allowed the automatic construction of space stations and their resupply with unpiloted ferry craft. If necessary, however, astronauts can take manual control when they are aboard.

A politically motivated docking between an Apollo and a Soyuz spacecraft in 1975 included a new docking system that was to be universal, allowing craft from both nations to link up whenever necessary. While that design was short-lived, it did lead to the development of a similar docking system by the Soviet Union that was installed on some space shuttles in the 1990s and used for dockings with the Soviet space station *Mir* and the International Space Station.

A CLOSER LOOK

THE LUNAR ROVING VEHICLE

Astronaut Eugene Cernan boards the Apollo 17 *Lunar Roving Vehicle.*

The idea of taking a surface vehicle to the Moon was a key part of the Apollo program from the outset, but the contract for developing the Lunar Roving Vehicle (LRV) was not awarded to Boeing until after *Apollo 11*'s successful mission in 1969. In just two years, the vehicle was designed and built, and three LRVs were taken to the Moon on board *Apollo 15, 16,* and *17*. The final LRV design was simpler than some of the alternatives considered, some of which were for fully pressurized mobile laboratories.

The vehicle was built principally out of lightweight aluminum and fiberglass and had a mass of only 460 lb (210 kg). Among its special features were wire-strung wheels capable of absorbing shocks as the vehicle raced along at speeds of up to 11 mph (18 km/h) and an inertial guidance system similar to those used in spacecraft (a compass would have been useless, because the Moon has no magnetic field). A communications antenna allowed the astronauts to communicate directly with Earth, while a television camera relayed pictures and allowed scientists on Earth to see the surroundings and direct the astronauts to areas of interest (see ANTENNA AND TRANSMITTER).

A CLOSER LOOK

ticularly in lunar exploration. These included the first spacecraft to fly around and return images of the far side of the Moon, in 1959, and, in 1966, the first spacecraft to land safely on the surface of the Moon.

NASA also achieved important successes, including the first successful planetary mission *Mariner 2*, which flew past Venus in December 1962, and *Mariner 4*, which took the first close-up photographs of Mars in 1965. The Mariner and Pioneer probe series continued into the early 1970s, with return visits to these planets, as well as a flyby of the planet

Mercury. *Pioneer 10* and *11* were the first probes to travel beyond Mars, returning pictures and other important data from the outer planets.

Race for the Moon

In 1961, U.S. president John F. Kennedy (1917–1963) committed the United States to putting a person on the Moon by 1970. Although the Soviet Union was more secretive about its lunar program, the race for the Moon was intense.

As the Vostok and Mercury missions came to an end in the mid-1960s, the missions that replaced them were designed to test technologies and techniques for a mission to take people to the Moon. NASA's two-person Gemini series tested people's ability to conduct missions lasting as long as two weeks, and to accomplish difficult tasks in space, including space walks. Gemini missions also tested spacecraft navigation and were the first crewed spacecraft to switch between orbits and dock with other vehicles (see the box on page 1233).

The Soviet *Voskhod* ("Sunrise") *1* preempted Gemini by putting three astronauts into space together, while *Voskhod 2* saw the first space walk by Soviet astronaut Alexei Leonov (1934–). After these flights, Voskhod was abandoned and the Soviet Union used its new Soyuz ("Union") spacecraft to continue working toward reaching the Moon.

Meanwhile, Wernher von Braun was designing a huge rocket, powerful enough to send a three-person NASA mission to the Moon. The 363-ft (111-m) Saturn 5 is still the largest rocket ever built. While it was being built, other teams were working on the design of the lunar mission itself.

Named Apollo, the U.S. lunar spacecraft consisted of a conical command module in which the three astronauts spent most of their journey. The command module was attached to a cylindrical service module, which contained the power, life-support, and communication systems. The service module also contained the engine that was used after the Saturn 5 had completed its job of sending the craft on the way to the Moon. At the pointed end of the command module cone was a docking clamp that would attach to the lunar module, which was the spacecraft that would descend to the lunar surface.

The Apollo program had a tragic start, with a fire that killed the crew of *Apollo 1* on the launch pad during a test in January 1967. Crewed missions restarted with *Apollo 7* in October 1968. In December 1968, the crew of *Apollo 8* became the first people to orbit the Moon, and on July 20, 1969, the *Apollo 11* lunar module *Eagle* touched down on a lunar plain called the Sea of Tranquillity, making U.S. astronauts Neil Armstrong (1930–) and Edwin (Buzz) Aldrin (1930–) the first humans on the Moon.

As the Apollo program continued through the early 1970s, the Soviet Union denied that it had planned a lunar mission, but this was found not to be the case. As early as 1962, Soviet space mastermind Sergey Korolyov (1906–1966; see the box on page 1236) had planned a mission that would have sent astronauts to orbit the Moon. In the late 1960s there were several uncrewed tests of the Zond ("Probe") spacecraft that could have done something similar. But both these programs were dogged with problems, and their true purpose was kept secret. Similar setbacks occurred with the Soviet N-1 rocket developed for the planned lunar landing, and in 1972 the project was quietly dropped.

After Apollo

As the Apollo program came to an end, so did the space race. Relations between the superpowers were easing; in 1975, an Apollo command module docked with a Soviet Soyuz capsule in orbit for a historic handshake in space. Gradually, NASA and the Soviet space program developed different goals.

The Soviet Union had already put its first Salyut ("Salute") space stations into orbit, and NASA launched its own short-lived *Skylab* in 1973. Until after Apollo, the space program's purpose was to produce political propaganda, despite it resulting in many scientific breakthroughs. In the 1970s, doing science in zero-gravity, and making money from satellite launches, became the reason for space travel.

Other countries began developing their own space programs. France launched a few satellites with its own Diamant rockets from 1965 on, and became the leading partner from 1975 in the European Space Agency (ESA). It developed the Ariane rocket, which became an important commercial satellite launch vehicle. Japan became the fourth nation to launch its own satellite on its own launch vehicle in 1970, and it has continued with two nearly independent space agencies—one focusing on space science and the other on developing commercially useful space technologies. Also in 1970, China launched its first satellite, *Dong Fang Hong* ("The East is Red"). Although at first the Chinese program was purely devoted to national satellites, this policy changed in 1985 when satellite launches on the Long March rocket were first offered for sale.

In the late 1970s, NASA's most spectacular successes were with space probes. The Viking missions of 1976 mapped Mars from orbit, landed, and conducted extensive surface investigations, including a search for life. *Voyagers 1* and *2*, both launched in 1977, visited the outer giant planets of the Solar System. There were no crewed U.S. space missions at all in the late 1970s, as NASA concentrated its resources on building a new type of spacecraft.

The space shuttle

The space shuttle was originally intended as one part of a larger project—one that has only recently begun to become a reality. The original plan was for a space transportation system consisting of a fleet of reusable shuttles servicing a space station. However, with the conclusion of the space race and shifting priorities, the U. S. government authorized NASA to build only space shuttles, and not the space station they were designed to service. Robbed of its original purpose, the shuttle proved its versatility in other ways.

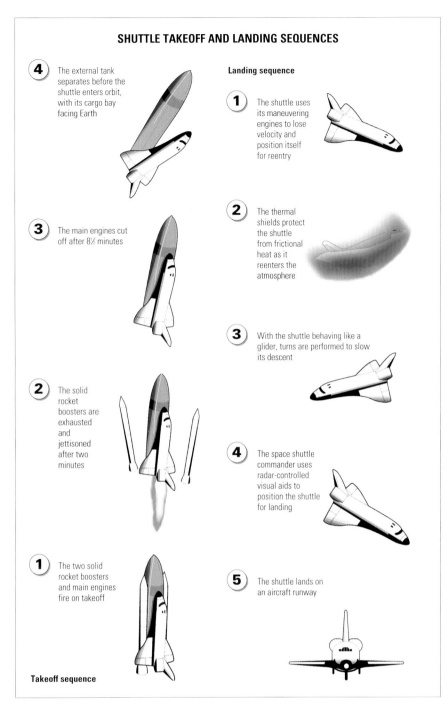

SHUTTLE TAKEOFF AND LANDING SEQUENCES

Takeoff sequence

4 The external tank separates before the shuttle enters orbit, with its cargo bay facing Earth

3 The main engines cut off after 8½ minutes

2 The solid rocket boosters are exhausted and jettisoned after two minutes

1 The two solid rocket boosters and main engines fire on takeoff

Landing sequence

1 The shuttle uses its maneuvering engines to lose velocity and position itself for reentry

2 The thermal shields protect the shuttle from frictional heat as it reenters the atmosphere

3 With the shuttle behaving like a glider, turns are performed to slow its descent

4 The space shuttle commander uses radar-controlled visual aids to position the shuttle for landing

5 The shuttle lands on an aircraft runway

The space shuttle system consists of the 122-ft (37-m) orbiter spacecraft, two solid rocket boosters, and an external tank to carry liquid oxygen and hydrogen. At launch, the entire assembly weighs 2200 tons (2000 tonnes), with the orbiter accounting for around 83 tons (75 tonnes), excluding its payload (the load essential to the mission).

The boosters are exhausted and jettisoned around two minutes after liftoff. They fall back into the ocean on parachutes. The external tank, however, remains attached to the orbiter almost all the way into orbit before it falls back into the atmosphere and burns up. Once the orbiter has completed its space mission, it reenters the atmosphere, glides back to Earth, and lands on a runway.

In orbit, the shuttle maneuvers using small rocket motors around the orbiter, called the reaction control system (RCS). Once the shuttle reaches orbit,

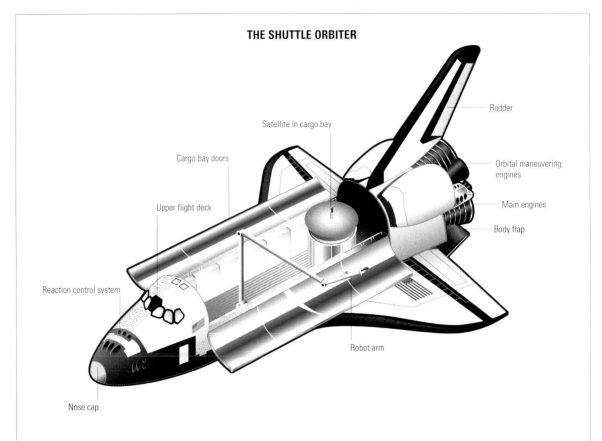

THE SHUTTLE ORBITER

Rudder

Satellite in cargo bay

Orbital maneuvering engines

Cargo bay doors

Main engines

Upper flight deck

Body flap

Reaction control system

Robot arm

Nose cap

Half the length of the 122-ft (37-m) shuttle orbiter is taken up by its cargo bay. This can carry objects for deployment or retrieval such as communication satellites. The bay can also be used to house the ESA's Spacelab.

it opens the doors to the cargo bay that occupies most of its interior. This maneuver exposes radiator panels that help release heat from the orbiter into space (see the diagram above).

The orbiter can carry a crew of up to eight, and missions typically spend around 10 days in orbit. The orbiter cabin, at the front of the spacecraft, has two decks: an upper flight deck and a lower mid-deck where the crew spends most of its time. As well as the controls for piloting the shuttle itself, the flight deck has instrument panels to operate various other shuttle systems, including the Remote Manipulator System (RMS) robot arm. Many shuttle flights have involved the deployment of satellites. These are released by the crew from the cargo bay, and then use rocket motors to reach their final destinations. After the destruction of the space shuttle *Challenger* in 1986, the United States decided to conduct fewer routine satellite launches with space shuttles.

As well as launching satellites, shuttles can also retrieve and service them. One highly publicized example of this was the servicing mission that gave the Hubble Space Telescope a new optical system. Satellites to be serviced are approached very slowly using the RCS motors, and then grabbed using the RMS, which has a specially designed hand that locks on to the satellite's docking target. Space-suited astronauts can work on satellites in the cargo bay, and the satellites can be released back into orbit or returned to Earth.

Space shuttles can carry various experiments on the cabin mid-deck, and valuable information is obtained as the astronauts' actions and reactions are monitored in zero-gravity and during exercise. The cargo bay can also carry the Spacelab module. Spacelab has a variety of configurations; the cargo bay can be filled with a pressurized laboratory used for science experiments, or a half-length lab can be used to operate telescopes and other instruments.

SERGEY KOROLYOV

Soviet aircraft designer Sergey Pavlovich Korolyov (1906–1966) was the mastermind behind the program that put the Soviet Union ahead of the United States in the early days of the space race. Ukrainian-born Korolyov trained as an aircraft designer but was fascinated with space travel from his youth. In 1933 he led a team that launched the first Soviet liquid-propelled rocket. He moved on to work on jet propulsion, but was jailed for treason and forced to work in a scientific labor camp during World War II (1939–1945) as part of Soviet leader Joseph Stalin's (1879–1953) great purges of his alleged enemies.

Once released from prison, Korolyov was put in charge of Soviet efforts to exploit the captured German V-2 rocket technology. In the early 1950s, Korolyov developed the first Soviet intercontinental ballistic missile—the rocket that was used to launch *Sputnik 1* and other early Soviet satellites.

As chief designer of carrier rockets and spacecraft, Korolyov went on to design many spacecraft, including the Vostok, Voskhod, and Soyuz spacecraft that put the first Soviet astronauts into space. He died during a routine operation in 1966, and was honored by burial in the Kremlin wall in Moscow.

PEOPLE

The 1980s and 1990s

The period after the introduction of the space shuttle was one of change for the U.S. and Soviet space programs. The Voyager probes continued to send back spectacular pictures and other important data from the outer Solar System, while an international fleet of spacecraft rendezvoused with Halley's Comet in 1986. NASA planned a series of probes as long-term orbiters that were intended to send back information from planets over several years—*Magellan* to Venus, *Galileo* to Jupiter, and *Cassini* to Saturn.

Crewed space flight, however, was coming under increased pressure as NASA faced budget cuts. The planned U.S. space station *Freedom* faced cutbacks and constant delays, while the destruction of the space shuttle *Challenger* in January 1986 grounded NASA's crewed program for two years. A month later, the Soviet Union launched *Mir*, its most sophisticated space station yet, and was setting a series of new space flight endurance records.

The early 1990s saw a number of embarrassing failures for NASA, including the Hubble Space Telescope having a flaw in its mirror in 1990; the *Galileo* Jupiter probe failing to open its main antenna dish in April 1991; and a *Mars* probe failing in 1993.

However, with the collapse of Soviet communism and changing political and economic conditions throughout Europe, the world's space programs began to change. They focused more on cooperative ventures and activities, to support and stimulate subsequent commercially profitable undertakings. A shuttle repair mission to Hubble was successful, and the recovered *Galileo* finally entered orbit around Jupiter. The last of NASA's great space probes, *Cassini*, should arrive at Saturn in 2004. Meanwhile, the first of a new generation of less expensive Discovery probes are already returning information about the Solar System. The *Lunar Prospector* mission has found ice on the Moon and the *Pathfinder* mission to Mars has returned color images of the red planet using its remotely-controlled *Sojourner* rover.

Meanwhile, the changing political situation has turned the U.S. space station into an international project, with contributions from Russia, ESA, and Japan. An important part of the preparations for this project involved a series of link-ups between space shuttles and the *Mir* space station—a feat that had been unthinkable only a few years before.

Future developments

Since its beginning, the exploration of space has been driven by money and politics as much as by science, making the future of the space program hard to predict. Construction of an International Space Station is under way, and NASA's new space probes are sending back exciting results. News stories such as the possibility of fossil evidence of life on Mars have continued to fuel public interest in space.

Close to Earth, the demand for inexpensive satellite launches has led NASA and private industry to begin research into reusable single-stage launch vehicles. Although they are currently only at the

prototype stage, these could dramatically reduce launch costs (see LAUNCH VEHICLE). Various aerospace companies are also developing designs for space planes. These are passenger aircraft that combine conventional and rocket engines to reach hypersonic speeds.

Once the International Space Station is completed, NASA may well turn its attention back to the Moon. It is hoped that the continuing interest in Mars may eventually result in a mission to put people on its surface. The most exciting discoveries, however, are still likely to be made by the new generation of space probes and Earth-orbiting satellites.

G. SPARROW

See also: SATELLITE; SPACE FLIGHT; SPACE STATION.

A computer artist's impression of an astronaut exploring the surface of Mars. A manned mission to Mars would require funding and technology of a far higher level than for the Apollo lunar missions.

Further reading:
Aeronautics and Space Transportation Technology: Three Pillars for Success. Washington, D.C.: NASA, Office of Aeronautics and Space Transportation Technology, 1997.
Brown, C. *Spacecraft Mission Design.* Reston, Virginia: American Institute of Aeronautics and Astronautics, 1998.
Cernan, E. *The Last Man on the Moon: Astronaut Eugene Cernan and America's Race in Space.* New York: St. Martin's Press, 1999.
Gurzadian, G. *Theory of Interplanetary Flights.* Amsterdam: Gordon and Breach, 1996.

SPECTROSCOPY

Spectroscopy is the analysis and characterization of matter using electromagnetic radiation

A system of particles can be promoted to a higher energy level, called an excited state or level, by absorbing energy such as electromagnetic radiation (see ELECTROMAGNETIC RADIATION). Likewise, energy can be released when molecules and atoms relax from an excited state back to the ground state (the lowest energy level of a system).

The key principle behind spectroscopy is that electromagnetic radiation is also quantized: it consists of photons—packets of radiation with an amount of energy that is proportional to their frequency. Hence, when a system drops from an excited state to a lower one, a specific frequency of radiation is given out that corresponds exactly to the difference in energy between the two states. Conversely, if a complete range of frequencies is shone through a substance, those photons with frequencies that have the exact amount of energy to raise a system to higher energy levels will be absorbed. Therefore, studying the frequency of radiation emitted and absorbed by a substance can tell scientists what makes up that substance.

TYPES OF SPECTROSCOPY

The means by which the many types of electromagnetic radiation are generated vary according to frequency, and this has a bearing on the nature of the equipment used for spectroscopy in different parts of the electromagnetic spectrum. Nevertheless, most spectrometers have certain elements in common: a source of radiation, a means of selecting frequencies, a container for sample material, a radiation detector, and a means of processing the information from the detector to produce a spectrum.

The different types of spectroscopic techniques are classified by the frequency of the radiation, the nature of the transitions between different energy levels in the sample material, and the types of materials under investigation, either atomic or molecular. Atomic spectroscopy techniques focus on individual atoms and give information on the behavior of subatomic particles within a given type of atom. Molecular spectroscopy techniques study complete molecules and provide information about molecular structure and the motion of bonded particles.

A scientist operates a nuclear magnetic resonance (NMR) spectrometer, which can detect the constituent elements of a substance.

The revolution in physics and chemistry that resulted in quantum mechanics was started when scientists sought to understand the interaction of electromagnetic radiation with matter. As well as providing a very complete picture of atoms, molecules, and bulk matter, the study of the absorption and emission of radiation gave rise to a collection of spectroscopic tools and techniques that could be used for chemical analysis, eliminating the need for much tedious laboratory work. The applications of spectroscopy extend to many areas, including medical practice, food production, and quality control.

PRINCIPLES OF SPECTROSCOPY

Molecules, atoms, and their component subatomic particles are constantly in motion: the electrons in an atom or molecule move in orbitals (see the box on page 1241); each electron exhibits a characteristic spin (as do many varieties of atomic nuclei); and each molecule vibrates as the bonds between atoms expand and contract or change their angles.

Each type of motion is quantized: it can only occur if a fixed amount of energy in the form of electromagnetic radiation is introduced or released (see the box on page 1240). The size of the packets of energy needed to produce motion are determined by the nature of the particle that is in motion and by its circumstances. As a consequence, the packets of energy emitted by substances are fingerprints that can be used to gather information about their constituents (molecules, atoms, or subatomic particles).

CONNECTIONS

● Many types of spectroscopy are used to monitor **POLLUTION** levels.

● **RADIATION DETECTION** devices are integral to spectrometers.

● Some **TELESCOPES** have spectrometers attached to them.

CORE FACTS

■ Electromagnetic radiation includes radio-frequency, microwave, infrared, visible, ultraviolet, and X-ray radiation. These are all used in spectroscopy.
■ Each type of electromagnetic radiation interacts with molecules and atoms in characteristic ways.
■ The frequency and intensity of a certain type of radiation is used to determine concentration, structure, and other properties of sample substances.

Radio-frequency radiation

The most important spectroscopic technique in the radio-frequency band is nuclear magnetic resonance (NMR). Certain atomic nuclei exhibit a property called spin. Since an atomic nucleus contains the positively charged protons of the atom, all nuclei have a positive charge. As a result of the nuclear spin, this charge appears to rotate around the nucleus, constituting a tiny loop of electric current. Because electric current generates a magnetic field, the nucleus will thus behave like a tiny bar magnet (see ELECTRICITY AND MAGNETISM; MAGNET).

If a hydrogen nucleus (single proton) is placed in a magnetic field, the laws of quantum theory dictate that it has two possible spin states: a ground state in which its own magnetic field is aligned with the external field, and an excited state in which its magnetic field is not aligned with the external field. The energy difference between these states is proportional to the strength of the magnetic field (flux density). A typical NMR spectrometer uses a magnetic flux density of 7 tesla (T)—some hundred thousand times Earth's magnetic field—which produces an energy difference between the two spin states that corresponds to a radio frequency of approximately 360 MHz.

NMR spectra are particularly useful for determining the structures of organic molecules, which often contain several hydrogen atoms. The precise frequency of the signal from each proton is determined by the strength of the magnetic field the proton experiences. Since molecules contain electrons, which also behave like magnets, the magnetic field experienced by each proton will vary according to the density of electrons around that proton. The magnetic field will also be affected by the proximity of other nuclei that possess spin, such as carbon-13, fluorine-19, phosphorus-31, and oxygen-17, as well as by the other protons present in the same molecule.

Most NMR spectrometers use a pulse of radio-frequency (RF) radiation, which is mathematically equivalent to hitting the molecule with a range of frequencies all at the same time. The pulse knocks the protons into their excited state, and a radio antenna then detects the signal emitted by the sample as the protons fall back to their ground state. This is the equivalent of hitting a bell with a hammer: the hammer passes energy to the bell, which gives out energy as sound waves. The pitch of the sound could be used to identify the size of the bell. Similarly, if the signal from the sample were converted to sound waves and played through an audio output, the molecules could be heard to ring like a badly tuned bell. All of the different frequencies are emitted together, and a processor is used to separate the signal into its constituent frequencies. In practice, the signals from several pulses are usually added together to average out random noise and give a clearer spectrum.

NMR forms the basis of magnetic resonance imaging (MRI), a three-dimensional noninvasive imaging technology used in medicine, primarily for imaging tissues and organs inside the body. For example, the hydrogen nuclei in water display a different spin resonance behavior in cancerous cells than in normal body cells, and tumors can be imaged from outside the body (see MEDICAL IMAGING). MRI can be performed using the signals from a variety of nuclei that exhibit spin.

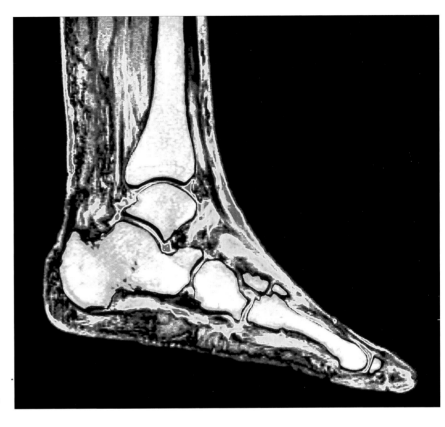

A magnetic resonance imaging (MRI) scan of an ankle and foot. MRI is mainly used in medical applications and uses NMR technology.

Microwaves

Microwave spectroscopy, using wavelengths of approximately 4 to 1 mm, is used to study the rotational motion of molecules. A photon consists of oscillating electric and magnetic fields, and it is the electric field that can stimulate the rotation of a molecule, provided the molecule has an electric dipole—a distinct separation of positive and negative charge across the molecule.

The transitions of molecules between rotational energy levels are determined by their moments of inertia—their opposition to a change in rotational motion brought about by a force (see ROTATIONAL MOTION). The laws of energy and motion can be used to give an understanding of the shape of molecules (see MECHANICS). The precise geometry of a molecule can be calculated by using values for the amount of energy emitted and absorbed (in the form of microwave radiation) by a molecule and for the masses of the bodies in the molecule.

Infrared light

Molecules that undergo a change in electric dipole when they vibrate are those that absorb infrared (IR) radiation. This technique is very versatile, since practically every compound absorbs IR photons except single gaseous atoms, such as helium, and gas molecules of two identical atoms, such as nitrogen and

The enormous Canada-France-Hawaii Telescope fitted with an infrared spectrometer took images of a comet colliding with Jupiter in 1994.

hydrogen. The most commonly used wavelengths are in the mid-infrared region, from 16 to 2 um (millionths of a meter).

All molecules vibrate in several ways, or modes. Each of these modes has a different frequency and appears separately in the spectrum. As the complexity of a molecule increases, so does the IR spectrum.

QUANTIZATION

Each type of motion has an amount of energy associated with it. A hydrogen chloride molecule comprises one hydrogen and one chlorine atom that are joined by a chemical bond. When this bond is vibrating (stretching and contracting) with the least possible energy, the molecule is said to be in its ground state. Quantum mechanics dictates that it can never be completely at rest. Energy can be put into the molecule to make it vibrate with more vigor, but there is a restriction: only certain frequencies of vibration are possible.

To visualize how this can be, it helps to think of a jump rope lying on the floor with one end fixed in place. By moving the free end from side to side, the whole rope can be made to move from side to side, forming an arc at each extreme of the motion. By moving the rope with increasing vigor, the movement of the rope becomes jumbled until a point is reached where the two halves of the rope are moving in opposite directions and the rope forms an S shape at each extreme. The point halfway along the rope does not move and is called a node. Increasing the vigor still more, the movement of the rope becomes irregular again until a point is reached where there are two nodes and three arcs, then three nodes and four arcs, and so on (see WAVE MOTION). The points at which the rope settles into a regular motion correspond to the allowed energy levels of the vibrating hydrogen chloride molecule. These energy levels are called excited states, and the molecule has a series of excited states of increasing energy.

By adding a quantum (a discrete packet) of energy that corresponds to the difference in energy between two points in that series, the molecule can be made to pass from the lower-energy state to a higher one. This transition between states is known as quantization.

A CLOSER LOOK

Hence, IR spectra tend to be used as fingerprints, and there is a vast database of standard spectra that can be used to identify a sample by its IR trace.

IR spectroscopy is commonly used in environmental analysis of atmospheric compounds. The concentrations of carbon monoxide and residual hydrocarbons in vehicle emissions can be determined with IR. The presence of compounds such as chlorofluorocarbons (CFCs), ozone, and carbon dioxide have been routinely measured by balloon and aircraft using IR absorption in a method called atmospheric trace molecular spectroscopy (ATMOS).

Ultraviolet and visible light

Ultraviolet-and-visible spectroscopy, which is frequently shortened to UV-visible, is used to study the transitions of electrons within atoms. These occur in the region of 1 mm to 10 nm; visible light covers only 400 to 750 nm (billionths of a meter), so in fact UV-visible also extends into the infrared region.

Atomic UV-visible spectroscopy. The UV-visible spectra of atoms are produced when electrons move from one orbital to another. The atomic orbitals that are permitted by the theory of quantum mechanics are very exactly defined, and the energy absorbed or emitted during a transition between two orbitals is similarly very precise, giving a spectrum of very sharp, well-defined bands of radiation. In the most common form of spectroscopy—atomic emission spectroscopy—a sample of material is fed into a very hot flame or even hotter plasma. This has two consequences: the material splits up into individual atoms and the heat excites some of the electrons to high-energy atomic orbitals.

When the atoms relax back to lower energy levels, photons are emitted that are unique to that element. Atomic spectra are valuable because their intensity can be used to determine the quantity of trace elements, even in the parts-per-billion concentration range. The presence of lead, mercury, and other heavy metals in groundwater can be detected by these methods, and forensic scientists often use atomic spectra to determine the origins of hair, synthetic and natural fibers, paints, gunshot residues, and many other samples. Also, the atomic spectra of elements that are in the atmosphere of distant stellar objects can be detected and used to supply information about the composition of these objects.

Molecular UV-visible spectroscopy. The UV-visible spectra of molecules are produced by electron transitions between orbitals in a molecule. The most striking difference between atomic and molecular spectra is the broadness of the lines in molecular spectroscopy (they are often several hundred nanometers wide, compared with less than one nanometer for atomic spectra). This is because the molecules are constantly vibrating and colliding, which changes the geometry of the molecule temporarily and blurs the energies of the orbitals. Since UV-visible spectra are so blurred, it is difficult to obtain detailed structural information about the molecules. Certain groups of atoms can be identified, but the main use of UV-visible spectroscopy is in measuring the concentrations of materials.

Some molecules exhibit luminescence, that is, they emit radiation at a lower frequency than the UV-visible light they absorb. This is because the molecule is first stimulated into an excited state by the light source, but then drops into a lower excited state rather than relaxing back to the ground state. If this occurs immediately, the process is called fluorescence. If there is a delay in the emission after the light source has been removed, the process is called phosphorescence. Luminescence spectra are more sensitive than absorption spectra, since the absolute intensity of emitted light can be measured, which is more accurate than measuring the fraction of light that is absorbed by a sample. These techniques are used to measure the concentration of polycyclic aromatic hydrocarbons (a type of pollutant) in environmental samples. Chemiluminescence is emission of light after a chemical reaction. The gaseous oxides of nitrogen are measured by the luminescence emitted after reacting nitric oxide with ozone gas, which produces molecules in an excited state.

X rays

The electrons near the nucleus of an atom, called inner-core electrons, are very strongly attracted to the nuclei. These electrons can be knocked away from the core by high-energy X-ray photons, which give the electrons more than enough energy to escape from their orbital. The energy of the fugitive electron after leaving the atomic core is called its kinetic energy. X-ray photoelectron spectroscopy (XPS) measures the binding energy of core electrons by subtracting the kinetic energy of the ejected electrons from the energy of the original X-ray photon. The resulting spectrum identifies the material pre-

sent. XPS is mainly used for identifying small amounts of solid impurities that are present on the surface of other solid materials.

A related technique is X-ray fluorescence (XRF). After an inner-core electron has been ejected using an X-ray photon, the electrons that are left will rearrange themselves to replace it. Low-energy X-ray photons are emitted as these changes take place, and their spectra can be used to determine the composition of a substance.

M. BRYANT

See also: CHEMICAL ENGINEERING; CHEMICAL INDUSTRY, INORGANIC; CHEMICAL INDUSTRY, ORGANIC; LABORATORY EQUIPMENT; LIGHT AND OPTICS.

Further reading:
Contemporary Chemical Analysis. Edited by J. Rubinson and K. Rubinson. Upper Saddle River, New Jersey: Prentice Hall, 1998.

ATOMIC AND MOLECULAR ORBITALS

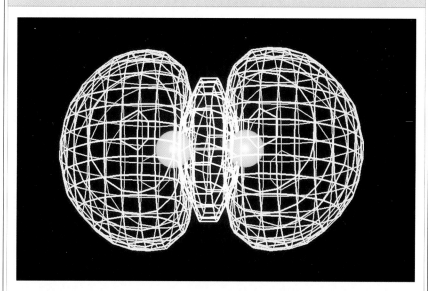

A representation of a nitrogen gas molecule. The electron orbitals are shown as yellow and white, and the atomic nuclei are blue.

A basic tenet of quantum mechanics is that a small, fast-moving object such as an electron in an atom behaves as if it were a wave and can be described by a mathematical wave equation. It is impossible to calculate the exact motion or location of an electron at any point in time. However, the wave equation of an electron makes it possible to calculate a three-dimensional envelope of space that contains the electron. This is called an orbital. There are many solutions to the wave equation, and in each one the electron has a different energy. The energy of an orbital depends on how far the electron is from the nucleus, to which it is attracted, and from other electrons, from which it is repelled.

In a molecule, each electron is attracted to all of the nuclei in the molecule and repelled by all of the other electrons. Approximate molecular orbitals that spread throughout the molecule can be calculated by mathematically combining the electron orbitals of the individual atoms. The mathematics of these calculations is very complicated, but with the aid of computers, chemists are able to estimate the position of the orbitals in increasingly larger molecules.

A CLOSER LOOK

SPORTS EQUIPMENT

New materials and designs have enhanced sports equipment to add to enjoyment, performance, and safety

Hollow aluminum baseball bats, which are very light and resilient, are used by players in the United States Little Leagues.

CONNECTIONS

● **PRODUCTION ENGINEERING AND PROCESS CONTROL** have improved the quality of sports equipment by producing working prototypes and testing the materials at every stage of production.

● New **TEXTILES AND THEIR MANUFACTURE** and **PLASTICS** have accelerated improvements in high-caliber sports equipment.

Humans are competitive by nature. They have been vying to determine who could run fastest and throw farthest since prehistoric times. These contests helped to hone the skills needed by early humans to hunt for food and fight for survival.

With the growth of early civilizations, sports began to be recognized as an attraction for festivals and other social gatherings, and athletic skills started to be regarded as something to be developed for their own sake. In ancient Greece in 776 B.C.E., the Olympic Games were established, but except for the discus and javelin events, very little or no sports equipment was required.

Over the centuries, more sports and games were invented, and with them came different types of equipment. Sports equipment tends to fall into a few basic categories. There are projectiles such as balls, arrows, and horseshoes; and devices that propel these projectiles, including bats, bows, clubs, and racquets. In some sports, the participant propels him- or herself by one of a variety of means, including skis, skates, boats, and sleds. Another very important category of sports equipment is protective clothing—such as helmets, masks, gloves, and body padding—which is specially designed to prevent injury (see BODY PROTECTION).

Tradition and innovation

All competitors try to use equipment that will maximize their chances of success. They want balls that fly farther and faster, bats and racquets that hit with more force, and protective gear that is lighter and more comfortable. But every game has rules, and equipment must be made to accommodate these. A person can probably throw a baseball farther than a cast iron shot, but baseballs are not allowable in a shotput meet. Most sports have organizations that regulate the equipment that is used in formal competition. As advanced materials and manufacturing methods are developed and different designs are tried, these organizations must decide whether the new equipment is still within the bounds of the particular sport (see MATERIALS SCIENCE).

When aluminum baseball bats were introduced, they were soon adopted by Little Leagues and

---

CORE FACTS

- Technology has affected not only the equipment used for sports and recreational activities, but also protective gear and even the surfaces that sports are played on.
- Equipment innovations are evaluated by governing boards of organized sports to determine whether they will be allowed in official competition.
- Synthetic materials such as plastics, fiberglass, and composites have largely replaced wood, leather, and other natural products because they offer good performance and less weight.
- For some applications, natural materials are still preferred over synthetic materials and are sometimes used for the sake of sporting traditions.

schools all over the United States. Being hollow, aluminum bats can be made very light and resilient while maintaining a reasonably large cross-section. The result is a bat that is easier for young players to swing and achieve a satisfying rebound on the ball. They are also more durable, which makes them an economical choice. However, professional baseball has stuck with traditional wooden bats, although many rookies in the minor leagues have never used them. Players in the big leagues would be able to hit the ball so far with aluminum bats that stadiums would have to be rebuilt and batting records could not be compared meaningfully. Aluminum bats also change the game by making it easier to hit inside pitches, which are pitches that are closer to the batter. Wooden bats tend to break when the ball impacts the thinner area close to the batter's hands.

In tennis, speed is far more important than distance. Managing to hit the ball into the designated area of the court faster than the opponent can reach it is the object of the game, and hitting the ball out of the park is penalized. Racquets are therefore made as light as possible—within the allowable size limits—with traditional wood largely giving way to metals, plastics, fiberglass, or composite materials. Although distance is not an issue, the lighter racquets have in fact changed the character of the sport. Some observers complain that professional tennis, especially the men's game, has gotten so fast that rallies do not develop. With more points being made on the serve, the game can be less interesting to watch. In some cases, traditional materials are still the best, and many serious tennis players insist on racquet strings made of gut, which is derived from the intestines of cattle and goats. Gut strings are more resilient than the more modern nylon types, but they do not last as long and are more expensive.

In 1894, the first basketballs were put on the market to replace the soccer balls that were initially used to play the game. These balls were 32 in (81 cm) in circumference and weighed 20 oz (0.5 kg). The official size was set at 30 in (76 cm) in 1949, and the modern molded ball replaced the laced version. The size of basketball courts was standardized in 1903. Before this, basketball games were played wherever there was room, often in irregular-shaped areas. The hoop and net were first used in 1893. Initially, balls were removed from the net using a ladder, pole, or chain. In 1913, a net with a hole in the bottom was introduced.

The science of skis

Nonskiers would probably be surprised at the enormous number of design variations it is possible to obtain in what looks like a pair of straight boards. Varied skiing conditions, different skiing activities and styles, and the size and ability of the skier must all be taken into account when selecting a pair of skis.

Skis are not perfectly flat. They have a camber (arch), the shape of which controls the distribution of the skier's weight along the skis' length. Dampening is the ability of the ski to absorb vibration, and this is determined by the type and design of the core material used inside the fiberglass ski coating. The core is generally made of wood or polyurethane foam, which is surrounded by carbon fibers or a synthetic material called Kevlar.

Bindings are the mechanisms that hold the booted foot to the ski. Originally, bindings were simple clamps, but these proved to be dangerous in falls, because the foot was forced to turn whichever way the ski turned. Following many broken bones, bindings were eventually developed that would release the boot when a predetermined force was exceeded.

Skis are made from vibration-absorbing materials and are shaped to evenly distribute the skier's weight along the length of the ski. This assists the skier's balance and control in making the sharp turns required for slalom racing.

RUNNING SHOES

Olympic running shoes are cushioned for shock absorption and padded for support.

Special shoes are worn for most sports to accommodate the surface upon which the sport is being played and the expected types of motion. For example, basketball shoes are designed to support the players' ankles, which are put under a lot of strain during a typical match. However, few activities put as much strain on the feet as running. Running is a very popular way to exercise, and shoe manufacturers have been encouraged to develop a variety of ways to support and cushion the feet.

Designing good running shoes begins with studying the forces that are encountered during a runner's stride. The foot lands on the heel, with an impact of up to three times the weight of the body. As the runner's body weight moves forward, it is supported by the entire sole. This is the point at which instability can occur, either in the form of pronation, where the foot tilts toward the inside, or supination, where the foot tilts toward the outside. The body's weight continues to move forward toward the ball of the foot, in preparation for pushing off for the next stride. The front of the foot experiences a force that is four to seven times the body weight at this time.

The obvious way to deal with the forces on the foot is to cushion the shoe for shock absorption, and indeed cushioning is an important part of running-shoe design. But there is a tradeoff, because the softer the shoe, the more difficult it is to provide good stability. To find the proper balance, manufacturers have engineered shock-absorbing pads that reduce side-to-side motion. Padding may be molded of materials with multiple densities so that they are stiffer in some areas than others. Another technique is to use an insert of a different material, which helps to hold the shape of the shoe as the padding compresses.

A CLOSER LOOK

This was a big safety improvement for falling skiers, but a threat to those farther downhill who might be overtaken by runaway skis. To keep the ski near its owner, bindings are now designed so that when they release, a pair of brakes protrude into the snow (see SNOW AND ICE TRAVEL).

Watching the clock

Many sports involve the measurement of time. In team sports such as basketball, football, soccer, or hockey, there is a set amount of time allowed for each period of play. Racing events must also be timed. In most cases, timekeepers use stopwatches or other clocks, which can be paused to account for timeouts and other breaks in the action. In a running race, the times are taken from the starting pistol flash to the moment when the first runner's torso crosses the finish line. Depending on the length of the race, times are recorded to tenths of a second.

In the Olympic Games and other major athletic competitions, automated electronic timekeeping equipment is used. This allows times to be accurately recorded to the nearest hundredth of a second. Automated timekeeping systems are based on laser beams. When the beams are broken by the passing of a contestant, a signal is sent to a computer, which records the results.

Synthetic surfaces

Although grass is a pleasant surface for outdoor sports, it is not durable under the assault of cleated sports shoes. It is also subject to the vagaries of weather and requires a great deal of mowing and other maintenance. Practicality, economics, and an increase in the number of indoor stadiums have all driven the development of synthetic turf products.

Synthetic turf is laid on top of layers of gravel and stone dust, which serve to provide adequate drainage. It is made of tufts of plastic or nylon fibers that are supported by a brushed-in top-dressing of silica and/or rubber granules. Turf products are optimized for the requirements of each sport by adjusting the material, height, and density of the fibers and the depth of the silica. In golf, the aim is to simulate the performance of grass as closely as possible so that the expected path of the ball is not altered by the synthetic surface. Football fields need a sturdy turf that supports the pounding of feet but does not have so much "grab" that it causes injuries.

Synthetic turf is durable but not permanent. Debris such as mud, leaves, and dust infiltrates the top-dressing over time, and the turf becomes hard and compacted, unable to absorb impact.

Synthetic surfaces are also widely used for running tracks. On these, an asphalt substrate is topped with an aggregate of rubber granules that are bonded with polyurethane. The result is a more resilient and durable surface that can withstand any weather conditions and that cushions impacts for safer training and competition.

S. CALVO

See also: CLOTHING MANUFACTURE; COMPOSITE; ERGONOMICS; FIBERS AND YARNS; FOOTWEAR MANUFACTURE; LEATHER; RUBBER; SAFETY SYSTEMS.

Further reading:
Design for Sports: The Cult of Performance. Edited by A. Busch. New York: Cooper-Hewitt National Design Museum, Smithsonian Institution, and Princeton Architectural Press, 1998.
Rules of the Game: The Complete Illustrated Encyclopedia of All the Sports of the World. Edited by Diagram Group. New York: St. Martin's Press, 1990.

STEAM ENGINE

A steam engine converts the heat energy in steam into mechanical energy

The **Mississippi Queen** *paddle steamer powers down the Mississippi River at Vicksburg.*

The steam engine is an invention that fundamentally changed society. As the motive power behind the Industrial Revolution, steam engines began to transform the rural society of the 18th century into the industrial, urban society of today. Back in the 18th century, the steam-driven future may have seemed as exciting and uncertain as the future seems today. In 1792, English physician Erasmus Darwin (1731–1802), grandfather of the evolutionary biologist Charles Darwin (1809–1882), captured a vision of what that future might have been like:

Soon shall thy arm, unconquer'd steam!, afar
Drag the slow barge, or drive the rapid car;
Or on wide-waving wings expanded bear
The flying chariot through the field of air.

CORE FACTS

- Water vapor (steam) occupies around 1500 times more space as the equivalent liquid at atmospheric pressure.
- Steam engines use expanding steam to push a piston in a cylinder, converting heat energy into useful work.
- Early beam engines comprised little more than a boiler, a cylinder, and a piston. The piston simply rose and fell in a vertical cylinder, moving a heavy beam up and down like a seesaw about a central pivot.
- The steam engine was invented by English engineer Thomas Newcomen in 1705. An improved design was made by Scottish engineer James Watt in 1765.

Steam engines were the first heat engines—machines that convert the energy locked in fuels such as coal into useful, mechanical work (see ENGINE). When fuels are burned with oxygen in the air, they give off large amounts of heat. In a steam engine, this is used to boil water and make steam (water vapor), which is allowed to expand and do work.

Steam is still used in power stations to convert heat generated by coal, oil, gas burners, and nuclear reactors into rotational motion, and then into electricity (see POWER STATION). However, today's power stations carry out that conversion not using steam engines but with highly efficient steam turbines (see STEAM TURBINE). Despite the important position they occupy in the development of society, steam engines are now considered little more than a historical curiosity and rarely used today.

HOW STEAM ENGINES WORK

The basis of every steam engine is a useful property of water: water vapor (steam) occupies around 1500 times as much space as the equivalent liquid at atmospheric pressure. The energy released as water expands into steam can be used to drive a machine.

All steam engines have certain key components. First, and most importantly, they need a boiler (see the box on page 1249). This is effectively a giant kettle that is kept supplied with water and generates a steady supply of steam to the engine. Because steam engines generate their heat from fuel burned outside the cylinder, they are known as external

CONNECTIONS

- A key component of the steam engine is the flywheel, which undergoes **ROTATIONAL MOTION**.

- **A GAS ENGINE (STIRLING ENGINE)** also relies on the expansion of gas to generate useful mechanical energy.

CYCLE OF A SINGLE-ACTING STEAM ENGINE

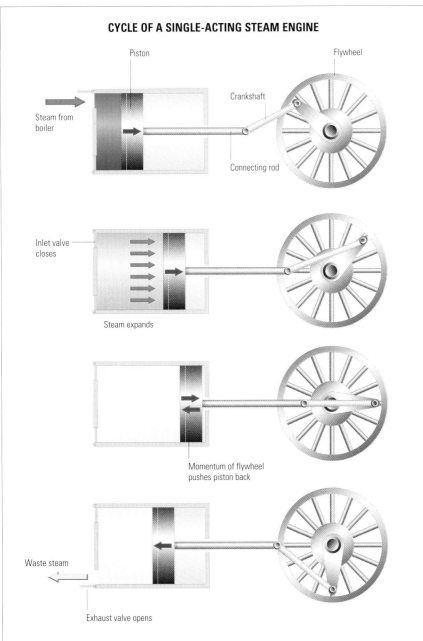

The single-acting steam engine uses the expansion of steam to push a piston to the end of a cylinder. This in turn pushes a crankshaft and flywheel. The momentum of the turning flywheel then pushes the piston back to its original position.

As the piston reaches the end of the cylinder, there is no more room for the steam to expand. Meanwhile, the crankshaft and connecting rod have pushed the flywheel around as far as they can. The flywheel has acquired momentum and keeps turning, pushing the crankshaft and connecting rod and driving the piston back through the cylinder.

It might appear that simply repeating these steps (known as the engine's cycle) would keep a steam engine running indefinitely, but there are some problems. First, what happens to the steam as the piston is pushed back into the cylinder? In the engine described above, the piston would compress the steam only so far, and the flywheel would come to rest without making a complete revolution.

For this reason, practical steam engines have a system of inlets and outlets known as valves, which open and close in a coordinated sequence (see VALVE, MECHANICAL). To start with, an inlet valve between the boiler and the cylinder is opened, allowing steam to enter the cylinder and push the piston forward (see the diagram at left). This part of the engine's cycle is known as the power stroke. The inlet valve closes as the piston moves part way along the cylinder. The piston is pushed to the end of the cylinder, not by more steam entering from the boiler, but by the steam that has already entered the cylinder and is expanding naturally.

As the piston begins to return, the inlet valve remains closed, but an outlet valve (called the exhaust) opens up. The piston pushes the waste steam through the exhaust and returns to its original position. This is known as the exhaust stroke. For an engine to operate efficiently (that is, to convert as much energy stored in the original fuel into useful mechanical work as possible), the steam must be exhausted at as low a pressure as possible. This is achieved by liquefying it at as low a temperature as possible (see the box on page 1250).

The first steam engines achieved this by squirting a jet of water into the cylinder while it was full of steam. This caused the steam to contract, which created a partial vacuum that helped draw the piston back through the cylinder. Later engines expelled the steam first and then liquefied it in a separate cooler called a condenser. Instead of the main cylinder being alternately heated and cooled, it could be kept permanently hot and the condenser kept permanently cold; this made the engine much more efficient.

TYPES OF STEAM ENGINES

Most steam engines share the key components outlined in the previous section. However, there are some important variations on the basic design. These are largely a reflection of the way engines evolved into increasingly efficient machines designed to drive different types of machines. Although there is no precise classification, steam engines can be described by their various mechanical attributes: reciprocating or rotary; single-acting or double-acting; single or compound; low pressure or high pressure; counterflow or uniflow; horizontal or vertical.

combustion engines. Gasoline and diesel engines, on the other hand, burn fuel inside their cylinders, so they are called internal combustion engines.

The steam from the boiler is allowed to expand into a large metal cylinder that contains a well-fitting plunger called a piston. As it expands, the steam pushes the piston along the cylinder, and the piston in turn pushes a two-part rod connected to a heavy wheel. The part attached to the wheel is called the crankshaft. The part attached to the piston is called the connecting rod. As the crankshaft and connecting rod move outward, they turn the wheel. The wheel, called a flywheel, is specifically constructed to have a large proportion of its mass around its circumference. For this reason, it acquires a great deal of momentum as it spins, which means it naturally keeps turning of its own accord (see MECHANICS).

First and perhaps most obviously, steam engines are either reciprocating (moving back and forth) or rotary. The earliest steam engines, known as beam engines, comprised little more than a boiler, a cylinder, and a piston; they had no crankshaft, connecting rod, or flywheel. The piston rose and fell in a vertical cylinder, moving a heavy beam about a central pivot like a seesaw. On one side, the beam was connected to the piston; on the other, to a similar system that rose and fell in a mine shaft, pumping out water.

Later, rotary engines used a crankshaft and connecting rod to convert the reciprocating motion of the piston into the rotary motion of a heavy flywheel. In this article, *reciprocating engine* is taken to mean a beam engine, and *rotary engine* to mean a piston engine that drives a wheel.

Early steam engines were not particularly efficient: they produced relatively little mechanical energy compared to the energy in the fuel that they consumed. These early engines were single-acting: the piston was driven in the cylinder only on the power stroke; during the exhaust stroke, the momentum of the flywheel (or the weight of the beam) returned the piston to its original position. This meant steam from the boiler was driving the engine only half the time.

Using a system of alternating valves, engines soon became double-acting. In these designs the steam was admitted on one side of the piston and exhausted from the other side of the cylinder during one stroke; then the valves switched functions as the piston reversed direction, and steam was admitted to the other side of the cylinder and simultaneously exhausted from the original side. Thus, in a double-acting engine, steam pushed the piston in both directions, producing twice as much power.

Even with these modifications, steam engines were still inefficient. The power produced by a steam engine is directly related both to how much the steam is allowed to expand in the cylinder and to the extent to which it is condensed afterward—in other words, to the amount of energy usefully extracted. Early steam engines had only a single cylinder, which

CYCLE OF A DOUBLE-ACTING UNIFLOW STEAM ENGINE

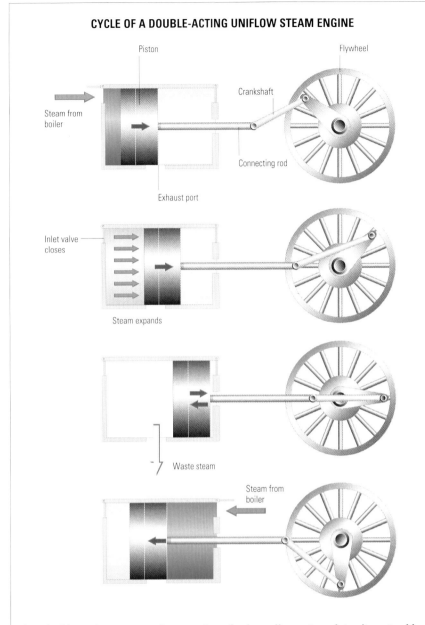

In a double-acting steam engine, a system of valves allows steam into alternate sides of the cylinder, pushing the piston back and forth. In a uniflow design, the steam on both sides of the cylinder leaves through a common central exhaust port.

A DOUBLE-ACTING UNIFLOW STEAM ENGINE

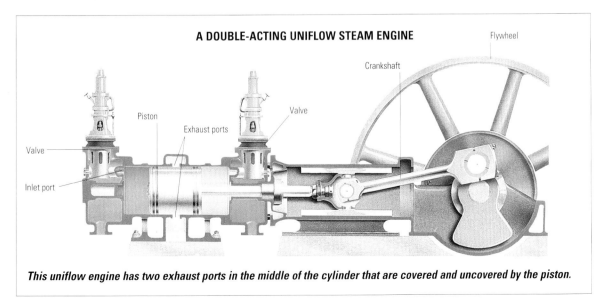

This uniflow engine has two exhaust ports in the middle of the cylinder that are covered and uncovered by the piston.

JAMES WATT

This beam engine, developed by James Watt, was made in 1788.

James Watt (1736–1819) was working as mathematical instrument maker to the University of Glasgow in Scotland in 1765 when he was asked to repair a model of a Newcomen steam engine. As he dismantled the model, he realized that it produced too little steam for the fuel it consumed. Watt wrote in his diary: "The idea occurred to me that as steam was an elastic vapor, it would expand and rush into a previously exhausted space; and that if I were to produce a vacuum in a separate vessel, and open a communication between this and the cylinder, such would be the result." So was born the separate steam condenser, which instantly transformed Newcomen's engine into a much more efficient machine.

In 1775, Watt went into partnership with English industrialist Matthew Boulton (1728–1809). Their firm in Birmingham, produced more than 500 steam engines, making them both very rich men.

PEOPLE

led to incomplete expansion and condensation. Later engines allowed steam to expand from the main cylinder through one or more auxiliary cylinders, which extracted more energy from the steam and made the engines more efficient. Thus engines are described as either single (having one cylinder) or compound (having multiple cylinders).

The first beam engines and steam engines were extremely large; typically a building the size of a house was needed just to contain them. This was because they operated at steam pressures not much above ordinary atmospheric pressure. The low pressure meant the steam did relatively little work, so much more steam had to be produced to do any useful work; hence the need for a large boiler, cylinder, and beam or flywheel. High-pressure engines, when they were developed, could be much more compact; they produced more power in a smaller space.

Another method of classifying steam engines relates to the way steam enters and leaves the cylinders. In a simple double-acting engine, there are inlet valves and outlet valves at each end of the cylinder. This is known as a counterflow engine, because steam enters in one direction and leaves in another. However, counterflow engines are inefficient because hot steam is always entering the cylinder very close to the place where cooled steam has just left it. An improved design, known as a uniflow engine, has steam inlets at the two ends of the cylinder and outlets near the center. The outlets are covered and uncovered by the motion of the piston (see the diagram on page 1247). Steam in a uniflow engine can enter the cylinder hotter and leave colder than the steam in a counterflow design, making a uniflow engine more efficient.

Engines can also be described as either horizontal or vertical, according to the direction in which the piston moves. Vertical engines were typically used as water pumps and for driving electricity generators; horizontal engines were used to drive factory machines and steam locomotives.

HISTORICAL DEVELOPMENT

Unlike some other technologies, which were developed as applications of pure science, the different types of steam engines evolved by trial and error. The theory of steam engines was worked out much later and only confirmed what the mechanical engineers of the 18th and 19th centuries had discovered by trial and error over the best part of 200 years.

Early development

The steam engine is usually thought of as an 18th-century invention, but experiments with steam power date back to Greek mathematician Hero of Alexandria (1st century C.E.), who developed a novelty steam-powered spinning sphere known as an aeolipile. In the 16th century, Italian architect Giovanni Branca (1571–1640) showed that a jet of hot steam could be used to rotate the blades of a spinning wheel, and so invented an early form of steam turbine (see TURBINE).

The early development of the steam engine was related to a growing scientific awareness of how gases expanded with temperature increases and turned to liquids with pressure increases. In 1680, Dutch physicist Christiaan Huygens (1629–1695) made the first piston engine using gunpowder. He exploded a charge of gunpowder in a cylinder underneath a vertically mounted piston, which caused an expansion of gas that was allowed to escape through a one-way valve; as the remaining gas cooled, it created a partial vacuum, which pulled the piston down.

Constantly loading gunpowder charges into a cylinder was no way to operate an efficient engine, as Huygens' French assistant Denis Papin (1647–c.1712) quickly realized. In 1690, he built a similar arrangement of a piston in a cylinder about 2.5 inches (6.4 cm) in diameter, but he replaced the gunpowder with expanding steam that entered from a separate boiler. The piston was not pushed up by the steam expanding, but pulled down by the partial vacuum created when the steam contracted.

Steam engines were initially developed purely to solve the problem of flooding in underground mines; they were little more than coal-fired water pumps. Thus, when English engineer Thomas Savery (c.1650–1715) produced his steam engine in 1698, it was called The Miner's Friend and patented as: "A new invention… for raising of Water, and occasioning Motion to all sorts of Mill Work by the Impellent Force of Fire, which will be of great Use and Advantage for Draining Mines, serving Towns with Water, and for the Working of all Sorts of Mills where they have not the benefit of Water nor Constant Winds." Savery's engine failed to live up to its promise—it could raise water no higher than 20 ft (6.1 m)—but his patent nevertheless gave a glimpse of a steam-driven future freed from the constraints of wind and water power.

Invention and refinement

The first practical steam engine was constructed in Dudley in England in 1712 by blacksmith Thomas Newcomen (1663–1729; see box on page 1250) and was used for pumping water from a coal mine. It was a large beam engine with a single cylinder that used steam at low (just above atmospheric) pressure. With the piston at the bottom of the cylinder, steam was allowed to enter from a boiler. This pushed the piston up, causing the beam to rise at the piston end and fall at the pump end. A jet of water was then squirted into the cylinder, causing the steam to condense. Atmospheric pressure was then greater than the pressure in the cylinder, and it pushed the piston back down, causing the beam to fall at the piston end and rise at the pump end.

Newcomen's engine was successful throughout Europe, but it was far from efficient: it converted only about one percent of the energy produced by its fuel into useful mechanical work. Without a number of improvements introduced by Scottish engineer James Watt (1736–1819), the steam engine would probably never have developed beyond its original limited application as an inefficient mine pump (see box on page 1248).

Watt realized that the steam in Newcomen's engine was doing too little work, and too much energy was being wasted. He introduced the insulated condenser (to reduce heat losses to the outside air), the separate cylinder for condensing steam (to prevent the energy losses incurred when the main cylinder was alternately heated and cooled), and the double-acting cylinder, in which steam pushed the piston both ways.

For patent reasons, Watt chose not to use a crankshaft and connecting rod. Instead he introduced the epicyclic (sun-and-planet) gear system for converting the back-and-forth motion of the piston into the rotary motion of a flywheel. The epicyclic gear system consisted of a gear at the center of the flywheel and another gear on the end of a rod attached to the engine's main beam. As the beam pitched up and down, its gear (the planet) cycled around the gear on the flywheel (the sun), which caused the flywheel to rotate (see GEAR).

Watt also introduced a device known as a governor for regulating the speed of his steam engines. This consisted of two heavy metal balls that spun around an axle, which was driven by a belt from the flywheel. As the flywheel and the axle spun faster, the metal balls were pushed outward and upward due to centrifugal force. They were connected to the engine's main steam inlet valve, and each time they moved up, they reduced the amount of steam entering the engine, thus slowing it down. This meant that they kept the engine working within a fairly narrow range of speeds.

Following Watt's improvements, the steam engine developed rapidly. Richard Trevithick (1771–1833), who was an English mining engineer, pioneered the high-pressure steam engine in 1797 and paved the way for the development of steam locomotives (see RAILROADS, HISTORY OF). U.S. miller Oliver Evans (1755–1819) was developing high-

BOILERS

A stoker adds coal to the boiler of a steamship.

A boiler is a device for generating steam at high pressures. The simplest boiler is a giant metal cylinder filled with water, something like an oversized kettle, which is heated by the flames from a burning fuel.

In a steam engine, the boiler supplies steam constantly to the cylinder through an inlet valve. The most efficient boilers expose as great an area of water to the flames as possible. In practice, this is achieved by running water through a number of thin tubes above the flames; by providing a constant supply of coal or other fuel to the furnace; and by keeping a strong draft of air moving through to keep the furnace hot.

Not all boilers are used for steam engines; domestic hot water systems and factories also use them. Most boilers are made from strong metal to withstand immense pressures, which may be as high as 5000 lb per sq in (350 kg/cm^3).

A CLOSER LOOK

THOMAS NEWCOMEN

Thomas Newcomen (1663–1729) invented the steam engine in 1705. He was a blacksmith from Devon, England, who had thought hard about the problem of pumping water out of flooded mines. Working with a friend, John Calley, who was a plumber, he developed his steam engine as an alternative to bailing out mines using horses and buckets.

It is not known whether Newcomen was aware of the earlier work of Thomas Savery, but the Newcomen engine was sufficiently similar to Savery's patent that the two men had to come to a business arrangement. Savery, whose own engine had been a failure, benefited more from the deal. But although Newcomen gained little financial compensation, history has rewarded him by recognizing his first practical steam engine of 1712 as one of technology's most important inventions.

PEOPLE

pressure steam engines at about the same time (see STEAM-POWERED ROAD VEHICLES). During his lifetime, Evans constructed about 50 engines working at pressures of up to 200 lb per sq in ($14 \, kg/cm^3$), including an amphibious steam-powered dredger.

THE POWER OF STEAM

Steam (water vapor) contains useful energy in three forms: the heat energy needed to raise water from room temperature to its boiling temperature of 212°F (100°C); the latent (hidden) heat of vaporization needed to convert boiling water at 212°F (100°C) into steam at the same temperature; and the energy needed to convert steam into superheated steam (steam well above its boiling point). The story of steam engines is the story of engineers competing against one another to achieve the maximum power and efficiency from steam.

The power output of a single-acting steam engine is given by the formula

Power = mean pressure × stroke (distance the piston travels) × area of piston × number of strokes per minute

For a double-acting engine, the power must be multiplied by two. This formula explains why engineers tried to produce engines capable of higher pressures and speeds; although they could have increased the area of the cylinder and the length of the piston to achieve the same effect, this was much less practical with the poor machine tools of the 18th century.

The efficiency of a steam engine is slightly more complex. A steam engine converts heat energy into useful mechanical energy, first by allowing the steam to expand and push a piston outward, then by condensing the steam into water. This transforms a certain volume of steam through a cycle.

In 1824, French physicist Nicholas Sadi Carnot (1796–1832) demonstrated how this cycle determines the efficiency both of an ideal engine and any practical engine. The efficiency of an idealized engine is given by the formula:

Efficiency = useful mechanical work / total heat supplied = $1 - T_F / T_I$

where T_F is the temperature to which the steam is cooled and T_I is the temperature to which it is raised (both expressed in Kelvin). This means a real engine is most efficient when T_F is as low as possible and T_I as high as possible. A typical engine with a boiler temperature of 393 K (248°F or 120°C) and a condenser temperature of 293 K (68°F or 20°C) has a maximum efficiency of only 25 percent. In practice, its efficiency will be much lower than this due to heat losses at various points in the cylinder (see HEAT, PRINCIPLES OF).

A CLOSER LOOK

Pioneers of American steam

Although the steam engine was invented in Great Britain, American engineers played a considerable role in its development. Oliver Evans, one of the pioneers of high-pressure steam, developed a steam road carriage in 1804, a few years after his English rival Richard Trevithick. American engineer Robert Fulton (1765–1815) ran the first steamboat service along the Hudson River in 1807 (see SHIP AND BOAT, HISTORY OF). Twelve years later, the American sail- and paddle-driven steamship *Savannah* crossed the Atlantic from New York to Liverpool in 29 days, using steam for 83 hours of the voyage.

The benefits of steam power were not confined to factories and transportation. Toward the end of the 19th century, steam engines were used to pump the domestic water supply from a site in Dunkirk, New York. In 1882, electrical engineer Thomas Alva Edison (1847–1931) opened the first major power station at Pearl Street in New York using high-speed, horizontal steam engines to drive the electricity generators (see ELECTRIC MOTOR AND GENERATOR).

The final days of steam

Later innovations included the compound (multiple cylinder) engine, patented in 1803 by English engineer Arthur Woolf (1776–1837); the horizontal engine pioneered in the mid-1820s by the London firm of Taylor & Martineau; the high-speed vertical engine developed by U.S. inventor George Westinghouse (1846–1914) and others in the United States; and the uniflow engine patented by British engineer Leonard Todd in 1885 and developed by the Skinner Engine Company of Erie, Pennsylvania.

However, with the invention of the efficient steam turbine in 1884 by English engineer Charles Parsons (1854–1931), and the simultaneous development of the internal combustion engine, the days of steam engines were numbered (see AUTOMOBILE, HISTORY OF; INTERNAL COMBUSTION ENGINE).

The development of the steam engine lasted centuries, from the late 17th century to the dawn of the 20th century. Although the steam engine was a landmark in the history of technology, the preoccupation with steam (a luxury permitted by an abundance of cheap coal) arguably hindered the development of cleaner, more efficient technologies.

C. WOODFORD

See also: COAL; ENERGY RESOURCES; ENGINE; GEAR; HEATING SYSTEMS; MECHANICAL ENGINEERING; MECHANICAL TRANSMISSION; POWER STATION; RAILROAD LOCOMOTIVE; SHIP AND BOAT, HISTORY OF.

Further reading:
Crowley T. *Beam Engines.* Princes Risborough, England: Shire Publications, 1999.
Hills, R. *Power From Steam: A History of the Stationary Steam Engine.* New York: Cambridge University Press, 1989.
Woodruff, E., and Lammers, H. *Steam-Plant Operations.* New York: McGraw Hill, 1992.

STEAM-POWERED ROAD VEHICLES

Steam-powered road vehicles predated automobiles powered by internal combustion engines

The urge to travel faster than walking speed has a long history. For centuries, *horsepower* literally meant the energy produced by one or more horses, usually attached to a wagon, cart, or carriage of some kind. It was not until the 18th century that viable alternatives to horses, using mechanical means, were developed to produce power.

The first such invention to use steam was the three-wheeled artillery tractor produced in 1770 by French artillery officer Nicolas-Joseph Cugnot (1725–1804). He followed this in 1797 with a four-passenger tricycle capable of going 4 mph (6.4 km/h). British engineering pioneers William Murdock (1754–1839) and Robert Fourness both developed vehicles using steam engines, but it was Sir Goldsworthy Gurney (1793–1875) who made real progress with a steam vehicle that carried six people at a top speed of 17 mph (27 km/h) over a distance of 84 miles (135 km).

In the early 19th century, Gurney's omnibuses operated successfully over fixed routes and to timetables and were very popular with the public (see BUS). Unsurprisingly, operators of horse-drawn coaches were very much against them and proved to have the greater influence. In England, the Road Trustees (members of the community who managed roads) imposed prohibitive tolls and did all they could to stifle the development of steam transport (see ANIMAL TRANSPORT). As a result, the impetus was lost in that country, while development continued elsewhere, particularly in the United States.

It was in the United States that the industrial pioneer Oliver Evans (1755–1819) developed a passenger vehicle in 1804, but there was little progress for most of the 19th century because very few suitable roads existed. Interest was rekindled when a method of fitting small steam motors to bicycles was devised around 1886. The steam-powered bicycle industry was short-lived in the United States, mainly because of the appalling condition of the roads, which made cycling hazardous.

A steam carriage developed in the 1890s for two or more passengers by George D. Whitney was improved by Francis Stanley (1849–1918) and his twin brother Freelan (1849–1940). It was demonstrated to the public in the fall of 1898 at Charles River Park in Boston. Stanley vehicles differed from most other contemporary designs by having the motor geared directly to the back axle, rather than connected by a chain (see GEAR). Because the Stanleys had not patented their design it was copied by many other manufacturers. Carrying two passengers at a top speed of 20 mph (32 km/h), it was produced in large numbers and became very popular. But it was complex, not very stable, and had a short wheelbase (distance between the front and rear wheels), which made the ride bumpy; and it had

A group of passengers is carried by a L'Obeissante steam carriage. This 5-ton (4.5-tonne), 12-seat vehicle was manufactured in France in 1872.

many fragile parts. Road conditions made it necessary to design machines with high ground clearance and large wheels to protect the mechanism from rocks, mud, and dust.

Steam power was used not only for public omnibuses or private cars. Amazingly, more than one thousand steam-powered vehicles were known to be working in the United States as late as the 1960s. Steamrollers were a common sight on roadworks, where they were used to compress the surface of newly poured roads. Many fire engines were powered by steam in the early part of the 20th century, as were a range of farm vehicles, especially tractors and threshing machines (see AGRICULTURE, HISTORY OF).

Manufacturers such as Charles Duryea (1861–1938) and his brother Frank (1869–1967), who had developed a vehicle that used gasoline as the fuel, began to make inroads into the industry in the 1890s. German engineer Gottlieb Daimler (1834–1900) developed a one-cylinder air-cooled internal combustion engine around the same time. These engines' greater potential for speed was soon recognized, and interest in steam gradually waned.

F. HAMILTON

See also: ELECTRIC ROAD VEHICLE; INTERNAL COMBUSTION ENGINE; STEAM ENGINE.

Further reading:

Bacon, J. *American Steam-Car Pioneers*. Exton: Newcomen Society of the United States, 1984.
Hardenberg, H. *The Oldest Precursor of the Automobile*. Warrendale, Pennsylvania: Society of Automotive Engineers, 1995.

CONNECTIONS

● At first, the **CIVIL ENGINEERING** technology used for **ROAD BUILDING** and the construction of **BRIDGES** was not very suitable for carrying heavy steam-powered vehicles.

STEAM TURBINE

A steam turbine is a machine in which a shaft is rotated by the impact of steam flowing over blades

The Mauretania *(pictured here) and its sister ship,* Lusitania, *were the first transatlantic passenger liners to be fitted with steam turbine engines. Both ships were launched in 1906.*

A flow of air, hot gas, water or some other fluid is enough to rotate the shaft of a turbine. However, by far the most widely used and most powerful turbines are operated by steam.

The steam that drives a steam turbine is produced by evaporating water in boilers using fuels such as coal, oil, or natural gas (see FUELS AND PROPELLANTS). The steam turbines used in nuclear power stations typically run on steam produced using heat removed from the reactor core by a coolant, normally water (see NUCLEAR POWER). The hot steam is allowed to expand rapidly inside the turbine. This expansion converts heat energy into kinetic energy (motion). Most of this kinetic energy is subsequently used up as the fast-moving steam transfers its energy to the blades, making them turn the disk or drum to which they are attached.

There are two main types of steam turbine: an impulse turbine and a reaction turbine. Impulse turbines use a nozzle to direct fluid onto the turbine's blades. The fluid in a reaction turbine accelerates over the movable blades of the turbine as the pressure is decreased. This creates a reaction force that cause the turbine to rotate (see MECHANICS).

However, in practice the turbine design may be a combination of both. In many types the steam is directed onto the moving (rotor) blades by a ring of stationary (stator) blades, which act as nozzles. The reaction between the steam and the rotor blades causes the rotor to spin. The steam expands progressively as it passes through alternate rows of fixed and moving blades, which continuously move and absorb more and more of the steam's kinetic energy.

Development of the steam turbine

The principle of the steam turbine was first demonstrated by the engineer Hero of Alexandria in the first century C.E. In Hero's device, water in a boiler was heated by a wood fire. Steam from the boiling water was forced through pipes into a metal sphere fixed above the boiler. These input pipes were positioned along a horizontal axis of the sphere. The sphere also had two other pipes from which the steam exited. These were positioned on an axis that was perpendicular to that of the input pipes. In addition, the output pipes had a slight bend in them that directed steam out to the side. The sphere turned as a reaction to the escape of the steam. The device was, therefore, a reaction turbine. But it was not powerful enough to be used to perform useful work.

The development of the modern steam turbine was another step on the ladder of engine development, which began in 1712 when English inventor

CONNECTIONS

● The steam in most steam turbines is produced by burning **COAL**, oil, or gas.

● Steam turbines revolutionized **BOATBUILDING AND SHIPBUILDING**.

CORE FACTS

■ Steam turbines are used to drive machines needing rotational mechanical power.

■ In a steam turbine, steam is allowed to expand, causing an increase in kinetic energy, some of which is transferred to the moving blades of the turbine.

■ Propelling ships and driving electric generators are the two most important applications of steam turbines.

■ A modern nuclear power station generates about 2 billion shaft horsepower (1500 MW) of electricity using just one steam turbine.

Thomas Newcomen (1663–1729) built the first practical steam engine using a cylinder and piston (see STEAM ENGINE). Around 1859, Belgian-born French engineer and inventor Jean-Joseph-Étienne Lenoir (1822–1900) developed the first working internal combustion engine fueled by coal gas (see INTERNAL COMBUSTION ENGINE). In 1883, the first gasoline engine was built by German engineer Gottlieb Wilhelm Daimler (1834–1900). The following year, English engineer Charles Algernon Parsons (1854–1931) invented the steam turbine.

There were two applications ripe for Parsons' steam turbine: the generation of large amounts of electricity and the propulsion of ships. Before the steam turbine, electric generators were powered by ordinary steam engines that could not rotate the generator coils fast enough to produce large amounts of electricity. Parsons showed that the high speed of his steam turbine (it could rotate 18,000 times per minute) and the uniformity of its running (its vibrations were so small that it did not require bolting to the floor) made it ideal for electricity generation. With high speeds of rotation, high voltages could be obtained from a relatively small generator, and the turbine itself was smaller than a steam engine of the same power (see ELECTRIC MOTOR AND GENERATOR).

The first steam turbine built by Parsons produced only 6 horsepower (4.5 kW). The development of bigger turbines was delayed for six years because the validity of the patent was questioned. Nevertheless, within 30 years steam turbines of 35,000 horsepower (26,000 kW) were operating using relatively small amounts of steam. The steam turbines now working in nuclear power stations are equivalent to 1.7 million horsepower (1300 MW).

Until 1884, steamships were fitted with reciprocating steam engines. These engines contain heavy components—such as pistons and connecting rods—that change direction frequently. In turbines, a rotary force is applied directly to the shaft.

Steam turbines can run much faster than steam engines, increasing the power available from a device of the same size and weight. They also run very smoothly, almost without vibration. Also, the condensed steam from a steam turbine is not contaminated with oil and can be fed back to the boiler for reuse without much cleaning.

To demonstrate the advantages of his steam turbine, Parsons fitted it into a launch, the *Turbinia*, which was demonstrated at the Royal Naval review at Spithead, England in 1897. The vessel reached speeds of nearly 40 mph (65 km/h). The Cunard Company fitted four huge steam turbines into the transatlantic liner the *Mauretania*, which crossed the Atlantic in 1907 in a record time of five days. Today, most merchant vessels and many warships are powered by steam turbines (see MARINE ENGINEERING).

The operation of a steam turbine

Inside the casing of a steam turbine, the rotor blades are attached to a drum (rotor) that is free to rotate. The rotor is connected to a rotating shaft that

CHARLES PARSONS

English engineer Charles Parsons invented the steam turbine in 1884.

Charles Parsons, the inventor of the steam turbine, was born in London in 1854. In 1877, he began work at an electrical engineering factory in Newcastle upon Tyne in northeast England. In 1884, Parsons invented a multistaged steam turbine, which could extract the greatest amount of kinetic energy without causing blades to spin at an uncontrollable speed and shake the apparatus to pieces.

In 1889, Parsons established his own engineering business, which manufactured steam turbines, dynamos, and other electrical apparatus. The basic turbine design was altered in 1891 when a steam condenser was added for use in power stations (see POWER STATION). As well as running his own business, Parsons was heavily involved with several other large electrical and engineering companies. He became a fellow of the prestigious Royal Society in 1898 and was knighted in 1911.

In addition to the turbine, Parsons also invented a mechanical reducing gear system, which greatly improved the efficiency of turbine-driven propellers (see MECHANICAL TRANSMISSION; PROPELLER). He also came up with the idea of using chains to improve the grip of automobile tires in icy conditions (see TIRE), and he designed and developed optical instruments. Parsons died in 1931.

PEOPLE

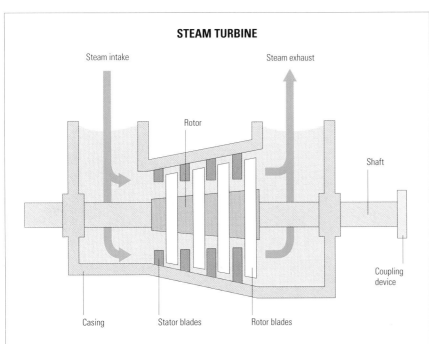

STEAM TURBINE

Steam intake

Steam exhaust

Rotor

Shaft

Coupling device

Casing

Stator blades

Rotor blades

A diagram of a steam turbine. The superheated steam flows through a series of fixed (stator) and movable (rotor) blades, causing the shaft to rotate. The stator blades act as nozzles directing the expanding steam onto the rotor blades. The acceleration of the expanding steam creates a force that causes the movable blades to spin.

extends out of the turbine along its horizontal axis. The fixed (stator) blades are attached on the inner surface of the turbine casing. All the blades are arranged in rings around the axis of the turbine. Rings of rotor blades and stator blades are positioned alternately through the turbine (see the diagram above). The distance between each ring is very small to ensure that the flow of steam is accurately focused onto the next ring of blades in the turbine.

Steam is injected through a valve onto the first ring of the fixed stator blades and is focused by these blades onto the first ring of the moving blades. The kinetic energy of the steam is transferred to the blades, causing them to spin. The stator blades are shaped so that the steam impacts the moving blades at exactly the right angle to transfer as much of its energy as possible. The steam then passes on to the next fixed ring, and so on along the length of the turbine. After passing the last ring, the steam exits through the steam outlet and is condensed and returned to the boiler.

The rings of blades on the drum are of different diameters. The diameter increases along the drum, and the pressure decreases. The varying diameter is necessary for the operation of a steam turbine. This is because the steam passing through the larger and larger spaces between the rings rapidly expands to fill these spaces, thus reducing the pressure of the steam. This expansion releases the kinetic energy in the steam that is used to turn the rotor blades.

The shaft is supported by bearings attached to the casing and transmits the mechanical energy of the turbine to a coupling device that connects the turbine with the machine being driven. Originally, turbine speed was controlled by a governor—a mechanical control device that opened and closed valves. A second governor was normally provided for emergency use. Modern turbines are controlled by pressure and speed sensors (see PRESSURE MEASUREMENT; TRANSDUCER AND SENSOR). These control devices serve to prevent the speed of the turbine from becoming so high that destructive vibrations cause the machine's materials to fail (see MATERIALS SCIENCE).

Turbine ratings

Steam turbines are used to drive machines that need rotational mechanical power. They can drive them at either constant or variable speeds and can provide fine speed control. Their most important applications are the propulsion of ships and the driving of electric generators. Other uses include driving pumps and compressors (see PUMP AND COMPRESSOR). The power of steam turbines has increased with demands for larger outputs.

Turbine characteristics usually have to be matched with the requirements of the application. Ships use turbines of up to 80,000 shaft horsepower (about 60,000 kW); ship propellers rotate at speeds of up to 250 revolutions per minute, and turbine speeds are typically 20 times higher than this. Reduction gears are used to match the speed of the turbine to the desired speed of the propeller. Steam pressures of about 600 lb/sq inch (42 kg/cm^2) and temperatures of about 930°F (500°C) are typical.

Electric power stations require much more powerful steam turbines than ships need. A modern nuclear power reactor provides about 2 billion shaft horsepower (1500 MW) of electricity using a steam turbine with a speed of about 1800 revolutions per minute. Most nuclear power reactors produce steam at a pressure of about 1000 lb/sq in (70 kg/cm^2) and a temperature of about 570°F (300°C).

Conditions in fossil-fueled power stations are different. Steam pressures are typically about 1080 lb/sq in (76 kg/cm^2) and steam temperatures are about 1000°F (540°C). The steam can be reheated in the boiler (superheated) to increase its kinetic energy and reduce the amount of water condensing inside the turbine itself. Turbines in nuclear power stations are larger and more expensive than their counterparts in fossil-fuel stations.

Steam turbines operate at high speeds and high temperatures; some components are subjected to powerful centrifugal forces. Machines must be constructed from materials that are strong enough to withstand these conditions.

S. FLETCHER

See also: AERODYNAMICS; GAS ENGINE (STIRLING ENGINE); GAS TURBINE; HEAT EXCHANGER; HEAT, PRINCIPLES OF; HYDRODYNAMICS AND HYDROSTATICS; POWER STATION; TURBINE; WATER POWER; WAVE POWER; WIND POWER.

Further reading:
Bloch, H. *A Practical Guide to Steam Turbine Technology.* New York: McGraw-Hill, 1996.

STEERING SYSTEMS

Steering systems are mechanical arrangements used to steer road vehicles easily, accurately, and safely

Kart drivers negotiate a sharp bend in a racetrack. The rotational motion of the steering wheels and steering shafts produces linear motion of steering rods and linkages that changes the angle of the pivoted front wheels.

In the days when locomotive energy was provided by horses, steering was largely a matter of ensuring that the horses moved in the appropriate direction. This was achieved by pulling on the bit (mouthpiece) by way of the reins to indicate to the horses which way to turn. Modern steering systems for road vehicles use steering wheels that are usually coupled to the front wheels of the vehicles. However, a few modern automobiles use a more complex four-wheel steering system, which improves the handling of the vehicle (see the box on page 1257).

Historical development

The earliest road vehicles tended to mirror the steering systems used in existing carriages and other vehicles (see HORSE-DRAWN TRANSPORT). Many of the earliest automobiles used some kind of boat-type tiller linked to the front wheels. Some of these vehicles had a single front wheel, which was steered in a similar way to the front wheel of a bicycle—many of these designs even featured handlebars. Steering arrangements were greatly simplified by using a single front wheel or a single rear wheel.

In many early vehicles, the solid axle for the two front wheels was attached to a small turntable that could be rotated for steering. Effectively, the axle was pivoted at its center, but this meant that the vehicle skidded when it went around corners because the wheels on the inside of the turn were forced backward against the direction of their rotation. This problem was recognized at an early stage in primitive road vehicles and solved as early as 1820 by the system known as Ackerman steering (see page 1257).

As automobiles evolved away from earlier influences, steering systems improved. However, not all designs resembled modern systems; one design even had a steering wheel that had to be rotated to the right to make the vehicle turn to the left. By 1900 most road vehicles were being steered by a steering wheel. They used one solid front axle, and, like modern systems, many, including the 1908 Model T Ford, used separately pivoted wheels and rods that turned the wheels on their pivots.

Principles of modern steering systems

The steering gear is the part of the steering system that converts the rotary motion of the steering wheel into the linear (straight-line) motion that is trans-

CORE FACTS

- Steering systems change the angle of the front wheels and provide the driver with a mechanical advantage so that less force is needed to turn the steering wheel.
- Front wheels do not remain parallel during a turn because the wheel on the outer side of the turn is describing a larger radius than the other wheel.
- Power steering has long been a feature of many modern vehicles and is usually operated by hydraulics.
- A few commercially available automobiles use a complex four-wheel steering system.

CONNECTIONS

- **TRACKED VEHICLES** such as **TANKS** are steered by changing the relative speed of the **WHEEL**s on either side of the vehicle.

AUTOMOBILE STEERING SYSTEM

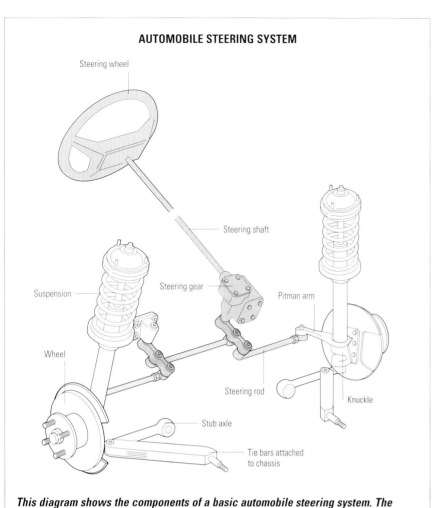

Steering wheel

Steering shaft

Suspension

Steering gear

Pitman arm

Wheel

Steering rod

Knuckle

Stub axle

Tie bars attached
to chassis

This diagram shows the components of a basic automobile steering system. The steering gear in this system uses a worm-and-nut configuration.

low-pressure tires that exerted considerable resistance to changing direction, especially at low speeds and when parking. The amount of work required to turn the wheels was greatly reduced by using more efficient steering gears and fitting better bearings in all the mechanical linkages in the entire system.

A gearing system used in the steering gear also reduces the force required at the steering wheel in order to make manual steering practical. The steering gear ratio is the number of degrees the steering wheel must be turned to cause the road wheels to turn one degree on their pivots.

The higher this ratio, the lower the force required to steer the vehicle. As well as making turning easier, safety is improved by a high steering gear ratio, because bumps in the road that jerk the wheels suddenly cause the steering wheel to move much less than in a car with a low steering gear ratio.

On the other hand, the higher the ratio, the poorer the maneuverability of the vehicle at high speed. An alternative or supplement to a high steering gear ratio is to provide some kind of power-assisted steering in which the power of the engine is employed to move the wheels hydraulically (see page 1257).

Gearing systems

The steering wheel is firmly attached to the upper end of a strong shaft that rotates with the steering wheel. In modern automobiles, the steering wheel and the steering shaft are often designed to collapse under impact to keep the driver from being injured on the steering wheel in a collision (see AIR BAG; SAFETY SYSTEMS).

At the lower end of the steering wheel shaft is the steering gear—the mechanism that converts rotary motion to linear motion. This can take various forms, each of which must provide a mechanical advantage. The worm-and-nut system (also called the cam-and-peg system) provides gearing between the angular rotation of the steering wheel shaft and the sideways movement of the steering rods.

The worm is essentially a screw gear with a single spiral thread or tooth (see GEAR). The nut that is threaded onto the worm moves a short distance for each complete rotation of the worm. The worm is on the lower end of the steering wheel shaft, and the nut is coupled to the steering rods by a pivoting arm. Because of the large gear ratio between the worm and the nut, a greater movement of the steering wheel is required, with correspondingly lesser force, than the movement required of the rods.

Rack-and-pinion steering achieves a similar mechanical advantage. The rack is a long steel bar with straight teeth on one side that mesh with the teeth on a gear, or pinion, that is attached to the end of the steering shaft. As the pinion rotates, the rack is forced to one side. Because the number of teeth on the pinion is small, a complete rotation of the steering wheel causes only a small sideways movement of the rack. Rack-and-pinion steering systems are perhaps the most common type in use today.

mitted to the rod or rods that link the pair of front wheels together. These rods ensure that the wheels maintain an appropriate near-parallel relationship while turning to the right or left. The front wheels of modern vehicles are not mounted on a single axle. Instead, each wheel rotates on its own short horizontal stub axles. The stub axles, together with the wheels, are also free to pivot.

The part of the wheel assembly that pivots is known as the knuckle, and each knuckle is joined to the steering rod by a movable angled arm, known as a Pitman arm. The steering rods in turn are connected to the steering gear. It is the side-to-side movement of the steering rods that changes the inclination of the wheels.

Steering gear ratio

Road vehicle steering gears serve an additional purpose. Vehicles can be extremely heavy, so the force required to turn the road wheels to one side or the other, without a system of leverage to provide a mechanical advantage (an increase in the force applied by the driver), would be too great (see MECHANICS). At one time a maximum force equivalent to 30 lbs (13.5 kg) was considered acceptable for heavy vehicles, but experience soon showed that this figure put excessive strain on the driver. The difficulty was greatest with vehicles that used wide,

Variable-ratio systems also exist in which the ratio is high for slow-speed driving, parking, and cornering, but low for high-speed freeway driving. This is achieved by switching between different sets of steering gears when certain speeds are reached.

Ackerman steering

The steering movement of the two front wheels of a vehicle is not as simple as might be imagined. The wheels do not, in fact, remain parallel. The reason for this is that when a vehicle turns, the wheel on the outside of the turn moves along the arc of a larger circle than that along which the wheel on the inner side of the turn moves. To steer around a small circle requires the wheel to be turned through a greater angle than to steer around a larger circle. This means that if the steered wheels remained parallel, one or both would have to skid sideways a little whenever the vehicle turned. To avoid this, vehicles have universally adopted the Ackerman system.

Rudolf Ackerman (1764–1834) was a German fine-art publisher and bookseller who, in 1820, developed a system to turn the front wheels by different angles. His system ensures that the wheel on the inside of a curve turns more sharply—that is, through a greater degree—than the wheel on the outside. The difference between the angle of the two wheels, known as the toe-out, is greatest when the vehicle is performing its smallest turning circle.

The Ackerman system is achieved by angling the Pitman arms away from the center of the car. (In a non-Ackerman system these arms would be at right angles to the steering rods). Therefore, when a wheel in an Ackerman system is on the outside of the turn, it must be moved through an angle before it is even at right angles with the steering rods. Alternatively, when it is on the inside of the turn, its position is already past right angles with the rods before it has even begun to turn.

The rear wheels of a vehicle need not be angled on a turn; they are able to rotate at different speeds because of the differential gear at the center of the rear axle (see AUTOMOBILE).

Power steering

Power steering (or power-assisted steering) amplifies the force applied to the steering wheel by the driver, usually with a hydraulic system. Such a system requires a pump driven by the engine, a reservoir for hydraulic fluid, a control valve, and a power cylinder containing a piston. The pump is connected to the cylinder by high-pressure hoses. The power cylinder may be an integral part of the steering gear, or it may be separate and connected between the vehicle frame and the steering rods and linkages.

The essence of a power-steering system is that the control valve is linked to the steering shaft in such a way that it directs the high-pressure oil to one side or the other of the piston in the cylinder, depending on the motion of the steering wheel. The movement of the piston, which is being pushed by the oil, determines which way the wheels are pivoted.

Current power steering designs are controlled using a microprocessor (a computer on a single silicon chip) that measures the positions of the wheels and the rotation of the steering wheel. Electronic control of this kind is more flexible than a mechanical system and can produce variable degrees of assistance depending on vehicle speed. The greatest degree of power assistance is provided at the slowest speeds when steering-wheel rotation is greatest.

R. YOUNGSON

See also: AUTOMOBILE, HISTORY OF; BRAKE SYSTEMS; HYDRAULICS AND PNEUMATICS; MECHANICAL TRANSMISSION; SUSPENSION SYSTEM; TIRE; WHEEL.

Further reading:

Halderman, J. *Automotive Chassis Systems: Brakes, Steering, Suspension, and Alignment.* Englewood Cliffs, New Jersey: Prentice Hall, 1996.
Steering and Suspension Technology. Warrendale, Pennsylvania: Society of Automotive Engineers, 1997.

FOUR-WHEEL STEERING

The 1986 Nissan Skyline was the first automobile with four-wheel steering.

Most vehicles steer by turning only the front wheels. However, this limits the turning radius and hence the maneuverability of the vehicle. A steering system that angles all four wheels can overcome these disadvantages, making parking much easier and improving comfort and safety. High-speed driving is said to be safer because fishtailing (the sideways movement of the back of a car when it is steered) is reduced. Patents for a four-wheel steering system (4WS) were taken out by the Japanese Mazda car company in 1965, but the first commercial automobile to use four-wheel steering did not appear until 1986. This was the Skyline, produced by Nissan. The following year, Honda offered four-wheel steering as an option on its Prelude XX sports car.

Four-wheel steering can take two forms: all four wheels can turn in the same direction, or the front and rear wheels can turn in opposite directions. Four wheels turning in the same direction will reduce the chance of skidding while the vehicle is cornering at high speed because all the wheels are kept in contact with the road. Moving the rear wheels in the opposite direction to the front pair reduces the turning circle of the vehicle considerably, making parking easier.

A CLOSER LOOK

STOVES AND OVENS

Stoves and ovens fueled by electricity or gas are used for cooking food in modern kitchens

A modern stove allows food to be cooked precisely.

heat could be easily adjusted with the turn of a knob, and the introduction of thermostats around 1915 (see THERMOMETRY) allowed the cook to set the temperature without having to monitor it constantly during the cooking time.

Electric stoves became popular immediately because they were perceived as cleaner and safer than gas-powered cookers. However, when they were first sold in the 1930s, many houses did not have enough electrical current available to run them, so stoves burning wood or gas were more common. Today, although a great number of U.S. households cook with electricity, many people still prefer gas because it is less expensive and the heat of gas burners can be regulated more precisely than that of electrical coils. Gas and electric stoves and ovens come in many sizes and shapes, with features to fill every need. In some kitchens a range combines the oven and the cooktop. Other kitchen designs include a wall oven with a separate cooktop installed in a counter elsewhere in the kitchen.

While modern gas and electric stoves do not heat the entire kitchen in the way that the old cast-iron stoves warmed the room, they were introduced at a time when both electric and gas central heating systems were becoming popular, making this less important (see HEATING SYSTEMS).

Modern ovens

Ovens must accommodate both baking, with heat coming from below, and broiling, with the heat applied from above. Electric ovens have two heating elements in the oven cavity, one on top that comes on when the oven is set to broil, and one on the bottom for baking. With gas ovens, there is one gas-burning element, and the food is placed either above it in the oven cavity to bake or below it in a smaller broiling area. Some ovens have two separate compartments: one for baking, the other for broiling, each with its own heating element. Convection ovens are often found in commercial kitchens and are becoming more popular domestically. They have a fan to blow heated air around the food, which helps to cook it more quickly and evenly. Ovens can be difficult to

Until about 200 years ago, cooking technology had not changed very much from ancient times. Ovens, fueled by wood or coal (see FUELS AND PROPELLANTS), were used mainly for baking bread. Meat was generally cooked on a spit over a fire in an open hearth. Similarly, vegetables were boiled in water that was heated over an open fire. Coal-burning stoves made of cast iron became popular in the 18th century for heating the rooms of well-off families, and they were being designed as cooking ranges by the early 19th century.

Coal gas and electric supplies reached the majority of homes in industrialized countries by early in the 20th century, and new stoves were developed that were cleaner and easier to use (see COAL; ELECTRICITY TRANSMISSION AND SUPPLY; GAS INDUSTRY). There was neither fuel to be hauled into nor ashes to be hauled out of these new stoves. The level of

CONNECTIONS

● Stoves and ovens that run on **SOLAR POWER** have been developed for use in tropical countries with few **ENERGY RESOURCES**.

CORE FACTS

■ Wood- and coal-burning ovens and open fires were used for all cooking until a few hundred years ago.

■ The early 20th century saw the introduction of gas and electric stoves, the invention of the thermostat, and the separation of cooking and home-heating functions.

■ Cooktop heating elements may be gas rings, electric coils, or magnetic induction units.

■ Microwave ovens use microwave radiation to heat foods by vibrating their water, fat, and sugar molecules.

clean; removing the baked-on grease by hand requires noxious cleansers and a great deal of scrubbing. Self-cleaning ovens appeared soon after the introduction of electric cooking and quickly became very popular. They employ a special cycle in which the oven temperature is raised up to about 900°F (480°C) for a few hours, burning the soil into a small amount of white ash that can be easily wiped away. A safety interlock prevents the oven from being opened until it cools down.

In continuous-cleaning ovens, there is no self-clean cycle, but a special coating keeps the oven walls from getting too dirty. Running the oven occasionally at its maximum temperature while empty helps to burn off any buildup of grease. The small amount of grease that cannot be removed must be tolerated because the self-cleaning coating is ruined by soap, detergent, or other oven-cleaning products (see CLEANING AGENTS). Oven racks and parts of the door are not coated and must be cleaned by hand.

Types of cooktop elements

Gas burners are installed as the heating element in many cooktops. Electronic spark ignition systems have now eliminated the need for a constantly burning pilot light. Another very common heating element is the electric coil. Unlike gas rings, electric elements stay hot for some time after they have been turned off.

Elements that are easier to clean are attractive to most cooks. Many cooktop manufacturers offer electric elements with the coils positioned under a smooth surface. These may take the form of solid disk elements or a flat ceramic surface.

A more unusual type of cooktop element is the induction coil. This also works by electricity, but instead of using the coil element's resistance to generate heat, it takes advantage of the fact that a current moving through a coil creates a magnetic field. When a pan containing a magnetic material such as iron is set on the coil, a current is induced in the pan and its own resistance heats it up (see ELECTRICITY AND MAGNETISM; RESISTOR, CAPACITOR, AND INDUCTOR). Induction elements are comparatively safe because they do not themselves get hot, although of course there is still a hot pan to be wary of.

Another innovation that has become quite popular is the downdraft cooktop. With ventilation built into the cooktop itself, these eliminate the need for large overhead stove hoods to suck out the steam and smoke produced during most types of cooking (see AIR-CONDITIONING AND VENTILATION). The vents are efficient enough to allow indoor grilling—an activity that makes a lot of smoke—using grill elements that can be swapped with removable burners.

S. CALVO

See also: BAKING INDUSTRY; BREWING INDUSTRY; BRICK MAKING; CERAMICS; FOOD TECHNOLOGY; HOUSEHOLD APPLIANCES; POTTERY; PREHISTORIC TECHNOLOGY; TECHNOLOGY IN ANCIENT CIVILIZATIONS.

Further reading:
Cohen, D. *The Last Hundred Years: Household Technology.* New York: M. Evans and Co., 1982.
Emley, D. *Oven, Cooktop, Range, and Stove Repair.* Orange, California: E. B. Marketing Group, 1996.
Plante, E. *The American Kitchen, 1700 to the Present: From Hearth to High-rise.* New York: Facts On File Publications, 1995.
Rubin, S. *Toilets, Toasters and Telephones: The How and Why of Everyday Objects.* San Diego: Browndeer Press, 1998.

MICROWAVE OVENS

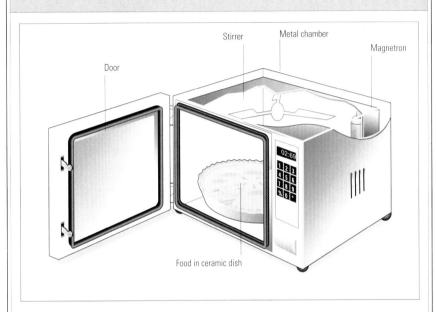

Microwaves are produced in the magnetron of a microwave oven. This radiation travels through a metal chamber and is directed onto the food by a metal stirrer.

In the fast-paced modern world, the microwave oven has become a necessity in many households, heating up meals in a fraction of the time it would take to cook them by conventional means. Microwave ovens heat food using specific frequencies of microwave radiation (around 2,500 MHz) that cause water, fat, and sugar molecules in the food to vibrate (see ELECTROMAGNETIC RADIATION; WAVE MOTION). As a molecule increases its vibration, it becomes hotter (see HEAT, PRINCIPLES OF). In addition, the vibrating molecules create friction inside the food, and this also raises its temperature, cooking the food. Microwaves are reflected by metal objects. Therefore food must be microwaved in glass or plastic containers, which are transparent to the radiation. Cooking with microwaves is very different from cooking with direct heat. The inside of a piece of food is cooked at the same time as the outside, so food is cooked evenly and quickly.

The microwave oven has its origin in a pocketful of melted candy back in 1946. Percy Spencer (1894–1970), an engineer working on a radar tube, found his snack melted inside a jacket that had remained cool (see ELECTRON TUBE; RADAR). He realized that it was the microwaves produced by the tube that had affected the molecules in the candy. Spencer quickly followed up on his discovery, but the oven he built was the size of a refrigerator and a great deal heavier. It took twenty years to build one that was small enough to fit on a counter, and then people had to be convinced that the ovens were completely safe. All microwave ovens have interlocks that prevent them from generating microwaves unless the door is firmly shut. The ovens were first used in the United States in 1947, in a hospital kitchen to heat large amounts of food. Today, they are found in nine out of ten homes in the United States.

A CLOSER LOOK

STRATEGIC DEFENSE SYSTEMS

Strategic defense systems use satellites, lasers, and other types of technology to destroy hostile missiles

This illustration shows how ground-based lasers could be reflected onto hostile targets by mirrors orbiting Earth.

CONNECTIONS

● **MEDICAL TECHNOLOGY** and **BODY PROTECTION** are the best defenses against **CHEMICAL AND BIOLOGICAL WEAPONS**.

system's first wave consisted of Spartan missiles, which would intercept as many attacking missiles as possible outside Earth's atmosphere at ranges of around 450 miles (720 km). The next wave of high-acceleration Sprint missiles would hit the remaining targets at ranges of about 25 miles (40 km).

Hitting a bullet with a bullet

Although President John F. Kennedy (1917–1963) described defending against missiles as like trying to hit a bullet with another bullet, he agreed to the development of the Sentinel system and the huge long-range radars needed to give the necessary warning of the launch of enemy missiles. These Ballistic Missile Early Warning System (BMEWS) radar sites—at Dundas (formerly Thule), Greenland, at Fylingdales Moor in northern England, and in Clear, Alaska—were to back up the Perimeter Acquisition Radar Characterization System (PARCS) radar, based in Grand Forks, North Dakota, which would detect any missiles that crossed U.S. borders (see the diagram on page 1261).

Both types of Sentinel missile carried nuclear warheads. The Spartan warhead was detonated by a ground-based computer when it was close enough to an incoming enemy missile to destroy it in the resulting explosion. The much smaller and faster cone-shaped Sprint missile reached an altitude of 25 miles (40 km) seconds after launch and carried a small nuclear warhead to destroy enemy missiles.

Only by the early 1970s were the Spartan and Sprint missiles able to intercept targets reliably. Even then, the possibility of meeting the original intention of defending all U.S. cities from missile attack proved to be impossible because of the huge cost and the ineffectiveness of the system. If only one hostile missile evaded the defenses, the system would have failed. Finally, in 1969, the U.S. government decided to use this antiballistic missile (ABM) defense systems to protect U.S. ballistic missile silos and remove

E ver since the invention of the nuclear ballistic missile (see NUCLEAR WEAPONS), the peace of the world has been maintained by a principle known as Mutual Assured Destruction (MAD). This states that, since there is no practical defense against a ballistic missile attack, the only way of avoiding one is to convince a potential aggressor that launching any missile strike would bring immediate and equally unstoppable retaliation.

Nevertheless, governments have been striving since the 1950s to find a way of destroying incoming ballistic missiles as a more reliable means of defense. The first U.S. antimissile system was Nike-Zeus, announced in January 1958. This consisted of the three-stage Zeus surface-to-air missile, which carried a nuclear warhead, and the Zeus acquisition radar system, an installation so huge that a single aerial weighed 1000 tons (910 tonnes).

Unfortunately, the final phase of steering the Zeus to its target relied on a radar system with a mechanical scanner, which proved far too slow to cope with the closing speeds of missile and target. Nike-Zeus was canceled in 1959, and attention shifted toward the Sentinel defense system. This

---

CORE FACTS

- The United States has an early warning radar that can detect missiles approaching from Europe, the Arctic, or across the Pacific and Atlantic Oceans.
- In an attempt to control space, Soviet hunter-killer satellites were developed to destroy enemy objects by exploding nearby or by launching a cloud of metal particles into the object's path.
- High-energy lasers would theoretically be able to destroy an attacking missile by focusing on a point on its surface and burning through it.
- Had the proposed SDI (star wars) system been implemented, it would have needed at least 100 orbiting space stations.

any possibility that a hostile first strike could eliminate the U.S. nuclear arsenal. Meanwhile, the Strategic Arms Limitation Talks (SALT) treaty limited the deployment of ABMs around just one area in both the United States and the Soviet Union.

Satellite warfare

Ever since the Soviet Union launched *Sputnik 1* in October 1957, satellites have developed into progressively more valuable military assets for surveillance and warning of missile attack. Since a weapon designed to destroy ballistic missiles or their warheads can also attack satellites, with devastating effects on an enemy's defenses, a hostile attacking force would include enemy satellites on its target list as well as targets inside enemy territory.

Soviet hunter-killer satellites were designed to destroy satellite targets by approaching them and then exploding or by launching a cloud of metal pellets into their path. However, these spacecraft were cumbersome, needed a powerful rocket to launch them into orbit, and were extremely limited in their height and speed. In contrast, U.S. antisatellite systems were based on missiles that could be deployed to destroy hostile satellites.

At first, these were ground-based missiles, but the administration of President Ronald Reagan (1911–) backed the development of a smaller missile that could be launched in the air from a modified F-15 fighter. With accurate sensors, the missile would destroy its target by direct impact, so no explosives were needed. This could be done more than 10 miles (16 km) above Earth, and because the F-15 was a U.S. Navy carrier-borne fighter, the system had a global reach. Like the Soviet hunter-killer orbiters, however, the missile could only hit satellites in relatively low orbits.

Star wars

To deliver a faster and longer-range response, the Reagan administration devised the Strategic Defense Initiative (SDI), otherwise known as star wars. SDI proposed reliance on space-based systems, including infrared telescopes and laser radars, intended to detect and track enemy missiles so that they could be attacked by a massive battery of space- and ground-based weapons systems.

Many of these weapons systems involved different types of high-energy lasers (see LASER AND MASER). Since bursts of laser energy travel at the speed of light, theoretically their responses would be fast enough to hit incoming missiles. Laser beams can be focused onto a small area over a large distance using mirrors, and they can be made to carry a lot of energy. High-energy lasers can damage a ballistic missile by burning a hole in its outer surface so that it weakens and splits, destroying the missile.

However, sheer scale along with the break up of the Soviet Union led to the abandonment of SDI. The system would have to destroy all enemy missiles and the independently targeted warheads and harmless decoys they released, without letting any genuine

FORTRESS AMERICA

Offshore early warning plane

Ballistic Missile Early Warning System

BMEWS Thule, Greenland

BMEWS Fylingdales Moor, England

BMEWS Clear, Alaska

Offshore early warning plane

Perimeter Acquisition Radar Characterization System

The United States is surrounded by a vast radar network that can detect incoming missiles from Europe, the Arctic, and the eastern and western seaboards.

warheads through. Experts estimated the Soviet nuclear arsenal could have launched as many as 100,000 nuclear warheads at once.

D. OWEN

See also: RADAR; ROCKETRY; SPACE STATION; SPACE TRAVEL AND TECHNOLOGY.

Further reading:
McMahon, K., and Warner, J. *Pursuit of the Shield: The U.S. Quest for Limited Ballistic Missile Defense.* Lanham, Maryland: University Press of America, 1997.

WOULD SDI WORK?

Many systems devised for the Strategic Defense Initiative are yet to be applied, chiefly because their task is too great for the technology available. For example, laser weapons would have to focus on one point on the skin of a missile to burn through it, and adding a heat-shield or simply spinning the missile in flight would greatly reduce the laser's effect. Very large mirrors, capable of reflecting a high-energy beam without being destroyed by it, would be needed to direct the laser, and imperfections on the mirror surface would again reduce its effectiveness. Space-mounted lasers could only intercept an attack during part of each orbit, so as many as 100 space stations would be needed to cope with a full-scale attack.

Other proposed weapons included X-ray, microwave, particle, and kinetic energy weapons (see WEAPONRY: SPECIALIZED SYSTEMS) and ground-based lasers. Ground-based lasers have several advantages. They can be more powerful than orbiting lasers, and they can be located in the right place to repel an attack. However, their beams would be affected by atmospheric turbulence, and even when placed on mountain peaks, complex compensating mechanisms would be needed to ensure accuracy. The lasers would also have to be 100 times more powerful than existing lasers and be able to change aim instantly.

A CLOSER LOOK

STREETCAR AND TROLLEY

Streetcars are horse-drawn or powered passenger cars that run along rails set in the roadways of city streets

This overloaded 1943 trolley car in Rio de Janeiro, Brazil, picks up power from overhead electric wires.

CONNECTIONS

● Some cable cars failed to survive because of problems with their **BRAKE SYSTEMS**.

● The **ELECTRIC MOTOR AND GENERATOR** revolutionized the development of the streetcar.

The first streetcars were introduced to New York's Bowery district in 1832. They were drawn by horses or mules and ran along rails that were set in the roadway. Because of the low friction caused by iron wheels on iron tracks, these early horsecars were large enough to carry as many passengers as a modern bus. The interior design was also similar—transverse bench seats arranged on either side of a center aisle, a platform at the front for the driver, and a platform at the back for the conductor. Some of the horsecars were open-top vehicles, but later designs had roofs, and some even had an upper deck for additional passengers.

Horsecars became very popular very quickly, and after New York, networks were soon set up in Boston, Philadelphia, and New Orleans. Within 50 years, there were around 18,000 horsecars on the streets of towns and cities in the United States. The use of horsecars also began to be developed in European cities such as London and Paris. However, the networks were not without their problems—the intense horse-drawn traffic proved to be a source of congestion and serious health problems. Every year,

thousands of horses died on the streets of U.S. cities. The working horses also caused human health problems. A city official in Rochester, New York, calculated that the 15,000 horses in the urban area there produced enough manure each year to fill a 1-acre (0.4-ha) plot to a depth of 175 feet (53 m).

The coming of electricity

The solution to the health problem from the horses already existed, although introducing it to the city streets took a long time. Just two years after the first horse-drawn cars appeared in the New York Bowery district, Vermont blacksmith Thomas Davenport (1802–1851) built a small, battery-operated electric car that ran on rails. In 1860, battery-powered electric streetcars were introduced to London and Birkenhead, where they were called tramcars.

The real revolution in changing from horsecars to electric vehicles came with the invention of the electricity generator. This made it possible to supply the streetcars with power while they were operating. Some streetcars—often called trolley cars—picked up electric power from overhead wires with a sprung collector pole with a bearing on the end called a trolley, or with an extending frame called a pantograph. Others used special collectors to make contact with conductor rails buried in slots in the road surface.

Between the 1890s and the 1920s, most horse-car services were replaced by electrically powered streetcars. At its peak, the United States had 14,000 miles (22,500 km) of streetcar lines, with the largest network in Los Angeles. Electrical power enabled larger, heavier cars with steel frames, supported on two four-wheel swiveling railway tracks, to carry more people more quickly. With these larger vehicles, lines were then extended from city centers to spreading commuter suburbs. As early as 1902, New York streetcars were carrying a billion passengers a year, and their services helped to increase the population of the Bronx district in New York from 90,000 to 200,000. They helped to provide fast and reliable transportation to and from work so that people could live in homes farther away from the commercial districts.

CORE FACTS

■ By the 1880s there were 18,000 horse-drawn streetcars in the towns and cities of the United States.

■ The United States used to have 14,000 miles (22,500 km) of electric streetcar lines, with the largest network situated in Los Angeles.

■ Today, San Francisco has 10 miles (16 km) of cable car tracks and 40 cable cars, compared with its 110 miles (177 km) of track and 600 cable cars of 1900.

Competition and decline

Streetcar lines were always vulnerable to competition because the fares for each network were fixed by the city authorities. When general living costs rose during World War I (1914–1918), fares failed to rise accordingly and profits gradually dwindled. Although the fares were eventually allowed to rise, by that time new competition from automobiles and buses put the future of streetcar networks in danger. In 1921, the 300 largest streetcar systems in the United States made a combined profit of just $2.5 million—an average of just over $8000 each—which was an extremely poor return on a total investment of around $1.5 billion.

To boost the industry, streetcar administrators tried various schemes to encourage leisure travel, such as building amusement parks at the outer end of streetcar lines. However, between 1922 and 1932 the increased use of buses and automobiles cut streetcar mileage by half. A company with oil and rubber interests, backed by General Motors, eventually bought several trolley lines and converted them into bus routes. By 1950, the old streetcar systems in more than 100 cities had disappeared, including those in Los Angeles, Philadelphia, Baltimore, and St. Louis. Within a few years, the last of London's tramcar routes had closed for similar reasons.

Rebirth of the streetcar

Ironically, the success of the automobile eventually brought about the revival of the streetcar in a slightly different form. Today, some cities seized by traffic gridlock are turning to new light rail transit (LRT) routes, which operate on a combination of under-used commuter rail tracks and traditional streetcar tracks in city center areas. These electric streetcars are much lighter and much more economical to operate than their predecessors, and they are often coupled in combinations of two, three, or more vehicles so that more passengers can be carried in much greater comfort.

New techniques for reducing noise and vibration—such as using rubber tires and suspension mountings—make the streetcar vehicles much quieter than their predecessors, and LRT projects are now in progress in an increasing number of U.S. cities, including Cleveland, Denver, Los Angeles, Minneapolis, St. Paul, Omaha, Portland, Sacramento, Salt Lake City, and San Diego.

One city in particular has kept even closer links with its streetcar past. Memphis operates historic trolley cars imported from cities such as Melbourne, Australia, and Porto, Portugal. The service follows the routes that were originally laid down for mule-drawn cars. There are 11 stations along Main Street and an additional five-stop riverfront loop that serves several popular tourist destinations. The city also plans LRT connections over a total of more than 60 miles (97 km) along three long-distance commuter routes to the north, east, and south of the city, at a cost of more than $1 billion.

D. OWEN

CABLE CARS

An operator turns around a cable car on a moving platform in San Francisco, 1984.

During the later years of the 19th century, the main competitor to the streetcar was the cable car. This was invented by Scottish cable maker Andrew Smith Hallidie (1836–1900), who settled in San Francisco. Instead of providing electric traction, his idea was to make a stationary steam engine drive an endless cable, which would run in a slot between the streetcar rails. Each car would be moved by engaging a pair of grippers that grabbed the moving cable. When the driver wanted to stop, a lever would be pulled to disengage the grippers from the cable.

The system was introduced on Sacramento and Clay Streets in San Francisco in 1873. Cable cars worked better than ordinary electric cars in hilly areas as the cable could easily run up steep gradients and by 1900, San Francisco had 110 miles (177 km) of cable car line and 600 cars. Another system served Seattle. However, cable car systems suffered from three major problems: cars could only run at a slow fixed speed; it was difficult to incorporate switches and crossings into the network for flexibility; and sometimes the grippers failed to disengage when a driver tried to stop. The whole system had to be shut down when there was a problem, such as a broken cable, and could only be restarted when the problem was fixed.

Eventually, more efficient electric cars replaced the cable car. The Seattle cable car lines closed in the 1930s, but one system still runs in San Francisco, with 10 miles (16 km) of line and 40 cars—the only survivor of this transport form.

A CLOSER LOOK

See also: ANIMAL TRANSPORT; AUTOMOBILE, HISTORY OF; BUS; ELECTRIC ROAD VEHICLE; RAILROADS, HISTORY OF; ROAD TRANSPORT, HISTORY OF.

Further reading:

Jewell, M. *Construction Costs and Operating Characteristics of Vintage Trolleys.* Washington, D.C.: U.S. Department of Transportation, 1992.
Middleton, W. *The Time of the Trolley.* San Marino, California: Golden West Books, 1987.
Molloy, S. *Trolley Wars: Streetcar Workers on the Line.* Washington, D.C.: Smithsonian Institution Press, 1996.
Morrison, A. *Latin America by Streetcar: A Pictorial Survey of Urban Road Transport South of the U.S.A.* New York: Bonde Press, 1996.

STRUCTURES

Structures are components of buildings or machines that support or resist loads

A group of men gather by the arched entrance to the Dome of the Rock, the ancient mosque in the Old City of Jerusalem.

CONNECTIONS

● **DEMOLITION** experts must understand the forces acting in a structure. They place **EXPLOSIVE** charges at the weakest points to ensure the building falls down.

● Strong **COMPOSITE** materials are used to make modern aircraft and other structures.

Almost all human-made objects, from airplanes to aqueducts and bridges to buildings, have a definite structure that enables them to stand up to the loads imposed on them. In many cases, this involves an internal or external framework made up of specific component parts, each one designed to carry particular kinds of stresses. These parts are arranged so that the construction is able to stand up under its own weight, as well as under the loads that are imposed on it by external factors such as high winds and extreme temperatures.

These loads can be divided into several different types depending on how they affect any individual part of the structural framework. Tension loads act along the axis of a framework component and stretch it; under a tensile load any material will tend to elongate in proportion to the load placed upon it (see MATERIALS SCIENCE). Compressive stresses work in the opposite direction by applying a crushing pressure to the component so that it tends to shrink as the load is increased. Shear loads act across an object and slide adjacent sections apart or produce a twisting motion in a single component. Bending loads also act across the axis of a component and change its shape by combining both tensile and compressive forces. If a load forces a component to bend downward, it will tend to stretch the upper part of the component and compress the lower part.

In elastic materials such as metal, increasing the load increases the change in shape of the component (see METALS). Heavier tension loads on a girder (a strong beam) will stretch it proportionately to the magnitude of the load applied, so that doubling the load will double the elongation, and trebling the load will treble the elongation. This continues until the material reaches what is known as its elastic limit. Up to that limit, releasing the load allows the girder to return to its original length. Any increase in load beyond the elastic limit produces permanent stretching: when the load is released, the deformed object will fail to return to its original length. If the load is increased still further, the object distorts more and more until eventually it breaks (fails).

Statics in structures

Because frame members fail when they are overloaded, from excessive deformation or from actually breaking, structures are usually designed to ensure that probable loads are within the elastic limit of each component. This involves using a branch of

CORE FACTS

- Many structures are based on triangles, since they are strong and efficient at resisting distortion.
- Timber-truss frames were first used in Bronze Age villages dating from some 4500 years ago.
- The arch is a structure that is much stronger than a beam or lintel of the same size and weight. A dome is a type of arch that has been rotated through 180 degrees around its vertical axis.

mechanics called statics, which concerns objects that are at rest as all the forces acting on them are in equilibrium: they cancel each other out (see MECHANICS).

Statics assumes that for each part of the structure, all the loads acting on it add up to zero. It also assumes there is no net torque (turning force) acting on the overall structure that would tend to turn it about an axis. These assumptions are independent of one another and they are the basic requirements of a static structure. They can be expressed as mathematical equations, which can then be used to solve up to three unknown quantities in analyzing the forces acting on any part of the structure.

The simplest structures require only three load-bearing elements for structural stability: additional elements are redundant. For example, a stool with three legs will be perfectly stable provided that the legs are adequately spaced and sufficiently strong. The fourth leg in a typical chair design is superfluous and introduces the problem of rocking if the chair is placed on an uneven surface.

In the same way, the basic element of any framework is the triangle. Under the basic assumptions of statics, a triangle undergoes small distortions because all the loads act along its sides in either tension or compression. Its shape will change significantly only if the loads are increased to the point where the triangle collapses through failure of the material of one or more of its sides. The stability of the triangle has led to complex trusses and girder frameworks being built up from networks of triangles, both for their inherent strength and their simplicity (which enables the forces acting on sections of the frame to be calculated).

Structural analysis

Engineers analyze the forces acting on structures by subdividing them mathematically into their simplest component parts. Take the case of a simple triangular framework made up of three interlocking girders, mounted vertically, supported at its two bottom corners, and with a load pressing down at its top corner (apex). The total upward force acting through the two supports at the bottom corners must be equal to the total downward force, which consists of the load acting at the top corner plus the weight of the triangular frame itself.

The load at the top corner of the triangle can be transmitted through the framework only by being split into two different forces, which act along the two girders that meet at the top corner. How the downward load is split between those girders will depend on their angles relative to the horizontal girder at the base of the triangle. If the two side girders are of equal length, they will be set at exactly equal angles to the base, and the downward-acting force will be split into two exactly equal components, each one acting as a compressive force down one of the sides. If one of these sides is nearer to being vertical than the other, this side will transmit more of the downward-acting force than the other (see the diagram above).

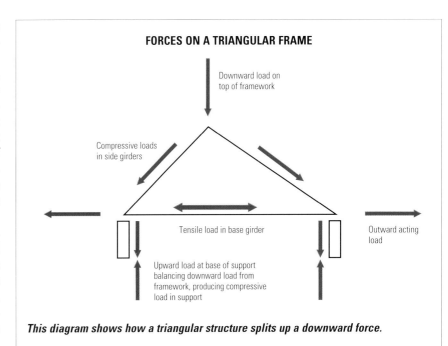

FORCES ON A TRIANGULAR FRAME

Downward load on top of framework

Compressive loads in side girders

Tensile load in base girder

Outward acting load

Upward load at base of support balancing downward load from framework, producing compressive load in support

This diagram shows how a triangular structure splits up a downward force.

Where each of the side girders meets the girder at the base of the triangle, the force acting down the side girder of the triangle produces forces acting in two directions. One force acts downward to balance the force acting upward through the support. The other force acts outward, and this produces a tensile load on the base girder of the framework. This is balanced by the outward-acting force at the opposite support, which tries to pull the base girder in the other direction. Thus the base girder is placed under a tensile stress acting along its length by these two balanced and opposing forces.

The result is that all these different forces acting on the triangular framework balance one another exactly, which is essential for a structure to be static and remain standing. If the three girders that make up the triangle are made of rigid material and distortions are small, the shape of the triangle is fixed in spite of the loads imposed on it. Geometry holds that a triangle, where the dimensions of the three sides are known, is fixed, and the angles between those sides can be calculated mathematically.

Since these angles are fixed by the relative lengths of the sides, the joints between the girders of the framework do not have bending loads imposed on them. This means they can be simple pin joints, where the sides are free to pivot until they are joined to the loaded structure. The triangular framework will remain in shape, even with these flexible joints, so long as the structure is not overloaded. In the 19th century, pin joints were deliberately used in complex structures to ensure that engineers could calculate the stresses involved in each section without the extra complexities that rigid joints would create.

Other framework shapes do not necessarily have this natural strength. For example, in a square framework, an out-of-balance force acting at an angle on one of the top corners would tend to cause the framework to collapse into a diamond shape and ultimately to be pressed completely flat, unless

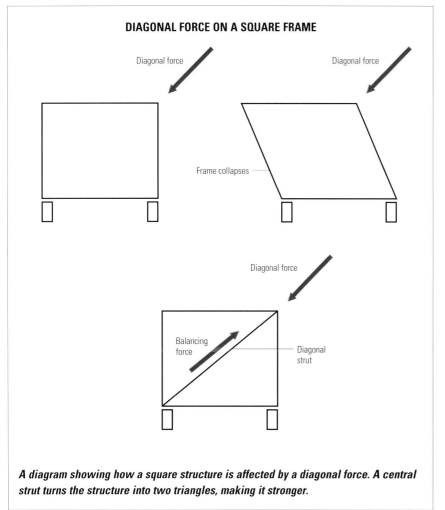

DIAGONAL FORCE ON A SQUARE FRAME

Diagonal force

Diagonal force

Frame collapses

Diagonal force

Balancing
force

Diagonal
strut

A diagram showing how a square structure is affected by a diagonal force. A central strut turns the structure into two triangles, making it stronger.

reinforcements were provided to prevent this from happening. The reinforcement could be an additional diagonal strut that would effectively transform the square into two adjacent triangles so that the framework could be held in shape with pin joints (see the diagram above). These would not transmit the turning forces created by the tendency of the square to collapse. Alternatively, the joints at the corners of the square could be reinforced sufficiently to keep them from distorting under the influence of an external load and to prevent the collapse of the square section under an out-of-balance force. However, this would complicate the calculation of the maximum stresses the structure could endure.

To carry out structural analyses, engineers make a series of additional assumptions. For example, the width or thickness of girders in a truss framework is often ignored, since the forces act along their length. In cases where a cable forms part of a structure, its weight may be ignored since it is likely to be insignificant when compared with the weights of beams and other structural members. Also, in cases where a strut supports a load by resting on a flat or curved surface it is common practice to assume that the surface is smooth and to neglect effects of friction.

For most of the 19th century, structures were designed using statics, which simplified structural analysis by applying basic assumptions. However, each assumption introduces a small error to the calculation of stresses; in more complex structures, the accumulation of these errors can make the result of such an analysis invalid. For example, the distribution of stresses in a particular part of a structure may not be as predicted. More powerful mathematical techniques have to be used to calculate the precise stresses involved and to predict the areas where stresses are likely to be particularly concentrated. Many modern buildings are also designed to stand safely even if one structural element fails unexpectedly. This requires extra structural elements and stress calculations for various failure scenarios.

Material strength
Calculating the load to be carried by a particular part of a structure is useful only if engineers know the strength of the material of which the part is to be made. This means testing samples of the material under carefully controlled conditions. Tension tests on metal samples usually involve stretching a cylindrical bar in a machine that applies an increasing load. The stress imposed on the sample is defined as the load on the bar divided by its cross-sectional area; the strain of the bar in response to the stress is the fractional increase in length under the load imposed on it (see MATERIALS SCIENCE). The ratio between the stress and the strain will remain constant up to the material's elastic limit, after which strain will stretch more than the increase in stress, up to the point where the material eventually fails.

Careful precautions have to be taken to ensure accuracy. The load imposed by the test machine is increased by hydraulic pressure or through gears and a screw drive (see GEAR; HYDRAULICS AND PNEUMATICS). The test sample is clamped between specially designed grips that hold it firmly in place without creating local stress concentrations, which would distort the results. In addition, the grips usually incorporate swivel joints to ensure that the load is applied directly along the axis of the bar without any tendency to bend the sample, which would also affect the measurements being taken.

Similar tests are carried out to measure strength in compression. In this case, however, the sample does not have to be gripped to hold it in the test machine. The problem here is that increasing force may cause the sample to buckle before it reaches its failure point. For this reason test samples in compression testing are usually shorter in comparison to their diameter than those used for tension testing.

Other tests can be carried out to measure shear strength to sideways forces, which try to bend or break part of a structure. Many of these tests involve sheets of metal or composite materials, or grained material such as wood, which will have a greater shear strength in one plane than in another, depending on the direction in which the grain fibers run.

Beams and cantilevers
In reality, of course, the width and depth of girders become especially important where bending stresses are involved. For example, early structures built by

the ancient Egyptians used mud bricks as a building material. In the predominantly dry climate, the bricks were strong enough to resist compressive stresses, but openings for doors or windows would subject them to bending stresses, which would cause them to break. Instead, a beam called a lintel was placed on top of the bricks on either side of an opening and used to bridge the gap so that it supported the courses of bricks directly above the opening (see BUILDING TECHNIQUES, TRADITIONAL).

Originally beams were made of large pieces of wood or stone, depending on the materials available and the size of the loads to be carried. In more complicated structures, where beams are used to form the floor of a building or a deck of a bridge, the longitudinal beams are often called stringers and are less heavily loaded than the more massive cross beams. Beams used in complex frameworks in three dimensions are usually called girders and are made from steel or concrete reinforced with steel. Steel girders are often rolled out to a particular shape or built up from smaller sections by welding or riveting.

In cases where beams are carrying bending loads, the bulk of the stress is imposed on the top of the beam, which is in tension for a load acting downward, and the bottom of the beam, which is in compression for a downward-acting load. This means the center of the beam is less highly stressed, so weight can be saved by making the center section narrower than either the top or bottom, resulting in the characteristic I shape of many girders (see the diagram below). In applications where weight reduction is particularly important, holes are often drilled along the center section of the beam to lighten it but not reduce its resistance to bending.

Cantilevers are beams that are supported firmly at one end so that the loads are carried by the unsupported end of the beam. These are used in building structures to carry partial floors, balconies, and other projecting portions of the structure, as well as galleries, roofs, and systems such as traveling cranes or elevated railroads. Large cantilevers are used in bridge structures to enable long spans to be sup-

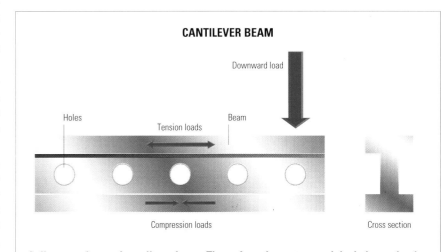

CANTILEVER BEAM

Downward load

Holes

Beam

Tension loads

Compression loads

Cross section

A diagram of a steel cantilever beam. The I-shaped structure and the holes make the beam lighter without making it weaker.

This wooden frame includes many beams and trusses to make the structure strong.

ported at a small number of points, where strong foundations can be established. This helps to maximize the amount of free space under the bridge.

Trusses and frameworks

Beams and girders are the basic units that are assembled into larger structural frameworks. Trusses, for example, are straight pieces of wood or metal arranged in a series of triangles, which are inherently resistant to distortion under loads. This arrangement produces a more stable frame than beams on their own; trusses can support heavier loads over broader spans. Each individual piece of the frame supports a load along its axis, where its strength is greatest either under tension or in compression.

Timber trusses have been used in building structures for centuries. The first remains of wooden truss frames were found in Bronze Age villages dating from some 4500 years ago. Timber trusses were also used in ancient Greece and in medieval buildings. From the early 19th century, trusses made from cast iron, wrought iron, and steel became increasingly common in bridge construction (see IRON AND STEEL PRODUCTION). Trusses made of aluminum alloy are used for airplane structures, such as wings, since they are both light and strong (see AIRCRAFT DESIGN AND CONSTRUCTION).

The longitudinal beams that form the top and bottom of a truss framework are called the upper and lower chords. The vertical and sloping beams that join the top and bottom chords together make up the web of the truss, and these are arranged in different ways depending on the type of truss used. The Warren truss uses sloping web members (struts) arranged in alternate directions to create a series of triangles along the length of the truss. The Whipple-Murphy (N-type) truss has diagonal web struts running in parallel directions, which creates a series of parallelograms, and vertical ties, which give the truss the inherent strength of triangles.

More complicated frameworks have been used in building structures since the Middle Ages. Houses and larger structures were often given greater strength and stability by putting up a timber frame to outline the walls, and then filling the spaces between the different struts of the framework with windows, doors, and courses of brickwork. At each additional floor level above the ground, horizontal timbers in

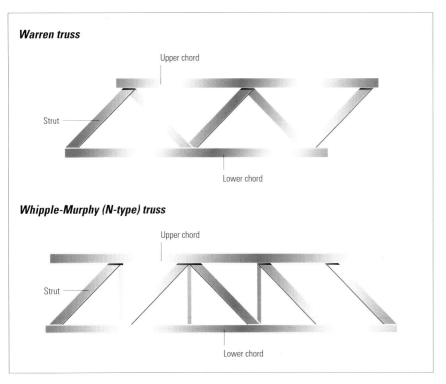

Warren truss

Upper chord

Strut

Lower chord

Whipple-Murphy (N-type) truss

Upper chord

Strut

Lower chord

the wall frame would be linked by cross timbers to the equivalent timbers in the opposite wall. This built up a framework of joists to carry the floorboards of the upper rooms.

These basic principles were used for building the mills and factories of the Industrial Revolution in the 19th century. Steel-girder frameworks enabled wider spans to be built to provide more room for storage or machinery (see BUILDING TECHNIQUES, MODERN). Stronger frameworks for buildings, relying on steel girders and concrete walls and floors, together with new inventions such as escalators and elevators, enabled structural engineers to build taller and taller buildings. This in turn enabled more efficient use of limited and expensive land (see SKYSCRAPER and the box on page 1270).

Arches and domes

Arches were developed as a means of supporting greater structural loads than horizontal beams or lintels. The curve of an arch is built up from a series of wedge-shaped blocks, called voussoirs, whose upper edges are wider than the lower edges. This enables the blocks to fit together tightly to create the curve of the arch, and also to transmit the downward force of the structure supported by the arch into a force that acts outward as well as downward.

The main advantage of arches is that they can be built stage by stage from fairly small blocks of material (provided these are held in place by a framework until the arch is complete), without all the trouble and expense of hoisting a single massive lintel into place. The main disadvantage is that the outward thrusts at the bottom of the arch call for massive supporting posts to transfer the loads safely down into the foundations. In cases where arches are arranged in rows, such as in churches, aqueducts, and arched bridges, the diagonal thrusts from adjacent arches tend to cancel one another out, so the foundation pillars can be lighter.

The level at which the curve of the arch begins from its vertical supports is called the spring line. Above this level the two sides of the arch follow symmetric curves until they meet at the keystone, which occupies the central position at the top of the arch. Roman arch builders tended to favor semicircular arches, where the curve follows an arc of a circle from the vertical at the springing line to the horizontal at the keystone.

In some cases, particularly in Gothic and Arab structures, the curves of the arch tended to meet in a point at the top. In the case of the Gothic cathedrals, this was an attempt to reproduce the curve of a catenary as closely as possible. A catenary is the curve adopted by a chain or cable hanging between two supports under its own weight, which when inverted is theoretically the most efficient shape for an arch.

Present-day arches, made from versatile materials such as steel or concrete, can be made in complex shapes for greater efficiency. Their strength enables them to be lighter so that the horizontal loads applied to the supports are much smaller. In some cases a tie

GEODESIC DOMES

The Science World geodesic dome at False Creek, Vancouver, Canada.

One of the most unusual types of dome was invented by U.S. engineer Richard Buckminster Fuller (1895–1983) in the late 1940s while he was developing lighter and simpler structures. Instead of a conventional framework of intersecting arches, a geodesic dome is supported by a complex framework of intersecting ribs running along a network of geodesic (great-circle) lines. A geodesic is a line on the surface of a sphere that forms the shortest connection between any two points. The result is a complex surface pattern of hexagonal or triangular spaces.

Buckminster Fuller's geodesic dome used the same principles as the geodesic airplane fuselage developed in the 1930s by British inventor Sir Barnes Wallis (1887–1979). This used a network of intersecting helical ribs to carry an outer skin made of a tough fabric. Because they were anchored together where they crossed, structural loads were carried as tension and compression loads in the different ribs, which tended to counterbalance one another. Not only did this leave the interior space free of framework, but it made airplanes much better able to absorb combat damage than conventional fuselage structures. Even serious damage to one part of a geodesic fuselage left other parts relatively unaffected and thus maintained the aircraft's airworthiness.

Geodesic domes have no internal framework to take up valuable space. Because the stresses are carried by the intersecting ribs, the skin needs to support only its own weight and provide insulation and protection, so the domes are much lighter than conventional structures of equivalent size. This means they can be carried on light supporting walls or even laid directly on the ground, which would be completely impossible for traditional domes. Geodesic domes have been used for many applications including theaters, exhibition halls, and greenhouses and even for railroad maintenance workshops.

A CLOSER LOOK

THE GREAT SKYSCRAPER RACE

A combination of steel frameworks that could support taller structures and soaring land prices resulted in high-rise buildings that transformed U.S. cities. The process started when Chicago was rebuilt after a devastating fire in 1871, which destroyed many timber-framed buildings. The tallest building at that time was Chicago's 10-story Home Insurance Building, constructed between 1883 and 1885, but by 1892 New York had taken the lead with the 390-ft (119-m) Pulitzer Building. By 1909, the Life Tower had reached 700 ft (213 m), and the Woolworth Building of 1913 reached 792 ft (241 m), with 58 floors and space for 14,000 offices.

This record was broken only by the construction of the Chrysler Building in 1930. This was planned to reach a height of 925 ft (282 m) when a rival company announced they were building a skyscraper just 2 ft (0.6 m) higher, at 40 Wall Street. So architect William Van Alen (1882–1954) constructed a stainless-steel art deco spire 123 ft (37 m) high inside the frame of the Chrysler Building. This was finally hoisted into position after the rival skyscraper had been completed. The 1046-ft (319-m) building with its 77 floors remained the world's tallest skyscraper until the completion of the Empire State Building a year later, with 102 stories and a total height of 1250 feet (381 m).

The Empire State Building was not surpassed until 1972, when the first tower of the World Trade Center was completed at a height of 1368 ft (417 m). The second tower, completed in 1973, reached 1362 ft (415 m). However, the record was broken just one year later by the Sears Tower in Chicago, which has 110 floors and a welded steel framework of vertical tubes. The total height of the tower is 1454 ft (443 m).

Outside the United States, few skyscrapers reached this kind of height, except for designs such as the Bank of China Tower in Hong Kong, completed in 1989 with a height of 1209 ft (369 m). Its unusual design changes in cross-section from a four-sided base to a triangular-section top. The intention is to transfer all vertical stresses to the four corners of the building so that it can stand up to fierce Chinese typhoons.

In 1996, the Petronas Twin Towers in Kuala Lumpur, Malaysia, became the world's tallest buildings at 1483 ft (452 m) in spite of a roofline over 100 ft (30 m) lower than that of the Sears Tower. Like the Chrysler Building, the overall height of the Petronas Towers was extended by two steel spires forming part of the overall structure.

A new landmark in building heights—the X-Seed 4000—has been conceived for construction in Tokyo, Japan. If built, its projected height of 13,129 ft (4000 m) will dwarf the skyscrapers of the 20th century.

A 33-story building nears completion in downtown Seattle.

HISTORY OF TECHNOLOGY

bar added across the ends of the arch at the springing level can carry most of this stress, which means the supports can be made lighter still.

Extending an arch into a deeper three-dimensional structure produced the barrel vault, which was used in the naves of churches and crypts beneath the ground floor of long buildings. Rotating the arch about a vertical axis down through the keystone produced the round dome, which offered a structure that could cover large open spaces with the supports kept to the outside boundary of the dome.

The first large domes built during the Roman Empire suffered because they needed massive circular foundation walls to support them. Eventually, engineers of the Byzantine Empire in and around Turkey from 395 to 1453 C.E. developed a means of supporting a dome on four piers using masses of masonry called pendentives. These were shaped like inverted triangles curved in both the horizontal and vertical planes. Each one transferred the weight of the dome from its curved base down to its point.

More recently, domes have been made much more versatile by the use of new materials. Metal-framed domes gave structural engineers new freedom to change the shapes and the foundations of domes. Later, the availability of reinforced concrete slabs, which could be formed to any degree of curvature, widened their options still further.

Tension structures

Just as a semicircular arch can support a heavier load than a flat lintel of similar size and weight, so a tubular structure is inherently stronger for a given weight and type of material than a structure of any other shape, since it can resist loads in any direction. When a number of these tubes are used to build a strong structure, the result is known as a space frame. These structures have been used in a range of different applications, from sports stadiums to airplanes. In race cars, for example, a space frame with sufficient strength to meet the demands of the different loads caused by braking, acceleration, and cornering can be made much lighter than with solid framework (see RACE CAR).

Not all structures involve loads being imposed from outside. Several types of structures, such as pipes, boilers, and pressure vessels, have to stand up to the pressure of their contents imposed from the inside. Tubular structures enclose the greatest possible volume for a given amount of material used. This has been invaluable in applications such as pipelines for carrying liquids, pressurized gases, and suspensions of solids over long distances (see PIPELINE). The great inherent strength of tubular structures has also led to their use in high-pressure steam boilers, where superheated steam is created at pressures of hundreds of pounds per square inch (many times more than atmospheric pressure) and at high temperatures (see STEAM ENGINE; STEAM TURBINE).

The high strength and economy of material in circular cross sections are even more important when extended into the third dimension. Where pressure loads are imposed at a particular place, rather than along the length of a pipeline that has to transport materials to a particular destination, the best structural shape for strength and economy of material is a sphere—hence the spherical shape used for most storage tanks for liquefied gases such as ammonia and liquefied petroleum gas (see GAS INDUSTRY).

Shell structures

Modern requirements for very large structures such as covered sports stadiums and aircraft maintenance hangars tend to involve developments of classic structural methods that use modern materials. Steel trusses have been developed from the basic two-dimensional Warren and Whipple-Murphy trusses into three-dimensional space frames. These have been combined into massive and extensive structures to cover very large areas. One of the largest structures to use a framework of three-dimensional trusses is the Narita Hangar at the Tokyo International Airport in Japan, where the roof span is 295 ft (90 m) across.

Other large area structures are often based on a dome, using arches made of steel trusses that intersect at the center and provide the strength of the structure. The actual covering of the dome is reduced to a thin, flexible skin, which is often made of plastic. This reduces the weight the structure has to support and cuts the need for massive internal support frameworks, especially in buildings such as stadiums where obstructions to the spectators' field of view need to be kept to an minimum. Domes have also been built with a network of trusses acting as stiffening ribs to carry a thin concrete skin. One of the largest and most spectacular of these structures is the King Dome sports stadium in Seattle, where the

An overhead view of the King Dome sports arena under construction in Seattle in 1977.

dome is curved in a shallow parabola (a type of curve that a projectile, such as a baseball, follows when thrown in the air), 660 ft (201 m) across.

The use of stretched steel cables to carry the loads of suspension bridges has also been extended to other large structures. Many of these designs use tall masts that rise through or around the roof of the structure. Cables attached to the masts support steel trusses that carry the roof shell itself. The Millennium Dome in London is a vast structure that uses cable supports to carry the weight of its shallow-domed roof's skin.

Some large structures use air to help support their roof panels. An intersecting network of cables is attached by continuous seams to light roofing fabric made of vinyl-coated plastic membranes, which is then inflated to a domed shape. The roof shape is maintained against outside air currents by keeping the air pressure inside the building slightly higher than outside atmospheric pressure, the necessary difference being as little as 2 percent. Because of the lightness of the materials and the relatively low cost of construction, these designs are becoming very popular for sports arenas and large exhibition pavilions, where very long and wide spans are needed. However, maintaining the air pressure differential requires air pumps to work constantly.

D. OWEN

See also: ALLOY; BOATBUILDING AND SHIPBUILDING; CEMENT AND CONCRETE; DEMOLITION.

Further reading:
Rossow, E. *Analysis and Behavior of Structures*. New York: Macmillan, 1995.
Salvadori, M. *The Art of Construction: Projects and Principles for Beginning Engineers and Architects*. Chicago: Chicago Review Press, 1990.
Zalewski, Z., and Allen, E. *Shaping Structures: Statics*. New York: John Wiley & Sons, 1998.

SUBMARINE

A submarine is a ship that can be operated either on the surface of the sea or underwater

The **Oklahoma** *is a Los Angeles–class nuclear submarine that is designed for high submerged speeds. Los Angeles–class submarines make up the backbone of the U.S. Navy's submarine fleet.*

Submarines have revolutionized marine warfare. A simple hand-propelled wooden vessel first launched in the 1770s has evolved into a highly sophisticated warship that forms the centerpiece of the world's nuclear deterrent (the possession of nuclear weapons that deters countries from waging war). Submarines can operate at considerable depths and stay underwater for months at a time.

Historical development

Although a simple underwater boat was constructed in England in 1620, the first real powered submarine was the *Turtle*, invented by U.S. engineer David Bushnell (c.1742–1824). It was made of wood and powered by hand, with one person on board cranking a propeller. The *Turtle* was used in the American Revolution in 1776 to attack the British warship *Eagle* in New York Harbor. The plan was to hand-power the *Turtle* up to the *Eagle* and drill a hole in its bottom with a vertical auger. The attempt failed, so the *Turtle* released a 155-lb (70-kg) cask of gunpowder. This exploded on the surface with dramatic effect—the British fleet in New York Bay scattered in panic. The first use of a submarine in naval warfare was therefore a considerable success.

In France, U.S. maritime engineer Robert Fulton (1765–1815) built a more practical hand-powered submarine; it made a six-hour dive at Brest, western France. In 1878, successful steam-driven submarines were built and tested in Sweden, Great Britain, and the United States.

The forerunner of today's cigar-shaped submarines was the 60-ft (18-m) steel-hulled *Gymnote*, built in 1886 in France and powered by electricity. It served for at least 20 years in the French navy. In 1900, the U.S. Navy bought its first submarine, designed by Irish engineer John P. Holland (1840–1914). Holland had emigrated to the United States in 1873 and launched his first experimental submarine on the Hudson River six years later.

Major advances in submarine design were made by the Germans during World War II (1939–1945). With streamlined shapes and powerful electric motors, fleets of German U-boats (*Unterseeboote* or underwater boats) were able to conduct true submarine warfare. They devastated ships that supplied countries such as Great Britain and caused around 90 percent of Allied shipping losses.

In 1954, the first submarine powered by a nuclear reactor, the 323-ft- (98.4-m-) long *Nautilus*, was launched in the United States. In 1958, it sailed from the Pacific to the Atlantic under the polar ice

CONNECTIONS

● Submarines have become a fundamental part of worldwide **MILITARY COMMUNICATIONS AND CONTROL**.

● The development of submarines has progressed in parallel with technological advances in **BOAT-BUILDING AND SHIPBUILDING**.

CORE FACTS

- The first submarine was the *Turtle*, which was used in 1776 during the American Revolution.
- In 1954, *Nautilus*, the first submarine powered by a nuclear reactor, was launched in the United States.
- The navies of 47 countries operate a total of 523 submarines, of which 187 are nuclear powered.

cap. In 1960, the U.S. nuclear submarine *Triton* traveled around the world underwater—a journey of around 49,000 miles (79,000 km). In 185 years, submarines had developed from simple hand-powered vessels to sophisticated nuclear-powered warships capable of staying submerged for months or years.

During this period, submarines revolutionized naval warfare. However, before nuclear submarines were developed, submarine warfare was confined to attacking enemy ships. Blockade was a crucial role for the submarines in limiting trade and military activity in and out of enemy ports.

Since the 1960s, submarines have taken on an increasingly strategic role. Long-range ballistic missiles can be launched up to high altitude from submerged submarines, and used to attack civilian and military targets in an enemy country (see MISSILE; NUCLEAR WEAPONS). A nation's navy is therefore a crucial element in its nuclear strategy. Nuclear submarines can remain submerged for long periods; with their relative invulnerability, they are a key element in nuclear deterrence.

Submarine construction

Submarines have double hulls (one inside the other) that are usually made from high-quality steel. Some former Soviet submarines have titanium hulls (a metal that is as strong as steel but as light as aluminum), which enable them to dive deeper and travel faster. However, titanium is a difficult material to work with and is expensive.

Most of the world's submarines are powered by diesel. Most of the others are nuclear powered. Diesel engines do not operate the propellers directly but drive a generator to charge batteries, which run an electric motor that turns the propeller (see BATTERY). The batteries may be lead-acid, silver-zinc, or silver-cadmium. Silver-zinc and silver-cadmium batteries are more efficient, smaller, and lighter than lead-acid ones. Given the premium on space inside a submarine, these are important advantages, but these batteries are more expensive and require more maintenance than lead-acid batteries.

Diesel-electric submarines are far less expensive to build than nuclear submarines, and they are simpler to operate. They must, however, periodically return to the surface, or near the surface, to expel exhaust gases and take on air for the engine to recharge their batteries. This makes them vulnerable to detection and attack. Nuclear submarines do not have to return to the surface.

Most of the nuclear submarines are powered by pressurized-water reactors. These are cooled by water under high pressure, which removes heat from the reactor and passes it to a heat exchanger. There the heat boils water in a separate circuit, producing steam to drive a turbine, which turns the propeller shaft (see HEAT EXCHANGER; PROPELLER; TURBINE).

The former Soviet Union navy powered some submarines with reactors cooled by liquid metal. Submarines powered by these smaller reactors were faster than submarines with water-cooled reactors.

MINIATURE SUBMARINES

The one-person miniature submarine, **Deep Flight, at Monterey, California.**

Miniature submarines have often been used to sink enemy warships. The most primitive were essentially person-carrying torpedoes, which the crew, who sat on top of the craft wearing diving suits, aimed at the target and then abandoned. In 1918, a two-person vessel sank the battleship *Viribus Unitis* at Pola, Croatia.

Miniature submarines in which one or two people were enclosed were also used in World War II. They were sometimes driven through security nets into harbors to attack enemy warships by attaching limpet mines to them—magnetic explosives that cling to a ship's hull and detonate on contact or signal.

Uncrewed miniature submarines known as submersibles are used to examine wrecks on the seabed, to perform scientific research, or to film the oceans.

A CLOSER LOOK

However, the machines that pump coolant around reactors are noisy, making nuclear-powered submarines vulnerable to detection by antisubmarine war systems (see WEAPONRY: SPECIALIZED SYSTEMS).

Submarines cannot dive as deeply as most people believe, due to the pressure of the ocean depths. Modern steel-hulled, nuclear-powered submarines can reach depths of 1500 ft (450 m), and the Soviet Alfa class could dive to more than 2300 ft (700 m). Nonnuclear submarines operate at depths of less than 1000 ft (300 m). However, the world's oceans can exceed 23,000 ft (7000 m) in depth, so submarines are confined to a just a small part of the seas.

Nuclear-powered submarines can travel at speeds of up to about 30 knots (equivalent to 35 mph or 56 km/h) submerged; diesel-electric submarines can travel at speeds up to about 20 knots (23 mph or 37 km/h) submerged. Because of increased turbulence, on the surface the maximum speed of a submarine is about one half of its submerged speed.

Submarines dive and surface using at least two rotatable fins known as diving planes and by flooding and emptying ballast tanks located between the two hulls. To submerge the vessel, the tanks are flooded and the planes pointed downward. When the submarine is at the desired depth the planes are leveled. To return to the surface, the submarine's tanks are cleared of water by filling them with compressed air and the planes are pointed upward.

Submarines in the world's navies

Submarine production boomed in World War II (1939–1945). The navies fighting the war operated 1800 submarines, of which more than 1000 were German-operated. Over half of these were sunk.

At the end of 1998, 47 navies operated a total of 523 submarines. Some countries, such as Albania and Cuba, had only one submarine. Others had many: the Russian navy had 98 submarines, the U.S. Navy had 84, and the Chinese navy had 63.

China, France, Great Britain, Russia, and the United States are the only nations to currently operate nuclear submarines. These five navies operate a total of 274 submarines, of which 187 are nuclear-powered. Only the U.S. and Great Britain operate exclusively nuclear-powered submarines.

Submarines are designed to be either tactical or strategic. Tactical vessels are used in a theater of war to target military threats with conventional weapons. Strategic submarines are intended to launch nuclear missiles against the whole of an enemy's territory.

An example of a modern tactical nuclear submarine is the U.S. Los Angeles class. Carrying a crew of about 130, a Los Angeles submarine is designed for high submerged speeds of up to 30 knots (35 mph or 56 km/h), and it can dive up to 1480 ft (450 m). One pressurized-water reactor and two turbines propel the submarine. The U.S. Navy operates 53 Los Angeles–class submarines.

A modern strategic nuclear submarine is the Russian Typhoon class. Displacing about 20,400 tons (18,500 tonnes) on the surface and 27,600 tons (25,000 tonnes) submerged, the 558-ft- (170-m-) long Typhoon is the world's largest submarine. A Typhoon is powered by two reactors and is designed to operate under Arctic ice. Carrying a crew of 150, it can reach speeds of 30 knots (35 mph or 56 km/h) submerged. A Typhoon carries 20 Sturgeon SLBMs, which have a range of 5300 miles (8500 km). A Sturgeon can carry up to 10 individually targeted warheads and has an explosive power equivalent to that of 110,000 tons (100,000 tonnes) of TNT.

A typical diesel-electric submarine is the Swedish Gotland class. A Gotland submarine is powered by two diesel engines and displaces about 1100 tons (1000 tonnes) of water on the surface and 1200 tons (1100 tonnes) submerged. Carrying a crew of 17, it has a maximum speed of 20 knots (23 mph or 37 km/h) submerged, and it can dive to depths greater than 1100 ft (330 m).

F. BARNABY

See also: NUCLEAR ENERGY; WARSHIP.

Further reading:
Van der Vat, D. *Stealth at Sea: The History of the Submarine*. London: Wiedenfeld & Nicolson, 1994.

ADMIRAL HYMAN GEORGE RICKOVER

Admiral Rickover (right) is shown here with Lieutenant Commander David Leighton (center) and British admiral Lord Louis Mountbatten at the controls of the submarine Triton's land-based prototype reactor in Schenectady, New York, in 1958.

U.S. admiral Hyman George Rickover (1900–1986) was the father of the nuclear-powered submarine, a weapon that revolutionized naval warfare and contributed greatly to the development of nuclear strategies. Rickover was born in Russia in 1900. At a young age, he emigrated with his family to Chicago and graduated from the U.S. Naval Academy in 1922 and three years later became electrical officer on the battleship *Nevada*. Rickover then received a master's degree in electrical engineering at the Naval Academy and took courses in advanced engineering at Columbia University. In 1929, he decided he wanted to work with submarines and went to the U.S. Navy's submarine school at New London, Connecticut. After training, he became engineer officer on the U.S. submarine *S-48*.

During World War II, Rickover was chief of the electrical section of the Bureau of Ships. In 1946, he went to Oak Ridge, Tennessee, to represent the U.S. Navy in discussions about the possible applications of nuclear energy. He came to the conclusion that nuclear energy could and should be used to power a submarine. He proposed this to Admiral Chester Nimitz (1885–1966), who was then chief of naval operations. The U.S. Atomic Energy Commission accepted Rickover's ideas in 1949. The commission established a naval reactors branch and Rickover was made its head. Working with the Electric Boat Company in Connecticut, he oversaw the project to build the first nuclear-powered submarine, *Nautilus*, which was launched in 1954. He continued to direct the construction of nuclear submarines and other nuclear warships.

When Rickover died in 1986, the U.S. Navy was operating 135 nuclear submarines, 9 nuclear cruisers, and 4 nuclear aircraft carriers.

PEOPLE

SUBWAY SYSTEM

A subway system transports people around a city by direct underground routes, bypassing traffic congestion

Passengers inside a New York City subway train in the early 1980s. Graffiti-resistant surfaces have since been introduced. The last graffiti-prone train was removed from service on the New York City subway system in 1989.

Usually a subway is an underground passenger railroad network that is part of an urban mass transit system. It is not always called a subway. In many countries the underground railway is called the metro. London's subway system is known as the Underground, and riders call it the Tube. Similarly, residents of the San Francisco Bay Area sometimes speak of "taking the BART train," referring to the Bay Area Rapid Transit system. The word *subway* is also used to refer to some other underground tunnel systems, such as a pedestrian tunnel under a busy street or a road traffic underpass, and subway trains sometimes run above ground.

The largest subway rail system in the world is New York City's, with 137 miles (220 km) of underground routes and another 93 miles (145 km) of aboveground routes; its 468 stations serve some 4 million passengers a day. The first subway in the United States was built illegally in New York City in 1870. It was only 312 ft (95 m) long and used trains propelled by compressed air. It was a novelty, rather than a practical transit system, and soon closed. The

first practical subway in the United States was opened in Boston in 1897. The first real subway in New York was not opened until 1904. Chicago and Philadelphia also had subway systems in operation by the early 20th century.

By the end of the 20th century, every major city in the United States had some sort of subway system either operating or under construction. Elsewhere in North America there are subways in Mexico City, Montreal, and Toronto. A great number of European cities have subways, including seven in Germany. Japan has six cities with subways.

The oldest subway system in the world, and the second largest, is the London Underground. The third largest is the Paris Métro.

Riding in a tunnel

Underground transit systems became a desirable form of transportation as soon as city streets grew crowded and congested from automobiles. In addition, surface land was too expensive for railroad development. An underground train can travel much faster than any aboveground mass transit vehicle, and more or less in a straight line to its destination. The same could be said of elevated trains, but the subway leaves valuable real estate on the surface free.

These advantages were obvious to city planners early in the 19th century. The obstacles were the cost and engineering difficulty of constructing underground tunnels. The technology of tunneling is ancient—it was used by the Romans in building their extensive road and sewer systems. Many military fortifications included underground tunnel systems, and

CORE FACTS

- Subways can reduce traffic congestion and air pollution, provided subway systems are efficient and inexpensive enough to persuade the public to use them.
- Modern technology has reduced the cost and time required to build subways.
- Planning for a subway must include consideration of passenger comfort, safety, and convenience.

CONNECTIONS

- To connect underground train platforms to the surface, subway stations are often equipped with **ELEVATORS** or **ESCALATORS AND MOVING WALKWAYS**.

- A subway **RAILROAD CAR** is designed to carry a great number of riders on short journeys.

This picture shows a subway tunnel under construction in Union Square, New York City, in June 1901.

tunneling has always been part of mining (see MIN-ING; TUNNEL). However, nearly all these tunnels were cut through solid rock or at least firm ground.

When the city of London decided, early in the 19th century, that it needed underground transportation, it was faced with the problem of tunneling through soft, often wet, earth. The first attempt was made in 1802, when a tunnel was started under the Thames River, dug by hand. It failed when the roof caved in and the tunnel filled with water.

French inventor Marc Brunel (1769–1849) conceived a device that came to be called the tunneling shield, which was based on his observation that the body of a worm supported the tunnel it made. In its modern form, the tunneling shield consists of a tube

the size and shape of the tunnel to be dug. Hydraulic jacks at the rear of the shield push it forward into the earth a foot or so at a time. While the shield supports the roof, workers cut away the earth inside the shield. Modern shields often have built-in conveyors that carry away the dirt. As soon as the shield is moved forward, a steel or concrete lining is erected in the exposed space behind the shield, which supports the roof and walls of the tunnel. The hydraulic jacks are then placed against the front of the lining as a base for the next push forward.

Using Brunel's first simple shield, a tunnel under the Thames River in London was begun in 1825 and, after much difficulty, opened in 1843. First used as a pedestrian tunnel, it became part of the London Underground. The city's first true rail subway—a 3.7-mile (5.9-km) line—opened in 1863 and used steam-powered trains for transportation.

The first London line was built by a cut-and-cover method, in which a trench is dug along the route, a tunnel—usually concrete—is built at the bottom of the trench, then the trench is filled in. Cut-and-cover can only be used when the tunnel passes under an open space, such as under an existing street. Cut-and-cover was used for nearly all the subway lines built in New York City, most of which were laid under existing streets.

While it seems simpler, cut-and-cover can sometimes be more expensive than tunneling, at least when it is used on existing streets. Extra work must be done to move electric and water lines running under streets, and surface traffic may be disrupted for months. Both cut-and-cover techniques and tunneling are still used in various combinations today to build new subway tunnels.

Tunneling technology

Power-driven tunneling machines have replaced hand digging in most situations. A tunneling machine has a tunneling shield, rotary cutters mounted in the

VENTILATION

In the early days of the London Underground, some passenger deaths were attributed to asphyxiation. People in confined spaces need a constant supply of fresh air, as they consume oxygen and exhale carbon dioxide—a gas heavier than air that can accumulate in underground tunnels if not flushed out.

In most underground systems, the pressure created by moving trains helps circulate air. Large vents connected to the surface are located throughout the tunnel. A moving train pushes air ahead of it, and as it approaches a vent, it drives the air up through the vent to the street above. After it passes, it creates a partial vacuum behind it that pulls fresh air down into the tunnel. These vents also reduce air drag on the trains, as trapped air would compress and build resistance, causing the train to use more energy to maintain its speed.

Engineers cannot always predict how much venting is needed. When the Toronto subway system first opened, so much air was forced into some stations by oncoming trains that patrons could not pull open the station exit doors until a train had passed. This was partially solved by widening the tunnels where they entered the station area. Many subway systems use powerful fans to circulate air. These are set to expel air from tunnels up to street level, which causes fresh air to be pulled down through other vents and the station entrances.

A CLOSER LOOK

front, and a conveyor system to carry out the spoil (dirt, rocks, and sand) that is produced by the tunneling process (see TUNNEL).

To tunnel through hard rock, the technique is the same as the one developed for mining—drill into the rock, then use explosives to break it up. A promising variation developed in France is to drill holes that shape the circular outline of the desired tunnel, fill the holes with concrete, then use directional explosives to blast the rock inside the circular outline.

When tunneling through wet soil—for example under a river—the tunnel is sometimes pressurized with compressed air to keep water from seeping in. Early tunnel workers who spent long hours digging in a pressurized environment had to undergo a lengthy decompression procedure at the end of their shift, similar to the steps that deep-sea divers must follow when rising from a great depth. Today, some tunnels are dug using special tunneling shields that can be pressurized separately at the front, where digging is taking place, while workers behind the shield can work in normal or near-normal pressure.

New tunneling technologies include abrasive jets that erode a tunnel into rock, and ultrasonics—high-frequency sound waves that shake rock to pieces. Another technique uses alternating extremes of heat and cold to crack rock.

The cost of tunneling has fallen significantly since the early days, partly because of improved tunneling technologies and partly because of a new approach to tunneling projects: whereas expensive custom-built machinery used to be made for each project and then scrapped, it is now usual to contract a specialist tunneling company that uses the same equipment for several jobs and thereby reduces costs. As the cost of tunneling falls and the value of land increases, it becomes more economically favorable to build highways, offices, and shopping centers underground.

Electric trains

Early subway trains were powered by steam locomotives, much to the discomfort of the passengers who had to breathe in smoke in the confined tunnels. The first London subway had periodic open cuts where smoke could escape and the locomotives could blow off excess steam. Subways became much more practical and pleasant to travel in when electric motors were introduced.

A modern subway train typically comprises a mixture of power cars and trailer cars. The power cars, also called drive cars, have motors and brakes; trailer cars have brakes only. When cars are linked in a train, they are wired together so that all the cars' brakes and motors can be controlled by a single operator at the front. A common pattern is to use a unit of two motorized cars with one or two trailer cars in between. These units can then be linked to form larger trains according to requirements. There is a control booth at each end of each train unit, and at the end of the line, the operator simply walks from one end of the train to the other, then drives off in the opposite direction.

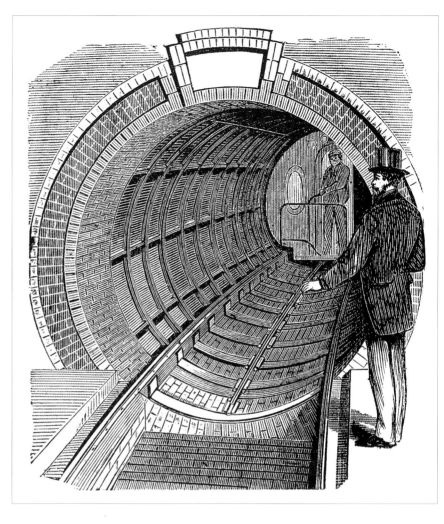

Power is usually supplied by a third rail by means of metal contact shoes mounted on the side of the train that glide along the third rail. The electrical circuit is completed by a return path that runs through the wheels to the regular rails. A few systems use overhead trolley wires (see STREETCAR AND TROLLEY).

Not all underground systems use trains. Some—often called light railroads—use single cars similar to underground streetcars. The Boston subway system consists of both high-speed trains and underground trolleys; each type runs in its own tunnel system. While most subway trains and light-rail cars travel on steel rails, a few—notably in the Paris Métro—use rubber-tired cars that travel on concrete guideways for a quieter, smoother ride.

Since the 1980s, there has been a gradual increase in the use of alternating-current (AC) motors. AC motors are more efficient, cutting electricity usage by up to 20 percent and reducing maintenance costs. DC motors use brushes called commutators to change the polarity of the current flowing through moving coils on the rotors. These brushes wear rapidly and need frequent maintenance, and they also release carbon particles into the air. It is, however, safer and more efficient to transfer electrical power along the third rail as direct current. The shift to AC motors has been made possible by the development of high-power solid-state inverters, which convert the DC from the rail to AC in the subway car (see ELECTRIC MOTOR AND GENERATOR).

An 1869 representation showing a passenger train in the entrance to the Broadway Pneumatic Tunnel in New York.

A train approaches a congested platform of the metro subway in Washington, D.C.

Newer AC motors allow the use of regenerative braking, where the motor is converted into a generator. This places a load on the motor shaft, which slows the car. The electricity generated is fed back into the third rail, reducing overall generating costs.

Computer control

Many subway systems control traffic in the same way as aboveground railroads, through signals operated from a central office. These signals typically have a green light that indicates to proceed at full speed, a yellow light to proceed with caution, and a red light to stop and wait.

More modern subway systems are computer-controlled, with human operators present only to operate the doors and make the signal for starting. Advanced computer controls enable trains to run safely at high speeds with a separation between trains of as little as 90 seconds. A central computer controls the entire system, communicating with computers on each train through inductive wire loops in the roadbed. In the case of a system failure, the door operator can override the computer system to drive the train to the next station.

Computers also handle fare collection. The BART system in San Francisco pioneered a new method in which riders pay in proportion to the distance they travel. Riders buy cards worth a certain dollar value, which is encoded on a magnetic stripe. The card is passed through a reading device in the turnstile when the rider enters and leaves the system, and the appropriate fare is deducted from the card value. More value may be added to the card in a machine at any station.

The London Underground's fare system is based on a series of zones that radiate from the center of the city. Riders buy tickets that are priced according to the zones through which they will travel, and these tickets are machine-checked for validity as the rider enters and leaves the system.

Other fare systems are being developed, including some that use smart cards, which need only to be held within a few inches of the reading device.

Convincing riders

Many commuters are reluctant to abandon the convenience of their private automobiles to ride a mass transit system. In order for the subway system to succeed, it must offer people a faster trip than a private car, in comfortable surroundings, at a noticeably lower cost. Subways can offer the speed; the newest air-conditioned, upholstered cars can offer adequate comfort. Keeping costs down is often difficult. One method is to reduce the number of employees needed to run the system, and this is the main reason that many systems are updating to use computers for control and fare collection.

Subway patrons are also concerned about crime and their personal safety. In order to build up the number of riders, transit systems have increased police protection and redesigned stations to provide more open spaces with greater visibility. Subway cars being used in New York City have glass partitions at the ends, allowing passengers and transit police to see from one car to another. Alarm and intercom systems are also being installed.

Modern cars are also being designed with provisions for disabled people, including wider doors and designated spaces inside the cars for wheelchairs. Some light-rail vehicles have ramps that extend to the ground when the car stops.

A subway can have a profound effect on the growth of a city. It can revitalize the downtown area by making it easy for shoppers to reach stores and recreational facilities, and residential areas continue to develop around many outer stations. But subways are not the answer for all transit needs. They work well in cities where population density is high and the layout of the city is compact, but they are not always practical in cities, such as Los Angeles, that have already experienced urban sprawl due to the automobile. There is no subway system in operation today that pays for itself in fare collections; in the United States the systems are subsidized by fares from other types of transit and by gasoline taxes.

To obtain the benefits of reduced traffic congestion and reduced pollution that subways offer, many cities have enacted measures to make driving less attractive, including restricted parking or high parking fees in downtown areas. However, some planners believe that the money spent on expensive underground systems would be better spent on other approaches, such as the promotion of car and van pools and the construction of bicycle paths (see POLLUTION AND ITS CONTROL).

W. STEELE

See also: AIR-CONDITIONING AND VENTILATION; BUS; ELECTRICITY TRANSMISSION AND SUPPLY; MASS TRANSIT SYSTEM; RAILROAD, HISTORY OF; RAILROAD LOCOMOTIVE; RAILROAD OPERATION AND SIGNALING.

Further reading:

Brooks, M. *Subway City: Riding the Trains, Reading New York.* New Brunswick, New Jersey: Rutgers University Press, 1997.

SURGERY

Surgery is the diagnosis and repair of injuries, deformities, and disease by means of medical operations

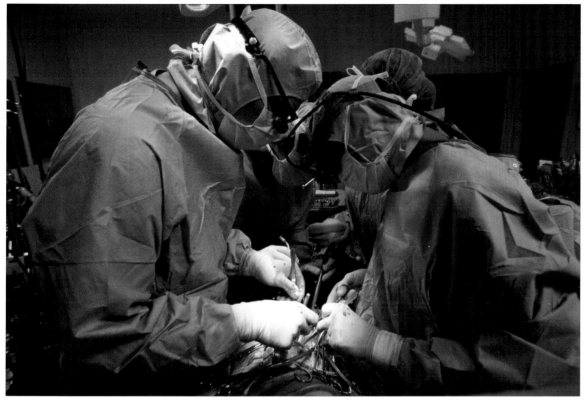

Surgeons at Temple University Hospital in Philadelphia perform the Ross switch procedure, which is heart surgery that involves exchanging two valves in the heart.

There are two main ways in which physicians can intervene to improve a patient's health: medical treatment and surgical treatment. Medical treatment involves the use of drugs, radiation, and other treatments that affect the workings of the body. With surgical treatment, the problem area is normally repaired or cut out. The two treatments are not always interchangeable—some conditions can only be addressed by either medical or surgical treatment. A dangerously inflamed appendix, for example, must be surgically removed urgently before it bursts, but strep throat (an inflamed sore throat that is caused by a *Streptococcus* bacterium) is cured with antibiotics (see ANTIBIOTICS). In other cases, there are both medical and surgical options for treating a particular condition, and factors such as the relative effectiveness of each method and the patient's general health must be taken into account.

Surgery in antiquity

Skeletal evidence indicates that primitive surgery was being performed as early as 35,000 years ago, during the Stone Age, in both the Old World and the Americas. The earliest known surgical procedure was called trephination, which involved drilling a hole in the patient's skull. While it is thought that this was probably done mainly for superstitious reasons—such as to provide an exit for evil spirits—it is likely that there were occasional recoveries because of the reduction of fluid pressure on the brain.

Circumcision—the removal of the foreskin that covers the tip of the penis—is another very early surgical procedure. It arose as a religious rite in the ancient Middle East and is today practiced almost universally among Jewish and Islamic people worldwide. In the 20th century, circumcision was adopted by other cultures when studies showed that the procedure virtually eliminated the risk of penile cancer, reduced the risk of infection, and aided in cleanliness. In the middle of the 19th century, most baby boys in the United States were circumcised within a few days of birth. However, the prevalence declined to about 60 percent by the year 2000, largely due to increasing opposition to a procedure that may not be medically necessary—especially since daily hygiene has improved, reducing the risk of infection.

CORE FACTS

- Many early surgical techniques developed in the context of military campaigns.
- In the 19th century, the development of anesthetics and antiseptics greatly increased the range of conditions that could be addressed by surgery, as well as the probability of surgical success.
- Modern surgery requires a team of highly skilled professionals and assistants.
- Advanced techniques have enabled surgeons to perform more extensive repairs than ever before; technology has also enabled them to reduce the invasiveness of a great number of surgical procedures.

CONNECTIONS

● Advances in **TELEMEDICINE** have allowed surgeons from across the world to direct or comment on surgical procedures.

● A number of **VETERINARY MEDICINE** operations use similar surgical procedures and anesthetics as human operations.

This engraving from English physician William Harvey's 1628 treatise, On the Motion of the Heart and the Blood, *demonstrates the circulation of the blood by showing pronounced blood vessels in two arms.*

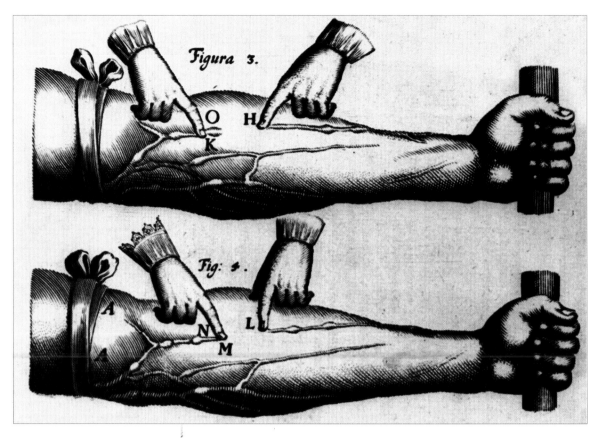

The variety and frequency of early surgical procedures increased among the organized armies of the ancient world, such as in Greece, Rome, and Babylon (present-day Iraq). Often in a state of war, these cultures had numerous occasions to patch people back together, and they also possessed the means of communication through which to spread surgical techniques. Amputations were common, as was cauterization—the burning or destroying of tissue with a hot iron or chemical agent in order to stop bleeding. Some of the most proficient ancient surgeons were to be found in India, where more than a hundred different surgical instruments were in use, and where cosmetic surgery was performed on badly injured noses and ears.

In medieval Europe—before the 16th century—physicians often avoided surgery, viewing it as a messy process that was beneath their station. As a result, simple operations such as pulling teeth and bloodletting—once a widespread procedure that was no doubt responsible for the death of many patients—were performed by barbers. This practice continued into the early 20th century in some European villages. The classic barber pole, with its red and white stripes, originally represented the blood and bandages that were the everyday tools of the barber-surgeon's trade.

The rise of scientific understanding

The European Renaissance, around the 14th to the 17th centuries, was a time of increased understanding about the workings of the body. Theories and methods that had been passed down from ancient Greek physicians gradually gave way to new knowledge that was gained through observation and experiment. The autopsy (examination of the body after death) became more common and allowed increasingly detailed study of human anatomy.

English physician William Harvey (1578–1657) described the principles of the circulation of the blood in his 1628 treatise, *On the Motion of the Heart and the Blood*, which is widely considered by medical

---

THE MAYO FAMILY

In Rochester, Minnesota, in 1883, a tornado killed 20 people and injured hundreds more. In the aftermath of the disaster, an order of Catholic nuns decided to build a permanent hospital on condition that respected local physician Dr. William W. Mayo (1819–1911) take charge. Mayo, who had emigrated from England to the United States almost 40 years earlier, led a colorful life, in occupations ranging from tailor to purser on a riverboat. A pillar of the community, the Protestant surgeon joined with the nuns to establish St. Mary's Hospital in 1889.

When Mayo's sons, William James Mayo (1861–1939) and Charles Horace Mayo (1865–1939), finished medical school, together they founded one of the first multi-specialty practices. Dr. William W. Mayo became especially skilled in dealing with women's health; his son Dr. William James Mayo became renowned for abdominal surgery; and Dr. Charles Horace Mayo specialized in thyroid, nervous system, and eye operations, including the removal of cataracts. Their reputations attracted patients from far and wide, and the Mayo Clinic eventually grew into one of the world's premier medical centers.

The Mayo brothers made many technological advancements in their respective surgical fields. But their greatest innovation—a major factor in their success—was their insistence on cleanliness, including the promotion of sterile operating conditions. This was considered eccentric at a time when the germ theory of disease was still in some dispute. It was word of the Mayo brothers' results, and the medical school and research foundation they established, that helped spread their procedures throughout the medical community.

PEOPLE

historians to be one of the most important books ever written about physiology.

Two developments in the 19th century were responsible for the growth of modern surgery. The first was anesthesia, which is the technique of pain relief through sedation and subsequent loss of sensation. Chemical anesthetics, such as ether ($C_4H_{10}O$), were discovered in the 1840s. Before this, surgeons relied on wine, opium, and fast work to block the pain of an operation. Prolonged surgery, with its attendant excruciating pain, was considered not only extremely traumatic for everyone concerned, but also likely to result in the death of the patient from shock. Under such conditions, surgery on the chest, abdomen, or brain was therefore rarely contemplated (see ANESTHETICS).

The other major 19th-century development in surgery was the germ theory of disease. With infection killing around half of all surgical patients, English surgeon Joseph Lister (1827–1912) revolutionized the operating room in 1865 by spraying a carbolic acid disinfectant around it and insisting that surgeons wash their hands and instruments with antiseptics (see ANTISEPTICS AND STERILIZATION). Lister's ideas were popularized in the United States by the Mayo brothers (see the box on page 1280).

In the 1950s, life-support systems enabled the pumping of the heart and lungs to be stilled so that surgery on these organs and on major blood vessels could be performed (see HEART-LUNG MACHINE). Organ transplants have given many patients whose conditions would previously have been hopeless a new chance at life (see TRANSPLANT SURGERY).

During the late 1900s, surgeons perfected techniques of targeting and performing many procedures with pinpoint accuracy. This is largely because of advanced diagnostic and surgical imaging systems and endoscopic techniques, which allow surgery to be performed with thin flexible instruments that are inserted through small incisions in the patient's body (see MEDICAL IMAGING; ENDOSCOPE).

Types of surgery

One way to classify the many types of surgical procedures is by their degree of urgency. In the United States, the usual three categories are elective, semi-elective, and urgent—or emergency—surgery.

Elective surgery is performed simply because a patient wants it. It is generally specific to a particular problem and does not have any effect on overall health. There are varying degrees of elective surgery, but none of the conditions that it is performed to correct or improve is life-threatening—the patient can choose either to live with the condition or to have the surgery. Examples of elective surgery include surgical sterilization and the removal of bunions. Cosmetic surgery, which is performed to enhance a patient's appearance, usually falls into this category (see the box on page 1284).

Semi-elective surgery, such as the removal of a troublesome gallbladder or the replacement of an arthritic joint, is performed to correct an existing

condition or to prevent further deterioration. However, the operation is generally not considered urgent and in most countries tends to be scheduled at the convenience of the hospital and the surgeon.

Urgent surgery is performed to correct a condition that threatens a patient's life or general health. Removal of a cancerous tumor falls into this category, as does heart-valve replacement. Certain procedures, such as coronary artery bypass or appendectomy, sometimes have to be performed as emergency surgery because the conditions represent an immediate threat to the patient's life. Severe bleeding; blockages in blood circulation, respiration, or excretion; imminent rupture of an abdominal organ; and fluid pressure on the brain are all emergency conditions that can often be successfully corrected by immediate surgical intervention.

Another way to classify surgery is by the part of the body upon which it is performed or by the type of procedure that is done. A very common category of surgery is the removal of a diseased or damaged organ. The names for surgery of this type usually end in the suffix -ectomy—for example, tonsillectomy, thyroidectomy, and appendectomy.

English surgeon Joseph Lister (1827–1912) is credited with introducing strict hygiene to the operating room. He sprayed carbolic acid disinfectant and insisted that hands and instruments be washed in antiseptics.

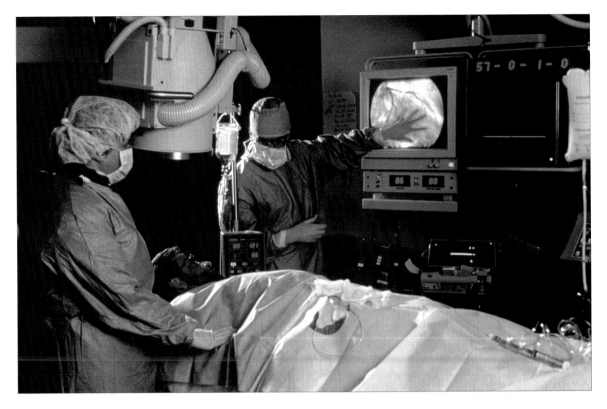

In the operating room, a surgeon uses a video screen showing a patient's interior to demonstrate to the patient what will happen during his surgery.

In the operating room

A common operation that can be used to illustrate general surgical procedures is an appendectomy, which is removal of the appendix. Surgery is a team effort, requiring the involvement of physicians, nurses, and orderlies. The surgeon who is performing the operation is in charge of the whole team for that particular surgery. The chief nurse in the operating room is in charge of all the nurses and orderlies working with the surgeon (see OPERATING ROOM).

Before an operation, orderlies wash down the walls and floors of the operating room, which is designed to be easily cleaned to keep it as germ-free as possible. They then wheel in any large equipment that is needed for a particular operation. Nurses lay out all the surgical instruments that are needed for the operation on a large side table. A smaller table at the surgeon's elbow holds instruments for immediate use. The full complement of surgical instruments is not necessary for every operation—surgeons who must work on or get past bone will use surgical drills and saws, but these are not required for performing operations on most organs.

The surgeon who is performing the operation is always assisted by another surgeon. Anesthesia is generally rendered by a physician called an anesthesiologist, although in some cases a certified nurse-anesthetist may be employed. The majority of abdominal surgery is performed under general anesthesia, which renders the patient unconscious. An increasing number of procedures are being found eligible for regional anesthesia, which blocks sensation only in one area of the body, such as a limb. For minor procedures, such as the removal of a skin mole, local anesthesia, which only numbs a small area, is generally used. Spinal anesthesia is the use of local anesthetic on the spinal nerve, which numbs the lower limbs or abdomen.

In operations where general anesthesia is used, it is sometimes administered in a nearby room and the patient brought into the operating room already

BLOOD TRANSFUSIONS

Replacement of lost blood is often required during surgery. Blood transfusion saves many lives, but it does involve risks (see BLOOD TRANSFUSION). The first is the risk of incompatibility, which has essentially been eliminated by defining the major blood types, and then by individually cross-matching the blood of the donor and the recipient to test for adverse reactions caused when the immune system rejects new blood (see IMMUNOLOGY AND IMMUNIZATION).

The other major risk involved in blood transfusions is the transmission of disease. The U.S. Food and Drug Administration specifies 12 tests for donated blood, of which 9 are to test for infectious diseases such as hepatitis and syphilis and for human immunodeficiency virus (HIV). But even the most rigorous of screening procedures cannot guarantee 100 percent safety. There are a number of options for surgical patients in particular to reduce their need for donated blood. Some surgeries can be performed in less invasive ways—such as endoscopic surgery—in order to reduce blood loss (see ENDOSCOPE). In other cases, the patient's blood pressure or temperature may be artificially lowered to cut down on bleeding. During many operations, the blood from the surgical wound is suctioned, filtered, and returned to the patient, which recaptures around a third of the lost blood volume.

When administration of blood during surgery is required, the safest blood is invariably that of the patient. If there is adequate time before surgery begins, and if the patient is in sufficiently good health, he or she can donate blood for use during the operation. This is called autologous transfusion. Many patients choose to use directed donations from family members who have compatible blood types. Not having to go to the public blood supply is reassuring to some patients and gives the family members the feeling that they can do something for their loved one. However, the actual percentage of directly donated blood that can be used is no greater than for outside donations.

A CLOSER LOOK

anesthetized. More commonly, the patient is brought in sedated and anesthetic gas is then administered in the operating room itself. Meanwhile, all of the members of the surgical team use antibacterial soap to scrub their hands and lower arms for eight to ten minutes, and then they all put on sterile gloves. Every person inside the operating room also wears a sterile gown, pants, mask, cap, and slippers.

To prepare for the operation, the patient is draped with sterile sheets so that only the surgical area—already shaved of any hair if necessary—is exposed. The area is wiped with antiseptic solution. Throughout the surgery, the patient is carefully monitored by the anesthesiologist, who tracks his or her respiration, pulse, blood pressure, and the critical blood-oxygen level that is necessary to nourish the brain (see MEDICAL MONITORING EQUIPMENT).

Scrub nurses anticipate the surgeon's needs, standing ready with the instruments and supplies that are required for each stage of the operation. Every effort is made to have all the necessary equipment ready in the operating room, but if extra supplies are needed, a circulating nurse is responsible for retrieving them. Because circulating nurses are exposed to nonsterile environments—anywhere outside the operating room—in the course of their duties, they do not take part in the surgery itself.

The surgeon performing an appendectomy, for example, begins by making an incision through the skin, and then through the abdominal fat, using a small, sharp knife called a scalpel. The assistant surgeon generally holds the retractors—an instrument that keeps the abdominal muscles and other tissues out of the way as the appendix and the part of the intestine to which the appendix is attached are exposed. The ends of any severed blood vessels are clamped with instruments called hemostats, which greatly reduce the loss of blood. Sponges, which are folded pads of gauze, absorb any blood seepage.

When the area has been thoroughly prepared, the surgeon removes the appendix, then stitches up the stump with a suture (stitch) and folds it back into the large intestine. Surgical assistants are heavily involved during the subsequent closing-up stage. First, they remove all the sponges, which are counted by a nurse before and after surgery to avoid leaving any of them inside the patient. They then unclamp and tie the severed blood vessels, remove the retractors, and allow all the tissues to fall back into their normal positions. The tissues are then carefully sutured, one layer at a time, until the skin surface is stitched back together.

Internal surgical sutures are commonly made using a fiber that dissolves inside the body when the sutures are no longer needed. Skin sutures are generally made of silk, and these must be removed a week or so after the operation. In some cases, surgical staples—fastenings made of nonallergic, nonirritating materials—are used in place of sutures. These can be applied quicker than sutures and do not need to be removed. When the wound is sewn or stapled, a gauze bandage is placed over it. Finally, the

DIAGNOSTIC SURGERY

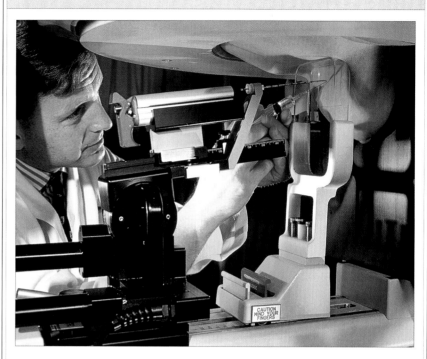

A physician performs a breast biopsy. A biopsy needle, guided by computer and X-ray coordinates, is fired into the breast to obtain a tissue sample for testing.

Not all surgical procedures are performed to solve a known problem; some are used to determine what the problem is. Exploratory surgery is not what it used to be: rarely does a modern surgeon open a patient's abdomen just to take a look around. Instead, a thin, flexible, illuminated fiber-optic instrument may be threaded through a small incision or a natural body orifice, revealing the area in question to the surgeon (see ENDOSCOPE). Alternatively, a catheter may be inserted to run radio-opaque dye through an area, which is then imaged by X rays. Often performed to examine coronary arteries, this process is called angiography.

Biopsy, in which a tiny sample of tissue is removed for analysis, is another important category of diagnostic procedure. Biopsies are commonly carried out via a small incision and an endoscope, but in some cases a needle biopsy may provide a large enough sample in a less invasive manner. The central goal in diagnostic surgery is to accurately obtain the required information with minimum stress and risk to the patient. Advanced imaging techniques (see MEDICAL IMAGING; DIAGNOSTIC TESTS AND EQUIPMENT) are increasingly allowing diagnostic surgical procedures to be dispensed with altogether.

A CLOSER LOOK

sterile draping is removed, and the patient is taken to a recovery room where he or she will remain until the anesthesia has worn off.

Surgery as a profession

All medical training includes some aspects of basic surgery, and any physician is therefore qualified to perform certain minor operations. Physicians interested in becoming surgeons require more extensive and specialized training, which generally takes place during a surgical residency at a teaching hospital after the surgeon has finished general medical school. In the United States, all surgeons must complete a specialized surgical internship, which is followed by a surgical residency that lasts for five years.

COSMETIC SURGERY

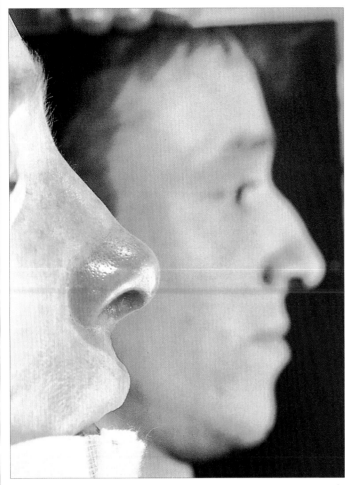

This patient has undergone rhinoplasty; the original shape of his nose is shown behind.

Cosmetic surgery includes some of the most commonly performed operations. While some people would never consider accepting the risks of surgery in order to improve their appearance, serious disfigurement due to birth defects, accident, or disease makes reconstructive surgery advisable for many people in order to restore self-esteem. Other people may have been unhappy about a particular physical feature since childhood and would like to change it to raise self-confidence. Some procedures, such as face-lifts, are performed to mitigate the effects of aging.

The simplest cosmetic procedures, such as the removal of a mole or birthmark, can be performed in a few minutes in a physician's office under local anesthesia. Others involve major reshaping of the body, removing pads of fat, or augmenting areas with implants. In general, the more extensive the surgery, the more significant the corresponding risk of complications.

One of the most common cosmetic surgery procedures is rhinoplasty (the "nose job"). This is usually performed via the nostrils so as to leave no external scars on the skin. Often the problem is a hump on the bridge of the nose, which can be sculpted with a surgical file. The shape of the cartilage at the tip of the nose is also frequently altered. Many patients seek cosmetic surgery for the restoration of their hair. One procedure involves transplanting plugs or strips of skin with functioning hair follicles onto bald areas. Another, the scalp reduction method, involves cutting out a bald patch and then gathering in and suturing the surrounding scalp.

A surgical scalpel is not a magic wand, and patients will generally not arise from cosmetic surgery looking like the models in glossy magazines. Before the final effect can be observed, black eyes and bruises must heal, and hair transplants must begin to grow. Neither does cosmetic surgery make time stand still—lifted faces and tucked tummies are gradually affected by aging and gravity just as they were before. Patients must be counseled to have reasonable expectations about how the surgery will change their lives and how it will not. But most people who decide that cosmetic surgery is right for them are satisfied with the results.

A CLOSER LOOK

Specialty surgical training can take longer than five years. Each of the major specialties has a board of qualified specialists who are responsible for certifying physicians in that particular field. Surgical specialties include heart surgery, neurosurgery, orthopedic surgery, urology, ophthalmology, gynecological surgery, thoracic surgery, and a number of others. Many surgeons work in subspecialties, where they specialize even further to concentrate on a particular type of surgery or surgical practice, on a very specific region of the body, or on pediatric (child) or geriatric (elderly) areas of work.

All surgeons must keep up to date with current research, new knowledge, and the latest techniques and technologies in their field. Most achieve this by reading relevant medical journals and attending surgical conferences and seminars.

S. CALVO

See also: AMBULANCE AND EMERGENCY MEDICAL TREATMENT; BIONICS AND BIOMEDICAL ENGINEERING; CANCER TREATMENTS; FORENSIC SCIENCE; INTENSIVE CARE UNIT; MEDICAL TECHNOLOGY; MICROSCOPY; OBSTETRICS AND GYNECOLOGY; PHARMACOLOGY AND DRUG TREATMENT.

Further reading:
Adams, G. *On Call: Surgery.* Philadelphia: W. B. Saunders, 1997.
Chari, R. *Surgery.* Philadelphia: Lippincott-Raven Publishers, 1996.
Computer-integrated Surgery: Technology and Clinical Applications. Edited by R. Taylor. Cambridge, Massachusetts: MIT Press, 1996.
Economou, S. *Atlas of Surgical Techniques.* Philadelphia: Saunders, 1996.
Essentials of Surgery: Scientific Principles and Practice. Edited by L. Greenfield and M. Mulholland. Philadelphia: Lippincott-Raven Publishers, 1997.
Inlander, C. *Good Operations, Bad Operations.* New York: Penguin, 1993.
Youngson, R. *The Surgery Book: An Illustrated Guide to 73 of the Most Common Operations.* New York: St. Martin's Press, 1993.

SURVEYING

Surveying is the practice of mapping the exact position of objects for construction and mapmaking

Surveying is the science of noting the relative location of points on the ground or of objects being built. When land boundaries are surveyed, this is called cadastral surveying. Roads, buildings, and tunnels are surveyed during construction (see ROAD BUILDING). In early civilizations, surveying kept ancient pyramids square and ditches draining downhill (see the box on page 1286).

Since the 1700s, when scientists and mechanics could make precise instruments, land surveying has consisted of measuring angles and distances. The early Greek scholars produced the fundamentals of geometry, or earth measurement, and trigonometry, which is measurement by triangles. Geometry has roots in Egyptian history, where it was first motivated by the need to survey land after the annual flood of the Nile River. Trigonometry was originally developed in connection with astronomy, but it was adapted to calculate precise locations from angles and distances measured in a survey (see BUILDING TECHNIQUES, TRADITIONAL).

CORE FACTS

- Surveying uses trigonometry to locate points from the measurement of angles and distances from other known reference points.
- The Global Positioning System (GPS) has improved the accuracy of surveys and made point location easier.
- Rapid changes to instrumentation technology have improved the accuracy of modern surveys.

Locating an object

Surveying describes locations in terms of their positions relative to two known points, which may themselves be defined absolutely—by their longitude, latitude, and height above sea level—or simply considered as reference points for the survey area.

The two known points form a triangle with any other point in the survey area, and the position of the unknown point can be calculated by triangulation (a form of trigonometry). Two of the points are marked to be visible at the third point, from which the angles between the two marked points in the horizontal and visible planes can be measured using an instrument such as a theodolite, which is described later. The position of the new point is then calculated from these two angles and the distance between the known points. For surveys over small distances—less than 12 miles (19 km)—the curvature of Earth's surface is usually considered to be negligible and relative elevations (heights) of the various points are quoted as X and Y coordinates, which define the point in the horizontal plane, and the Z coordinate (elevation, or height). This technique, known as plane surveying, is sufficiently accurate for small-area surveying.

Surveys over larger areas must be mathematically corrected to take into account the curvature of Earth's surface. This is known as geodetic surveying.

Most of the United States has been surveyed as a system of rectangles called public land subdivisions. Each state also has a plane-coordinate system that ties its plane surveys to a curved map projection, which approximates a geodetic survey.

CONNECTIONS

- Accurate surveying is essential for **ARTILLERY** units to hit their targets.

- **PRECISION FARMING** technology relies on land surveys in order to locate areas of high-yield land.

A hiker checks his location using a handheld satellite navigation receiver. The receiver instantly calculates its position from signals sent by Global Positioning System (GPS) satellites. These signals pinpoint the satellites' identities and positions and also give the exact time using atomic clocks.

Surveying equipment

Recent technological advances have largely replaced 300-year-old techniques of measuring distances with a tape measure and angles with a transit. Transits are devices that measure angles in two planes, vertically and horizontally, by moving a viewfinder up and down and side to side. They have a horizontal circular plate divided into a 360-degree scale and a similar vertical plate. A point is located through a viewfinder with crosshairs, then the angle that is turned between two points is read by lining up marks on the circle. Accuracy is limited to the diameter of the circular plates and the vernier, which is a device that

exaggerates small differences and can be used to read fractions of a degree. The theodolite, developed in the 20th century, is really a sophisticated transit. Prisms inside the device allow angles to be measured to great accuracy. A good theodolite reads to one six-hundredth of a degree.

Short distances can be measured using steel tape measures, which are typically 100 ft (30 m) long and measure to an accuracy of 0.01 ft (30 mm). Repeated measurements can yield an average to thousandths of a foot. Measurements made with a tape are considered too inaccurate for surveys that need to cover long distances, so these are done by triangulation, which forms a great chain of adjacent triangles with accurately measured angles (see the box on page 1287). The geodetic control points of the United States Geologic Survey were all first surveyed by triangulation.

The development of electronic distance measuring in the 1960s and 1970s greatly altered surveying. Electronic distance measuring devices (EDMs) are similar to radar and sonar (see RADAR): the time a signal beam takes to travel to and from a target is used to calculate the distance to the target. Early EDMs used beams of sound, but now laser beams are used. EDMs allow distances to be measured more accurately than with theodolite angles.

Surveying with satellites

Perhaps the greatest advance in surveying science in the 20th century was provided by the Global Positioning System (GPS). Initiated by the U.S. government in 1973, the GPS consists of 24 satellites and five ground stations (see GROUND STATION). The ground stations monitor the paths of the satellites and transmit signals to each one to inform its onboard computer of that satellite's exact trajectory. Each satellite uses this information, together with a cross-checked time signal from four onboard atomic clocks, to broadcast to Earth's surface a signal that identifies the satellite and advises its exact location and the exact time of transmission. The distance of a receiver on Earth's surface can be calculated from the time taken for the signal to reach that receiver. If signals are received from at least three satellites, and ideally four, the receiver can calculate its own position to within about 70 ft (20 m). In fact, the full accuracy of the system is only available to the U.S. military, which owns and operates the system. Civilians receive a signal that permits location only within 330 ft (100 m) to avoid misuse of the system by hostile forces—use of the full-accuracy system in conjunction with a known triangulation point allows missiles to be targeted with millimeter accuracy.

The main drawback of GPS is that it fails if fewer than three satellites' signals are available due to system failure or obstructions such as high buildings.

Three-dimensional surveys

For many purposes, such as street maps, a two-dimensional representation of a survey area is sufficient. In other cases, such as when planning

---

DEVELOPMENT OF SURVEYING

Little is known of very early surveying practices. The fertile fields of the Nile Valley in Egypt needed to have their boundaries replaced after annual floods. This was done using recorded property maps and measuring ropes. The Great Pyramid of Giza in Egypt has a square base, and the 750-ft- (228-m-) long sides vary in length by less than a foot, suggesting that accurate surveying was in use.

The Romans used a leveling frame, which consisted of a triangle with a string attached at the apex and weighted with a plumb bob that bisected the base. They used a *groma* made of two perpendicular boards with plumb bobs hanging from the ends to give a reference point. These tools simplified making square corners.

Transits and theodolites evolved when 18th- and 19th-century instrument makers combined a sighting telescope with circular plates for vertical and horizontal angles. Originally, theodolites had powerful sighting telescopes with long tubes and a large-diameter plate that enabled them to measure angles accurately over long distances (the larger the circular plate, the larger its circumference and the more divisions can be made).

HISTORY OF TECHNOLOGY

construction or landscaping, a three-dimensional description of the topography of a survey area is needed. Small sites can be surveyed using a theodolite and a measuring staff (a tall, square pole with heights marked on one face so as to be visible through the theodolite). The theodolite is secured with its sighting tube horizontal and the relative heights of the theodolite and measuring staff are read from the point where the theodolite's crosshairs intersect the markings on the staff. The distance between the two points can then be measured by using either a tape or an EDM device. The relative distances and elevations so obtained are then marked on the site plan.

For topographic maps of large areas, surveyors view aerial photos in pairs that form stereoscopic (apparently three-dimensional) images. Using a large stereoscopic viewer, a cartographer (mapmaker) can trace lines of equal elevation to create a map of valleys and hills. GPS can be used to produce topographic maps of limited areas: the location and elevation of a number of points can be measured and these data downloaded into a computer; the computer then processes the information and plots a contour map. When the survey is used for planning landscaping, the desired final landscape can be entered, and the computer calculates the amount of soil removal or fill needed to achieve the new landscape. Existing roads, buildings, or other utilities can also be included on the map.

Total stations

Conventional surveying with EDMs is very common, although theodolites and tapes are sufficient for mapping small areas. A total station is an electronic device that measures the distance and the angles in the horizontal and vertical planes between two points in survey. Total stations are sufficiently accurate to read distance and angle to thousandths of a foot and seconds of a degree.

Modern total-station devices include small computers that allow the surveyor to input the horizontal coordinates and elevation of the known point over which the total station is set. When an unknown point is sighted, the total station displays the angles and horizontal and vertical distances to the point, or calculates the X, Y, and Z coordinates at the targeted point. All this is recorded for mapmaking.

In addition to land surveys that locate property lines and topographic surveys that show Earth's natural features, there are route surveys that locate highways and power lines; mining surveys that are used to map underground tunnels and seams; and municipal surveys that record streets, sewer systems, and phone or gas lines. Construction surveys represent over 50 percent of surveys in the United States.

T. FINCH

See also: CIVIL ENGINEERING; PROSPECTING.

Further reading:

Kavanagh, B. *Surveying: Principles and Applications.* Englewood Cliffs, New Jersey: Prentice-Hall, 1996.

TRIANGULATION

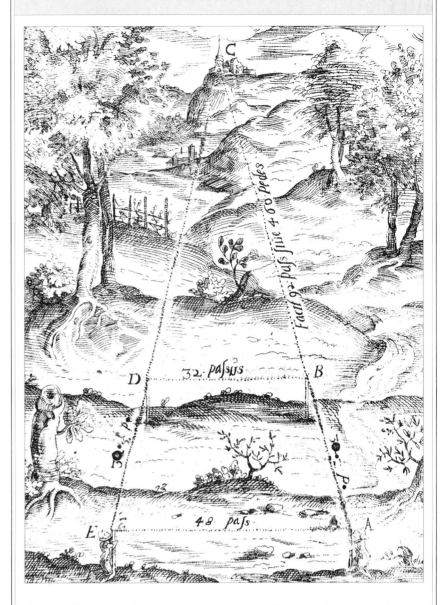

This 1605 illustration shows surveyors measuring a distance using triangulation.

The surveys that were used to map the United States over long distances were achieved through triangulation (angle measurement), because measuring long distances with a steel tape was difficult and inaccurate. A long tape is 100 ft (30 m), and using one would require 159,000 placements in order to cross the United States—assuming that it was only a flat plain with no rivers or mountains.

Triangulation requires a very accurately measured base (of a triangle) with the angles measured from the base to a single distant point. The lengths of the other sides and the location of the far point can be calculated from the base and angle measurements. This concept can be checked by creating a rectangle or trapezoid. The two far corners are sighted from both ends of the precise base. Direct sights of adjacent corners and diagonal sights divide the rectangle into four triangles, and the far side can be calculated using two sets of data to insure accuracy. Very long chains of triangles and trapezoids can measure distances over many miles. Where land is flat, towers can be used to take measurements over Earth's curvature.

Triangular data is also used by some electronic distance measuring devices. Using similar trigonometry as for triangulation, the angles between points can be accurately calculated in a process called trilateration, which measures the lengths of the three sides of a triangle.

A CLOSER LOOK

SUSPENSION BRIDGE

Suspension bridges comprise a roadway that hangs from anchored cables supported by towers

The Lions Gate suspension bridge in Vancouver, British Columbia, joins the northern suburbs to the downtown area of the city.

Suspension bridges are built on the same principle as a simple rope bridge, in that they are held up by tension from either end. In a modern suspension bridge, the heavy main cables run over support towers in an inverted arch (also called a catenary curve) and are held fast at anchorages on either side. The roadway, or deck, is held up by high-strength wires hanging from the main cables. Suspension bridges can span a greater distance between support towers than any other type of bridge, allowing river traffic to pass underneath unimpeded.

The first suspension bridges were built at the beginning of the 19th century, with rigid roadways hung from iron cables or chains. U.S. master bridge-builders John Roebling (1806–1869) and his son Washington (1837–1926) improved on these designs for the Brooklyn Bridge, one of the most famous bridges in the world, which was completed in 1883. For their ambitious project linking Brooklyn with Manhattan, the Roeblings used steel cables. The cables were made by wrapping together a number of strands, which were themselves bundles of hundreds of steel wires. Steel cables are stronger and more durable than iron ones and are used today for all suspension bridges. Towers are now generally made of composites of steel and concrete, which are more flexible and can carry much more weight than brick or stone structures (see MATERIALS SCIENCE).

The anchorages, which take most of the weight of the bridge, are embedded inside enormous reinforced concrete blocks or even solid rock. The earliest suspension bridges were prone to failure because their builders did not fully understand the engineering science of bridges, and their bridges were, to some extent, experimental. The tower foundations must be built deep enough to hold firm in the bedrock. Depending on the design and the site, they may be constructed on dry land or in underwater mud using caisson foundation structures that are sunk as the mud is excavated.

Longer and lighter

The decks of 19th-century bridges were often built with heavy trusses to accommodate railroad traffic. In the 20th century, automobile traffic became more important. This led to bridge designs that were lighter and less expensive to build since automobiles are not as heavy as railroad cars. With a lighter roadway, the structures could be built to span greater distances. Records were set and broken with regularity. But the race to decrease weight and increase spans was carried to extremes. Without the stiffening trusses, even a moderate wind could cause the bridge to sway dangerously. In 1940, a 42-mph (68-km/h) wind blowing across the narrow thin deck of the Tacoma Narrows Bridge in Washington set up severe oscillations and lateral twisting. The

CONNECTIONS

● Highly specialized **CONSTRUCTION AND EARTHMOVING MACHINERY** is used to sink the foundations of large suspension bridges into riverbeds and seabeds.

● When the position of a crossing is unsuitable or too long for a suspension bridge, a **TUNNEL** may be built instead.

CORE FACTS

■ Suspension bridges have a roadway or railroad hung from cables that are supported by towers near to each end of the span.

■ The first modern suspension bridges were built in the 19th century.

■ The growing importance of automobile transportation allowed suspension bridges to be made from lighter material than those needed to accommodate railroads, but the ability to withstand high wind speeds was also a critical design requirement.

■ Cable-stayed bridges look similar to suspension bridges, but their roadways are held up by cables attached directly to the towers.

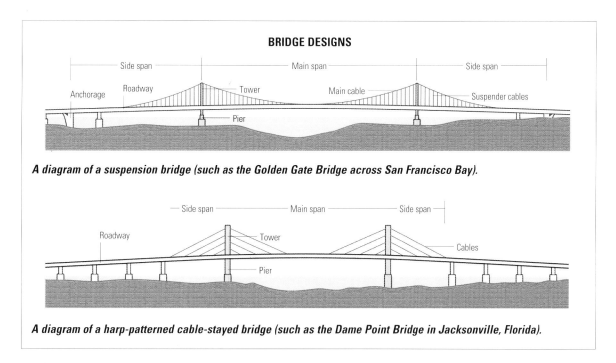

BRIDGE DESIGNS

A diagram of a suspension bridge (such as the Golden Gate Bridge across San Francisco Bay).

A diagram of a harp-patterned cable-stayed bridge (such as the Dame Point Bridge in Jacksonville, Florida).

dramatic collapse of the bridge was captured in a film that is still widely shown to illustrate the effects of poor bridge design. No major suspension bridge was built without trusses again until the late 1960s, when several bridges were designed with decks shaped like airfoils to reduce wind resistance. These included the Severn Bridge connecting Wales and England. The aerodynamic deck design used only half the weight of steel as comparable truss designs. However, this lightweight design turned out not to be up to the huge increases in traffic volume, and the Severn Bridge required a major overhaul just 15 years after it was built. (In 1996, a similar bridge was opened further downstream to cope with heightened traffic demands.) The Severn Bridge's aerodynamic deck was modified rather than abandoned, and the design was used in the Humber Bridge (4626 ft; 1410 m), in England—the world's longest when built.

Cable-stayed bridges

Another innovation of the mid-20th century was the cable-stayed bridge. In this design, a number of steel cables run directly from the towers to hold up the deck. Early suspension bridge builders, including John Roebling, used diagonal cable stays as an adjunct to main cables and suspension wires. Practical designs for exclusively cable-stayed bridges did not occur until developments in working with high-strength steel cables and stiffened steel decking were achieved during World War II (1939–1945). Spearheaded by German engineers, the design caught on most quickly in Europe, but today it is found worldwide in increasing numbers.

There is great diversity in cable-stayed bridges. The design is scalable from small footbridges to very long spans. The cable stays may spread out at different angles from the top of the towers (described as the fan configuration), or they may run in parallel from different heights (harp configuration). A hybrid arrangement is also possible. In any case, the cables connect to the deck at points distributed along its length. The number of towers may vary from one to several. The towers and decking can be constructed of steel, concrete, or a composite of the two materials. The largest single bridge in the United States, the Sunshine Skyway Bridge, has a central cable-stayed structure with several shorter spans either side supported by piles. The bridge was completed in 1987. In total the bridge spans 21,887 ft (6671 m) over Florida's Tampa Bay, with a high deck to accommodate a shipping clearance of 175 ft (53 m).

Into the future

The competition to build longer free-standing bridges has never stopped. Two giants, the Storebælt Bridge in Denmark and the current record holder, the Akashi Kaikyo Bridge in Japan (6529 ft; 1990 m), opened within months of each other in 1998. An even longer bridge linking Denmark with Sweden is being planned.

To design ever more challenging structures able to withstand heavy traffic, winds, and even earthquakes, engineers are continually looking for new construction techniques and materials. The limiting span for a bridge of any design is the maximum length at which it can support its own weight without collapsing. If a material could be developed that is both lighter and stronger than the high-strength steel currently used, the limiting span would be much larger. Materials being investigated include composites made with carbon or other fibers (see COMPOSITE; MATERIALS SCIENCE). However, cost is an issue, as is the need to thoroughly test new materials.

S. CALVO

See also: BRIDGE; BUILDING TECHNIQUES, MODERN; CIVIL ENGINEERING; DREDGING; STRUCTURES.

Further reading:

Brown, D. *Bridges.* New York: Macmillan, 1993.

SUSPENSION SYSTEM

Suspension systems on vehicles
provide a comfortable ride and
improve safety and road handling

The suspension system of this articulated truck allows it to flex about a central axis so that all the truck's wheels remain in contact with the ground—even on uneven surfaces.

CONNECTIONS

● Modern
AUTOMOBILE
designs incorporate
shock absorbers to
improve passenger
comfort.

● **RAILROAD
LOCOMOTIVES** do
not need elaborate
suspension systems
since railroad tracks
are relatively smooth.

Suspension systems in vehicles consist of mechanical linkages—generally springs—and shock absorbers that smoothen the motion of those linkages to minimize bouncing, which would otherwise be unpleasant or even dangerous. Suspension systems are designed to improve passenger comfort, maintain contact between the wheels and the road, reduce vibrational strain on other parts of the vehicle and cargo, and control the complex forces operating on a vehicle when it deviates from movement in a straight line. These requirements are greatly simplified in the case of railroad vehicles, which do not need complex suspension because railroads are smoother than roads (see RAILROAD CAR).

Suspension systems for automobiles have become highly sophisticated and varied. In spite of greatly improved roads, modern systems must still cope effectively with irregular terrain.

Early suspension systems
The people who made the earliest vehicles, such as animal-drawn sledges and primitive carts, were unconcerned with such luxuries as suspension. For well over a thousand years after the invention of the wheel, this situation remained the same (see WHEEL). But as horse-drawn transport improved and higher speeds became possible, the continual jolting caused by rutted roads became unacceptable, and springs were introduced (see HORSE-DRAWN TRANSPORT).

Initially a crude form of springing was achieved by exploiting the natural flexibility of wood. As the use of iron and steel grew during the 19th century, wooden springing was replaced by the flat single-leaf metal spring. One end of the leaf was firmly fixed to the body of the vehicle and the other was fixed to the axle, an arrangement known as a cantilever. Single-leaf cantilever springs were superseded by opposing-arch double springs: mirror-image arched strips of metal with movable linkages at each end. The center of the upper arch was attached to the body of the vehicle, and the center of the lower arch to the axle. The double arch would become flatter and wider under compression. Vehicle seats and the entire passenger-carrying body were sprung in this way, and the system proved highly successful and was widely used.

CORE FACTS

■ The first suspension systems were based on the natural springiness of wood.

■ Although suspension systems increase passenger comfort, they can make road handling poorer on rough terrain.

■ Modern shock absorbers dampen vibrations between the wheels and the body of an automobile using small pistons that move in oil-filled cylinders.

Development of automobile suspension

The earliest motor vehicles adopted many of the characteristics of horse-drawn carriages, including their suspension systems. Initially, leaf springing identical to that used in horse-drawn carriages was standard. Later, springs with several layers of opposed arches replaced springs with a single pair of arches. Leaf springs had one notable advantage for cars: they kept to a minimum the motion of the axles relative to the chassis or body. This was important because the axles were driven by relatively inflexible chain drives or shaft drives with differential gears (see GEAR; MECHANICAL TRANSMISSION).

Leaf springs have now largely been replaced by other forms of springing, especially coil springs and torsion-bar springs (see the diagram at right). Coil (or helical) springs, which are cylindrical in outline, are compact, easily accommodated into a car's design, and readily fitted with shock absorbers. They can also be made to compress more easily than leaf springs. The ratio between applied force and the amount of compression of a coil spring is relatively constant over a wide range of loads. This ratio, of the load in pounds to the deflection in inches, is called the spring rate. A constant spring rate can cause difficulties, however. For example, a spring with a large spring rate may be well suited to heavy loads, but less suited to lighter ones.

Soft springs—those with small values of spring rate—can increase passenger comfort by providing a smoother ride over bumps, but they bring their own disadvantages. They tend to produce undue vertical movement of the vehicle body on rough terrain, and they add to the amount of sway (body tilt) on corners. Soft front springs also increase the tendency of the front end of an automobile to sink toward the ground (dive) on sudden braking. Modern motor vehicles have lower body height than earlier carriages, so there is a limit on allowable vertical movement caused by springing. Modern automobile design has been greatly concerned with reconciling soft springing to stability and the avoidance of sway. These problems have been solved largely by stabilization bars and active suspension methods.

Torsion-bar springing is based on the use of a round spring-steel rod of uniform cross section. Torsion-bar springs take up very little room and are mechanically simple: one end is securely attached to the vehicle body, and the other is linked to the axle or wheel by a crank. When an upward force acts on the the wheel, a torsional (twisting) force acts on the bar along its long axis. The amount that a torsion bar will twist under a given torsional load depends on its dimensions and the elasticity of the steel from which it is made. The spring rate of a torsion-bar spring increases with the amount of twisting so that the greater the load placed on it, the greater is the resistance to further movement. This behavior makes for a suspension system that is well suited to a wide range of loads. Furthermore, torsion-bar springs react to changing loads more rapidly and with less tendency to bounce than coiled springs do.

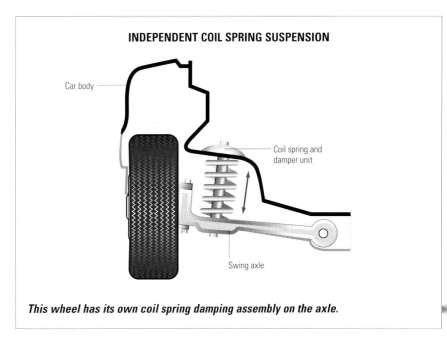

INDEPENDENT COIL SPRING SUSPENSION

Car body

Coil spring and damper unit

Swing axle

This wheel has its own coil spring damping assembly on the axle.

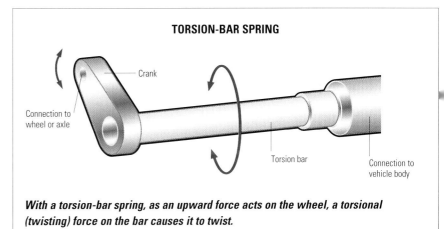

TORSION-BAR SPRING

Crank

Connection to wheel or axle

Torsion bar

Connection to vehicle body

With a torsion-bar spring, as an upward force acts on the wheel, a torsional (twisting) force causes it to twist.

Pneumatic or air springing depends on the compressibility of a gas such as air. The spring principle will be familiar to anyone who has pushed down the plunger of a bicycle pump while the air outlet is closed. The more the piston is pushed, the harder it becomes to pump. This is because the greater the pressure in the enclosed air, the greater the force required to compress it further (see HYDRAULICS AND PNEUMATICS). Air springs consist of two plates that are joined by a flexible membrane that seals the air between them. One plate is connected to the vehicle's body, the other to the axle. Air springs are often used in large trucks and railroad cars, sometimes in conjunction with automatic level control (see the box on page 1292).

Automobile shock absorbers

Spring bounce is reduced by a system of shock absorbers (also known as dampers or snubbers). These slow the reaction of the spring and reduce the size of the bounce. Early shock absorbers consisted of pads of flexible material—usually rubber—between metal plates that were pressed together by sprung bolts. One plate was fixed to the axle and the other to the body of the vehicle.

HYDRAULIC SHOCK ABSORBER

Connection to body of vehicle

Pressurized nitrogen (stops oil from foaming)

Free piston

Oil

Holes in piston allow oil to flow through slowly

Piston

Connection to axle

A hydraulic shock absorber consists of a piston inside a sealed cylinder, one attached to the chassis of the vehicle and the other to the axle. When the vehicle reaches an uneven road surface, holes in the piston allow the oil in the cylinder to leak from one side of the piston to the other, absorbing energy in the process.

Most modern shock absorbers dampen the relative movement between axle and body by means of a small piston that moves in an oil-filled cylinder. Various designs have been used. In one, the cylinder includes a small hole so that the oil is forced out slowly when the piston moves in one direction, and sucked back in when it moves in the other. Usually, the oil remains in the cylinder but passes through

valves in the piston from one side to the other. The swirling of the fluid that has passed through the holes becomes a random motion and the fluid becomes hot. Shock absorbers must therefore be designed allow for heat dissipation.

Independent wheel suspension

Until around 1930, almost all automobiles had rigid axles that were connected to the body by leaf springs. From the 1930s on, however, independent wheel suspension became more common. Independent suspension has separate springing and damping systems for each wheel on a flexible axle so that a vertical motion of one wheel when it strikes a bump has little effect on wheel at the other end of the axle.

Independent wheel suspension has a number of important advantages. It allows the use of softer springs, reduces wheel vibration, and improves road handling and steering. These advantages were found to be so beneficial that, from the 1950s on, independent suspension rapidly replaced rigid front axles.

Automobile stabilizer bars

When a vehicle turns, its inertia (tendency to continue in a straight line) causes the vehicle to sway out from the center of the curve. Vehicle sway cannot be effectively controlled by springs and shock absorbers alone. When a sprung vehicle is turning at speed, the whole body leans, so the springs outside the turn are compressed and those inside are stretched. This effect can be countered using a stabilizer bar. This is a U-shaped torsion bar extending across the vehicle's underside, with its center attached to the frame and its ends fixed to the respective springs. The method of linkage to the springs is such that compression of a spring twists the stabilizer bar in one direction and elongation of the spring twists it in the opposite direction. In the course of a turn, one spring compresses while the opposite one extends, and the torsion bar automatically tends to reduce body tilt.

Active suspension

Active suspension is a microprocessor-controlled system that uses information from acceleration sensors mounted at various points on the wheel supports and the vehicle's body. The microprocessor responds to the inputs by sending instructions to pumps and valves that adjust the pressure of fluid in hydraulic wheel-regulators—flexible, fluid-filled chambers that take the place of both springs and shock absorbers. Active systems can provide a higher standard of vehicle suspension than any conventional system, but they are expensive and require considerable power to operate the fluid pumps and valves.

R. YOUNGSON

See also: AUTOMOBILE; STEERING SYSTEMS; TIRE.

Further reading:
Birch, T. *Automotive Suspension and Steering Systems.* Fort Worth: Saunders College Publishing, 1993.

AUTOMATIC LEVEL CONTROL

Sometimes it is important for a vehicle's body to remain at a fixed height through a wide range of loads. This is the case for air-sprung passenger railroad cars, which must remain level with platforms as passengers board and leave the train. The height of the car body is kept within a narrow range by automatic level control: as the number of passengers in the car increases and the car starts to sink under their weight, a height sensor activates a compressor that supplies additional air to the springs (SEE PUMP AND COMPRESSOR; TRANSDUCER AND SENSOR). The compressor is deactivated when the car returns to its intended height. If passengers leave the train, the load on the springs decreases and the car starts to rise. When this happens, the height sensor opens a valve that releases air from the springs until the normal level is restored.

A CLOSER LOOK

TANK

Tanks are tracked armored vehicles that are used for artillery, infantry protection, or rapid assault forces

Originally, tanks were an extension of the armored car, of which the first model was a modified French Army staff car built in 1901. Like most prototypes, neither this vehicle nor the first tank designs were adopted, because military leaders thought that armored vehicles would have limited value on the battlefield.

World War I (1914–1918) changed military thinking completely. The first true tanks were fielded by the British Army in 1916. Originally called land-ships, the armored vehicles got the name *tank* because for reasons of secrecy the company developing them pretended that they were manufacturing water tanks for the army. At first, the British tanks had mixed success. In 1918, however, they played a major part in winning the Battle of Amiens in France, crippling Germany's military capability and hastening the armistice (the agreement that ended the war). Since then, generals have regarded tanks as a central component of land warfare strategy.

One of the most decisive battles of World War II (1939–1945), fought in 1943 at Kursk in Ukraine, involved more than 6000 tanks. Similarly, the Gulf War in 1991 was ended after the largest tank battle in history (see the box on page 1294).

Tank characteristics and use

A tank is an armored, self-propelled vehicle that runs on tracks, like a bulldozer, and carries machine guns and a main battery (artillery gun) that shoots explosive shells. The engine compartment, usually in the rear, and the driver's compartment make up the hull. Atop the hull, the fighting compartment comprises a revolving turret that houses the main battery.

On the majority of early tanks, the tracks circled the entire hull, but all later tanks have tracks that reach about halfway up the hull. Each track turns on between five and seven ground wheels; an idler wheel at the front, which angles the track up for climbing over obstacles; and a sprocket wheel at the back—a toothed drive wheel that engages with and moves the track around. The sprocket wheel is connected to the transmission system and to the engine (see TRACKED VEHICLE).

CORE FACTS

- A tank consists of a hull (which has a driver's compartment and an engine compartment) and a turret (which holds the main weaponry, gun crew, and tank commander).
- Tanks are classified as light tanks (under 25 tons), medium tanks (25 to 50 tons), and heavy or main battle tanks (more than 50 tons).
- A tank's armor may be metal, ceramic, or fiber-reinforced polymer. It is angled to deflect enemy shells and to be radar invisible.
- Main battle tanks carry cannons of 4.1–4.9 in (105–125 mm). They are aimed with laser and thermal (heat) sighting devices so that they are very accurate at thousands of yards (meters).

CONNECTIONS

- Modern tanks make use of the latest **NAVIGATION** aids, which are based on advanced **SATELLITE** technology.

- The development of the guided **MISSILE** and specialized weapons systems has changed the role of the tank in modern **LAND WARFARE**.

TANKS IN THE GULF WAR

A U.S. Army M-1A1 Abrams main battle tank lays a smoke screen in Kuwait during maneuvers in the course of the Gulf War in February 1991.

In 1991, the Gulf War pitted Iraq against a coalition of nations led by United States and under the authority of the United Nations. The land battle confirmed the effectiveness of tactics that use the mobility and firepower of tanks. The coalition had 3600 tanks poised at the Saudi Arabian border with Iraq and Kuwait on February 24, 1991. Facing them were more than 4300 Iraqi tanks.

The land offensive, named Desert Saber, began at 4:00 A.M. Just 100 hours later the battle was over, as the coalition armored forces cut through the entrenched Iraqis, raced behind, and surrounded them. The Iraqis lost an estimated 3700 tanks. The U.S. Army lost only two M-1A1 Abrams tanks to enemy fire—Iraqi shells, even from the powerful Russian-designed T-72 heavy tanks, simply bounced off the Abrams' armor. The U.S. Army and U.S. Marine Corps claim to have destroyed about 1400 Iraqi tanks, most in tank-to-tank battles. Other antitank weapons, tanks from other nations, and aircraft disposed of the rest.

A CLOSER LOOK

Tanks also carry radios, headlights, floodlights, and navigation instruments such as Global Positioning System (GPS) units, which allow them to pinpoint their positions using satellites (see MILITARY COMMUNICATIONS AND CONTROL).

Between three and five crew members operate a modern tank. The driver sits in the hull in front of the turret and guides the tank on orders from the commander in the turret. The driver may also have a machine gun. The commander finds targets or responds to radio orders from the unit commander and conveys instructions to the driver and gunner. On top of the turret, the commander has a machine gun for use when standing upright through the turret hatch. The gunner sights and fires the main battery and a machine gun that is mounted parallel to and beside it. Loaders may handle the ammunition for the weapons, although some modern tanks carry automatic loaders for the main battery.

Types of tanks

Tanks are classified by weight and function. Light tanks weigh less than 25 tons (22.7 tonnes), have thin armor, and are used for reconnaissance or to support fast-moving infantry. The U.S. Army's 17.5-ton (15.9-tonne) M-551A1 Sheridan is designed to be dropped from an airplane with paratroopers.

A medium or cruiser tank weighs from 25 tons (22.7 tonnes) to 50 tons (45.4 tonnes). They were first built during World War II for use in large armored formations. The heavy or main battle tank weighs over 50 tons (45.3 tonnes) and is heavily armored. Originally, heavy tanks were designed to support infantry, but during the cold war—the period of prolonged hostile relations between NATO (North Atlantic Treaty Organization) and the former Warsaw Pact countries (the former Soviet Union and Eastern European countries) from the 1940s until the early 1990s—battlefield doctrine called for large formations of heavy tanks that could spearhead an attack with infantry in support. The main battery varies from 3-in (75-mm) cannons on light tanks to 4.9-in (125-mm) cannons on heavy tanks.

The U.S. Army's M1 Abrams series exemplifies the main battle tank. Carrying a four-person crew, it has a 4.7-in (120-mm) gun aimed by laser and thermal sights, one 0.5-in (12.7-mm) and two 0.3-in (7.6-mm) machine guns on the turret, metal alloy-ceramic armor, and the ability to cross a ditch 9 ft (2.7 m) wide and climb over an obstacle more than 3.5 ft (1.1 m) high. Although it weighs as much as 68 tons (61.7 tonnes) and is 32 ft (9.7 m) long, the Abrams, propelled by a 1500 horsepower engine, can sprint as fast as 48 mph (77 km/h). The army's AirLand battle strategy requires the M1s to move very fast and carry communications gear capable of linking them to other ground and aircraft units. In this way, tank-led ground forces can burst through enemy lines immediately after airstrikes have destroyed command and supply centers.

Tanks of the 21st century will improve resistance to enemy fire by having either a lower silhouette or armor made from new materials. Experimental vehicles have tested designs without a turret; the main gun is either mounted in the hull or on a stand above it so that the tank presents a smaller target. Fiber-reinforced polymer armor, which can be shaped easily, will give tanks greater protection from armor-piercing shells than would steel or aluminum; weigh less; and be difficult to detect by radar or optical systems (see ELECTRONIC COUNTERMEASURES; MATERIALS SCIENCE). Called stealth tanks, these are likely to be built in the United States on a standard chassis that can be used for other types of armored vehicles and so reduce overall development and production costs.

R. SMITH

See also: ARTILLERY; MILITARY VEHICLES.

Further reading:
Gelbert, M. *Tanks: Main Battle Tanks and Light Tanks.* London: Brassey's, 1996.

INDEX

Page numbers in **boldface** type refer to main articles and their illustrations. Page
numbers in *italic* type refer to additional illustrations or their captions.